A SHEARWATER BOOK

Heatstroke

Heatstroke

NATURE IN AN AGE OF GLOBAL WARMING

Anthony D. Barnosky

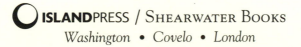

ISLANDPRESS / SHEARWATER BOOKS

Washington • Covelo • London

A Shearwater Book
Published by Island Press

Copyright © 2009 Anthony D. Barnosky

All rights reserved under International and Pan-American
Copyright Conventions. No part of this book may be reproduced in
any form or by any means without permission in writing from the
publisher: Island Press, 1718 Connecticut Ave., NW, Suite 300
Washington, DC 20009.

SHEARWATER BOOKS is a trademark of
The Center for Resource Economics.

Library of Congress Cataloging-in-Publication data.
Barnosky, Anthony D.
  Heatstroke : nature in an age of global warming / Anthony D.
Barnosky.
     p. cm.
  Includes bibliographical references.
  ISBN-13: 978-1-59726-197-5 (cloth : alk. paper)
  ISBN-10: 1-59726-197-1 (cloth : alk. paper) 1. Nature—Effect
of human beings on. 2. Global warming—Environmental
aspects. I. Title.
  GF75.B368 2009
  577.2'2—dc22
                                        2008033363

British Cataloguing-in-Publication data available.

The paperback edition carries 13-digit ISBN: 978-1-59726-817-2
and the 10-digit ISBN: 1-59726-817-8
Printed on recycled, acid-free paper ♲
Design by Joyce C. Weston
Manufactured in the United States of America

10 9 8 7 6 5 4 3 2 1

Contents

PART THREE. UNCHARTED TERRAIN   133

To the 2010 graduating classes of Henry M. Gunn
High School, Jane Lathrop Stanford Middle School, and
Nido de Aguilas International School,
and to young people of their generation everywhere.
You have the talent, the power, and the responsibility
to change the world for the better.

And especially to Emma and Clara.

Preface

IT IS no surprise that nearly seven billion of us (and counting) are redefining humanity's place in nature by replacing forests with houses, harnessing rivers for irrigation and flood control, turning deserts into farms and golf courses, moving mountains to find energy, and otherwise directly altering the world's ecosystems. The surprise of recent years comes in realizing the potentially devastating ecological effects of a new human impact: global warming.

The concept of global warming is not entirely new, of course. The idea has been around for more than a century, and over the past 30 years, in fits and starts, it has made its way out of scientific journals and into policy debates and, at least when the weather seemed unusual, into the news. But not until 2006 did global warming migrate from the minds of scientists into the public consciousness on a broad scale. That year a floodgate opened, with books, movies, and innumerable news reports all recognizing—more than that, publicizing—that our climate really is changing and that people are causing it. With that recognition comes a shift from the "if" and "why" questions—we've essentially answered those—to the "how" and "what" questions, especially: what does global warming mean for humanity and the rest of the world's species and what can be done about it?

While economic repercussions, sea-level rise, melting glaciers, and paralyzed politics have received lots of press, only recently have scientists begun to get a handle on one of the most important and far-reaching effects: how global warming will change the ecology of Earth. Even seemingly innocuous conveniences that we take for granted, such as air conditioning and driving to the store, when multiplied by billions of people, are making our climate hotter than humans have ever seen it, and heating it faster than life on Earth has experienced in millions of years, if ever. Couple that with ever-growing human populations and their needs and wants, and the ecological consequences promise to be profound. Will global warming be the coup de grâce to many already-stressed ecosystems? Are we, in effect, setting up a "perfect storm" for the destruction of key ecological processes that have evolved to keep Mother Earth healthy and the human species alive?

In searching for answers to these and related questions, I found isolated scientific reports about effects of global warming on this species or that. But there was no comprehensive synthesis that focused on explaining the overarching importance of those effects, the real reasons behind them, and how unusual they may be compared to the kinds of longer-term fluctuations—over years, decades, lifetimes—that we're used to. A critical question from my perspective as a paleobiologist was how, or even if, the kinds of changes we're beginning to see today really differ from the normal ebb and flow that ecosystems experience as they persist over thousands, even millions of years. And, just as critical from my perspective as someone who finds solace in wild country, I wondered what the ecological changes triggered by global warming might mean for the nature preserves the world has long sought to protect, the kinds of places that I and millions of others seek to keep our spirits whole. So I decided to write this book, which addresses those questions and more, as a means not only to consider the kinds of ecological transformations we and, especially, our children will see, but also to ponder how those transformations will affect humanity's concept of nature, and how we can continue to keep nature alive.

Many of the examples I use to illustrate my points in the pages that follow come from places that I have worked and species I have studied personally, and for that reason mammals from awe-inspiring landscapes take the spotlight in most chapters. For the many other examples cited I have relied primarily on the published, peer-reviewed research of scientists from around the world. Their dedication of years of their lives to finding out how nature works ultimately makes this sort of synthesis possible.

Specific acknowledgments are in order for several people who helped me as I was writing this book. I am tremendously grateful, more than words can say, to my soulmate and wife Liz Hadly, for the uncountable ways she contributed, among them: many impromptu brainstorming sessions, some at the weirdest times; feeding me relevant literature and news on a regular basis; being the resident expert on Yellowstone, mammalogy, and genetics; including me in thought-provoking classes she taught about the South American biota and on field trips to Monte Verde and Puerto Montt; educating me about salmon farming in Patagonia; critiquing the manuscript; and for her enthusiasm and support throughout this whole project. There is something of her in almost every chapter. Thank you Liz, for sharing your ideas, your scientific work, the good wine, and the hope of making the world a better place.

I thank Paul Ehrlich for passing the book proposal to Jonathan Cobb at Island Press, and Jonathan for his editorial help and for seeing the book through to publication. Researchers who read parts of the manuscript and provided helpful comments include Chris Bell, Rauri Bowie, Francis Chan, Chris Conroy, Todd Dawson, Inez Fung, Don Grayson, Larry Goulder, Rob Guralnick, Dale Guthrie, Liz Hadly, David Inouye, Brian Maurer, Craig Moritz, Steve Palumbi, Jim Patton, Mary Power, Terry Root, Bill Ruddiman, Steve Schneider, John Varley, and Jack Williams. Of course, any errors that may have crept in are my own.

For financial and logistical support during a sabbatical year when much of the writing was done, I thank the U.S.-Chile Fulbright Foundation and Department of Ecology, Pontificia Universidad Católica de Chile, Santiago. I am grateful to Pablo A. Marquet and Claudio Latorre for hosting my visit at the Universidad Católica. The National Science Foundation, especially programs in Sedimentary Geology and Paleobiology and Ecology, as well as the University of California Museum of Paleontology, contributed substantially to the financial support of my scientific research that helped to inform this book.

And for inspiring me to think more about the future of the Earth, I thank my children, my nieces and nephews, all their friends, and my students.

PART ONE

Recipe for Disaster?

Chapter 1

The Heat Is On

It's a different Earth; we might as well hold a contest to pick a new name.

—Bill McKibben[1]

ΛS RΛIN was spattering my tent high in the Colorado mountains, it didn't really seem like a different Earth to me, even though much of the world was reeling from one of the hottest summers yet recorded. This was the summer of 1988, the second year in a row of unusual heat. In fact, the average global temperatures in both 1987 and 1988 were the hottest on record up to then, fueling speculation in the news about whether global warming, a trend that climatologists had been talking about over the previous three decades or so, was to blame.

I had perhaps more reason than most to be thinking about global warming because at the time I was in the midst of digging fossil rats, mice, and other animals out of a cave in order to learn how mountain wildlife had been affected by climate changes that took place hundreds of thousands of years ago. For three summers I had been returning to the mountains, donning a headlamp and coveralls with the rest of my crew, and descending deep underground with shovels, trowels, screens, compasses, cameras, and assorted other gear. We were traveling back in time, peeling away the dirt floor of the cave—sedimentary layers of dust, clay, and rock—that encased hundreds of thousands of fossil bones. Determining the kinds of sediments in each layer—whether flowstone was present, for example, or compacted clay—told us something of the climate that had prevailed outside the cave in times past, and the bones told us what kinds of animals had lived in that climate. Each layer we peeled away essentially exposed a new snapshot of a long-gone ecosystem, and by analyzing all those snapshots and reassembling them in sequence, we would be able to track the ecological effects of past global warming events. We had dug deep enough to take us back nearly a million years, long before humans had any impact on climate, back to both past glacial ages much cooler than today and warmer periods resembling today's climate. The idea was to understand how ecosystems had responded to the extreme global warming events indicated by the glacial to interglacial shifts, so that we could better gauge what to expect with warming in the future.

But truth be told, for me, as for most of us in 1988, immediate problems felt more pressing than the effects of global warming, which only become evident over decades and centuries. I had sixty people to keep productively busy, and although we were spending mornings deep in a cave where the weather outside didn't matter, the afternoon rains were slowing us down. Each day after lunch, the morning's diggings were hauled out in canvas money bags and trucked to a nearby stream, where we used hoses and gasoline-powered pumps to wash the dirt through screens, leaving the fossils and gravel behind. Before the fossils could be separated from the gravelly matrix for identification, they had to dry. And that was where the rain was a problem. We were falling behind schedule.

In the soggy matrix clogging the screens, though, we did notice lots of fossil teeth and jawbones of marmots. They were so big they were hard to miss. Marmots are a kind of groundhog of the genus *Marmota*. The ones that live in the Colorado Rockies today are *Marmota flaviventris*, or yellow-bellied marmots. They are chubby, squirrel-like rodents (in fact marmots are members of the squirrel family) that we occasionally watched scampering around the boulders above the cave. They have puffy cheeks and buck teeth, like cartoon characters. They alternately hunch up their backs and then stretch out when they run, like a slinky whose ends you push together until it bends in the middle and the front end extends outward. They look at you first with surprise, then with a little bit of disgust, before they take off. The fossils we were picking off the screens were from long-dead *Marmota*, and showed us that marmots, in some form or fashion, had been a part of that Colorado mountain ecosystem for close to a million years. They were there during ice ages,[2] when most of the surrounding 3,000- to 4,300-meter (10,000- to 14,000-foot) mountains hosted vast glaciers. When the glaciers receded marmot populations persisted, even when the local climate became hotter and drier than it is today. What we were finding seemed to say that if any kind of animal should be able to persevere through dramatic climate changes, marmots should.

That ability to survive makes sense when you take into account what marmots do for a living. Like people, they hide from the weather. Unlike people (at least, most people), they hide in burrows. That means that a marmot's-eye view of climate is much like the view my crew and I had while we were crawling around inside the cave. Marmots construct elaborate burrow systems into which, in the Colorado Rockies, they disappear anytime the outside temperature gets colder than about 1°C (34°F) or hotter than 26°C (79°F). In the burrows, the temperature stays between 8–10°C (46–50°F), even though the outside temperature might be far colder or hotter. Marmots thus spend only about 20 percent of their lives outside their climate-controlled dwellings (If you have an office or factory job, the time you spend outdoors is probably a little less, maybe 10 percent of your year.). From the marmot's perspective, a problem with their climate-control system is that it forces them to spend all winter in their burrows without food (something we could never do)—and that's about 60 percent of their life.

To stay alive, yellow-bellied marmots in the Colorado mountains generally go into their burrows in early September to hibernate, reducing their metabolism to the bare minimum in order to conserve energy. They finally emerge sometime in the spring, April or May, when the fat reserves they accumulated during the previous summer begin to get low. As you might imagine, they're hungry. The cue that tells them to stay out of their burrows is warmer air, which in ideal circumstances has been melting the snow outside for some days prior to the marmots' emergence. When all that goes as it should, the sleepy, hungry marmots stagger out of their burrows and blink their eyes at what must be a welcome sight: fresh new shoots of nutritious vegetation poking up where only a few days before snowfields blanketed the ground. The salad bar's open. The delicate balance of each element in a marmot's life—a climate-controlled burrow, hibernation, a warm-air wakeup call, melting snow, and vegetation growth—seems to have served marmots well. This balancing act hadn't failed in nearly a million years in that mountain locale, and marmots seemed as much a part of the landscape as the rocks they trundled over.

Knowing this made me think that where I was camping and digging then was not a "different Earth" at all. Ecologically at least, things seemed to be chugging along pretty much as usual. What neither the marmots nor I knew at the time, though, was that their days there may be numbered.

Not far away, about 100 kilometers to the west as the crow flies, in the mountains above Gunnison, a team of researchers at the Rocky Mountain Biological Laboratory had for decades been painstakingly measuring temperatures inside marmot burrows and the air temperature outside, gauging snowfall and the timing of snowmelt, and recording when the first marmots emerged from each long winter of hibernation.[3] What the data made clear when the team published it in 2000 would have been disturbing to any marmot, had they only known, even as far back as twelve years earlier. In the spring of '88, the average marmot popped out of its burrow to look for something to eat around May 8, a week earlier than they were emerging in 1976. By 1999 marmots would be sticking their heads above ground near April 21, some 23 days—nearly a full month—earlier than they had in the mid-1970s. Meanwhile, more winter snow was falling each year and even the increasing spring temperatures were not melting the snow fast enough, as a marmot would see it—which meant that, year by year, more marmots were seeing snow instead of salad when they awakened, emaciated from hibernation. A higher percentage of the population, in other words, was spending too much energy awake when they should have been conserving energy asleep. Which means death. Something strange was happening to the climate, something that upset the natural balance that had been genetically coded into those climate-controlled marmots through their evolutionary history. For the marmots, it was beginning to look like a different Earth after all.

The summer of that same year, 1988, many of the eastern states were experiencing a heat wave, in the midst of which, coincidentally, the Senate Committee on Energy and Natural Resources was holding hearings about global warming. The scientists who testified there were facing a different kind of heat than people were suffering outside. They were trying to explain, in ways easy to understand, the long-term crises that could arise from global warming—no easy feat when you consider that the nature of climate science is computer models and probability calculations, just the stuff to make eyes glaze and heads nod, and the nature of people is to worry about what's happening today, not what might happen twenty or fifty or a hundred years from now. The task was complicated, too, because the easy way out—blaming the roasting temperatures outside the Capitol on global warming—was not scientifically sound: there was simply no way of knowing whether any particular weather event, like the hot summer of '88 or the gradual shift in the timing of snowfall versus warm spring temperatures in the Colorado Rockies over ten years, was the result of long-term global warming, or just a fluke.

But, specific weather events aside, some disturbing overall trends were becoming clear to the scientists, which led James Hansen, one of the pioneers in pushing for action to mitigate climate change, to state the case in no uncertain terms: "It's time to stop waffling so much and say that the greenhouse effect is here and is affecting our climate now."[4] Other respected scientists and climate policy advocates were offering future scenarios that seemed overly dramatic at the time, such as:

> [A] major hurricane . . . coming out of the Caribbean . . . of near-record intensity . . . [would] . . . hit . . . with storm tides as high as 4 meters (12 feet), bringing devastation. . . . Advance warning and prompt evacuation [would] keep loss of life to less

than a hundred, but property damage [would be] in excess of
$1 billion.[5]

That was a scenario offered by climatologist Stephen Schneider
in a book he published in 1989 to raise awareness on the climate
change issue. Think of Schneider as the Bob Dylan of climate science.
Just as Dylan was writing songs and rousing the civil rights crowds in
the 1970s, Schneider was studying how to calculate the probabilities
of specific kinds of climate events, and reaching out to policy makers with his conclusion: namely, that global warming was a threat
whose effects would become increasingly evident in the next couple
of generations. And, just as Dylan worked his crowds in the ensuing
decades, so did Schneider in congressional halls and meeting rooms
where national climate policy was discussed at the highest levels,
such as at that Senate committee hearing in 1988.

Seventeen years later, in fact, Schneider's scenario proved overly
optimistic. The prediction was pretty close on the storm tides (4.3
meters versus 4), but when Hurricane Katrina destroyed New Or-
leans (not to mention entire communities in Mississippi), there was
no prompt evacuation, nearly 2,000 people were killed, and property
damage was in excess of $81 billion—all from that one storm. Debate
ensued in the scientific literature as to whether or not the record
number of hurricanes that year—28—was attributable to global
warming, but a couple of facts were indisputable: warmer ocean
waters fuel more-extreme storms, and the ocean, as well as the rest of
the earth, had been getting on average warmer and warmer for five
decades, and especially the preceding decade. The ten warmest years
that thermometers had ever measured occurred from 1990 to 2005.
While there were some year-to-year ups and downs, on average each
year was successively warmer than the last, with 1998 claiming the
dubious honor of the hottest year ever known, and 2002, 2003, and
2001 taking second, third, and fourth place, respectively. In short, by
2005 global warming had not only arrived, it had literally taken the
world by storm and had given us a dramatic sneak preview of what to
expect from a different Earth.

What makes the Earth different now compared to centuries past
is that humans, primarily through burning oil, gas, and coal, have

changed the very air we breathe. While that may have been a point of debate in 1988, today it is as close as we get to fact in science[6]— meaning that atmospheric composition can be measured fairly precisely, that those measurements have been tracked with some precision over the past five and a half decades, and that a half century of measurements can be compared to what scientists have been able to discover about what the atmosphere was like hundreds, thousands, and even millions of years ago.

Details aside for now, the comparisons converge on disturbing conclusions that go beyond the immediate temperature rises themselves. First, today the air we breathe has more carbon dioxide, methane, nitrous oxide, sulfur dioxide, and other "greenhouse gases" than it has had for at least four hundred thousand years—longer than humans have been a species. They are called "greenhouse gases" because, as their concentration in the atmosphere increases, they prevent some of the heat that would normally radiate back into space—heat ultimately derived from the sun's rays striking the earth—from leaving the atmosphere. Just like a greenhouse, the Earth heats up as a result.

Second, the concentrations of those gases have risen—and are rising—so fast that it is staggering. By the time babies born today are in their fifties, even the best-case scenario predicts that more greenhouse gases will be in the air than has been the case in three million years—if we go on our merry way without any mitigation efforts. In just the years since 1950, we put approximately twice as much CO_2 into the atmosphere as we had over the previous 200 years, largely from burning fossil fuels. And those industrial-age additions may be on top of increased levels of greenhouse gases that prehistoric humans, through agricultural burning, land clearing, and coal burning, had begun dumping into the atmosphere as long ago as 8,000 years.[7] The net effect is that we've increased global concentrations of CO_2 by more than a third (~35%) with respect to normal, preindustrial levels.

Not only are we living at a time already warmer than Earth has experienced in at least four hundred thousand years, we are also living at a time when the climate is changing much faster than normal.

Earth has not experienced a similarly fast rate of climate change within at least the last 60 million years. The reason we tend not to notice is that the increase in greenhouse gases is incremental year to year, decade to decade, century to century, without a lot of discernable change within a human lifetime, until all hell breaks loose—which is now. Those ever-increasing levels of greenhouse gases are beginning to give us an Earth that not only is hotter, but one that also promises many other climatic changes: exceptionally violent storms more often, shortened growing seasons in some places and lengthened ones in others, droughts in some places, too much rain in others, and transformation of what used to be coastline (or even inland) into ocean.

Seen in that light, the scientific wakeup call about marmots in the Colorado Rockies, already evident by 1988 and getting louder by 2000, fit all too well into a bigger picture. Not only was our species' unwitting tinkering with the atmosphere inflicting collateral damage on this Colorado ecosystem where, for all practical purposes, the actual footprints of people were few and far between, but this atmospheric tinkering was actually beginning to disturb what we regard as "natural" ecosystems even in places where there are virtually *no* human footprints.

Places such as high in the Canadian Arctic. In April of 2006 a hunter from Idaho, Jim Martell, paid $50,000 for one of the many versions of a wilderness experience, the chance to shoot a polar bear near the top of the world on Banks Island, Canada. There's not much on Banks Island in the way of people. It's a big island—in land area around 67,000 square kilometers (26,000 square miles), a little bigger than West Virginia—but it has only one small settlement of around 114 native Inuit people. The rest of the place is ice, snow, tundra, shin-high willows, musk oxen, caribou, and, of course, polar bears. But that's not what Martell shot. Instead he bagged a pizzly, or a grolar bear, depending on what you want to call it. The bear looked enough like a polar bear to draw Martell's bead, but when he checked out his kill, he saw not only the cream-colored fur typical of polar bears, but also a hump on its back, long claws, a shallow face, and brown patches around its eyes, nose, and back. Those made it look

more like a grizzly bear than a polar bear. Later DNA tests showed
why it seemed like a little of both: Martell's trophy had a polar bear
mother and a grizzly bear father.

Something out of the ordinary had happened, something that
raised a host of questions. For starters, what were a polar bear and
grizzly bear doing in the same place? Polar bears are pagophilic,
which means they live almost exclusively on sea ice, especially the
annual ice that forms over the polar continental shelves and around
island archipelagos. Polar bears come onto land when sea ice melts
completely in the summer, or in the case of pregnant females, when
it's time to den and birth cubs in the winter. Even when on land, they
tend to stay within a few kilometers of the coast. Polar bears prefer
icy marine habitats because evolution has prepared them to specialize almost exclusively on a food source that is unavailable to other
terrestrial animals: seals (with an occasional narwhal or walrus for
variety). Most of their fat reserves are put on during the spring
breakup of pack ice, when holes and open-water corridors in the ice
provide a place for seals to come up for gulps of air and to bask. The
bears sniff out such breathing holes and employ a technique called
still-hunting: quietly waiting by the hole until dinner appears, at
which time they attack and, if they are lucky, pull out a desperately
wriggling seal.

Grizzlies, on the other hand, are today denizens of the terrestrial
arctic (and a few alpine or forested regions where people have
allowed them to remain). They amble across the hills, hunting and
scavenging prey like caribou, moose, ground squirrels, spawning
salmon and trout, as well as a wide variety of vegetation. Like you
and me, they are omnivores, cosmopolitan in their tastes, but firmly
rooted on shore. Grizzly range stops where the sea begins, which is to
say some 100 kilometers (62 miles) south of Banks Island. When sea
ice is at its greatest extent in the winter, polar bear range butts right
up against grizzly range, but there is little chance of interaction then
because grizzlies are hibernating and pregnant female polar bears are
denning (male polar bears stay active year-round). The ranges of the
two species near Banks Island are completely separated in summer by
100 kilometers of open water. That leaves only spring as a time,

potentially, for individuals of the two species to run across each other, during what is typically the mating season for both grizzlies and polar bears. The pizzly bear shot in 2006 suggests that a couple of years earlier, when pack ice was breaking up, an errant male grizzly awoke from hibernation and ventured out onto the ice, where he encountered a female polar bear. Or else the ice melted so fast that both were stranded on land by June, which is the latest month when the breeding seasons of the two species typically overlap.

Which leads to perhaps an even more perplexing question: why would any self-respecting female polar bear mate with a grizzly bear? Polar bear unions are not chance encounters. The courtship, if you want to call it that, typically begins where the polar bears are congregating to hunt seals, their main food. When male polar bears get interested, they are persistent, following a female up to 100 kilometers (62 miles). The female enjoys having several males vying for her attentions (on average there are around three males ready to mate for every available female). In the end she chooses the biggest and best of them, from her perspective, and then engages in multiple conjugal relations with the same male, over several days, which stimulates ovulation. Grizzlies have more of a hit-and-miss mating strategy, with a receptive female grizzly potentially mating with more than one male in a day. So where were all the male polar bears this time? Was this just one tough grizzly?

We can't know the answer to those questions for sure, but some things that we do know are suggestive. First, pack ice in northern Canada is breaking up substantially earlier than it did thirty years ago—some 2.5 weeks earlier in Hudson's Bay.[8] This means a greater chance that any grizzly that did wander out onto the ice would be caught there as ice floes shifted and would face two alternatives: turn around and swim back to shore, or keep walking north across the ice and end up on Banks Island or even farther north. Those sorts of unlikely events seem to be happening more and more. In 2003 and 2004, definitive photos, tracks, and hair samples of a grizzly were reported higher in the arctic than ever before—1,000 kilometers (620 miles) above the arctic circle, well into polar bear range on Melville Island and 100 kilometers (62 miles) northeast of Banks

Island.[9, 10] What seems to be happening is that grizzlies, along with species such as robins and sparrows—birds for which the indigenous Inuit have no name—have been expanding their ranges north onto Banks Island and farther in response to the last several decades of warming.

All of which means more chance encounters between grizzlies and polar bears. Couple that with the reduction in polar bear populations caused by early breakup of sea ice, and you have the recipe for a pizzly. The quicker the pack ice goes from fast ice (that is, ice anchored to the shore or seafloor) to no ice, the less fat a polar bear puts on to sustain it through the long summer of no seal holes to sit by. And, if the ice disappears earlier, then the summer is even longer and so is the time when a bear must subsist mainly on its fat reserves. Mortality correspondingly increases, and populations decline. Play that out over a few successive years and it is not hard to imagine a solitary female wandering around with no male polar bears in sight. Instead she sees that grizzly, caught on the ice floe, working his way north.

From there, ancestral genetics take over. As it turns out, polar bears descended fairly recently, in evolutionary time at least, from grizzly bears. The split between the two species is thought to have occurred somewhere between 70,000 and 1.5 million years ago,[11] during the Pleistocene, the epoch when climate changed such that the frozen north first became a relatively permanent feature of Earth's landscape. Those ice fields were new niches with new feeding opportunities, to which polar bears became specialized through what must have been some relatively rapid natural selection. Even so, polar bears have not diverged very far genetically from grizzlies. The blurry line between the two species of bears means that more pizzlies are possible, indeed even likely, as more and more grizzlies move into polar bear range, and polar bear populations become more and more depleted.

Of course, there are arguments that global warming has little to do with pizzlies, much as there were arguments in 1988 about whether global warming had anything to do with the hot summer. The pizzlies of 2006 are analogous to the weather of 1988 in that we

are still in the early days of observation, and we can't draw any conclusions with certainty. What we can be certain of, however, is that
polar bears are on the way out. The annual ice pack is getting smaller
and smaller, and when it goes, so will polar bears.[12] Anyway you look
at it, pizzlies or no, we've come full circle. A cooling global climate
stimulated the evolution of polar bears; global warming is taking
them away.

By 2008, the list of climate-caused ecological casualties was
growing far beyond polar bears, as we'll see in later chapters: species
ranging from golden toads in Costa Rica, to butterflies in England,
to forests from Alaska down into Montana blighted by tree-killing
beetles, and the inexorable march of species in all directions (but
mostly away from the equator, or uphill) as they race to track the
shifting climates they require for life. In the geologic past, there just
wasn't such a problem. New communities came and went as each
species adjusted its geographic range to follow the ever-shifting (in
geologic time) climates that sustained it. The geographic range of
each species was like a giant amoeba, projecting here, retracting
there, at a speed that more or less matched the pace at which their
habitats slid across the Earth's surface in response to natural climate
shifts—say, the change from an interglacial time to an ice age.
Where those amoebae overlap, you have an assemblage of species
that defines the communities and interactions that, in turn, define
an ecosystem.

Today, it is not an option, for a couple of very important reasons,
for many species to alter their range to follow their needed climate.
First, climate change is racing faster than it ever has during the evolution of living species and ecosystems—many species simply aren't
biologically capable of adjusting their geographic range at the speed
they would need to in order to survive. Second, "Los Angeles gets in
the way."[13] With cities, towns, large-scale agriculture, roads, and
other impediments, we have fragmented the natural geographic
ranges of many species and at the same time thrown barriers in the
paths that would otherwise make it possible for them move freely
around the Earth's surface, even if they could keep up with climate
change. As a result, whole communities and ecosystems may fail to

operate as they have evolved to do over thousands, even millions, of years. Under such conditions, species may not be able to adapt through natural selection as they have done in the past because the speed of climate change is simply too fast for evolution to keep up.

The net effect is double trouble for nature, double in the sense of a long-recognized threat, habitat fragmentation, now playing on a whole new field, accelerated global climate change. Under those circumstances, it is all too easy to envision many plants and animals being pressed against the boundaries of their already-diminished ranges. Where species are already confined to protected nature reserves—the plight of charismatic species like elephants, lions, tigers, pandas, grizzly bears, the great apes, and many, many others—changing climate pushes them inevitably out of the protected region (say, a national park) and into surrounding regions where their life is squeezed out because potential habitats there have been destroyed, or because their presence conflicts too much with people's other interests. Down that path lies extinction for many of the species, communities, and ecosystems we have spent decades trying to protect. The result would be not only a different Earth, but an impoverished Earth, with the overall effect much like taking a color portrait and rendering it in black and white, or stripping all the harmonic notes out of a symphony.

Luckily, there is something else different about Earth today: for the first time in humanity's history, we have both the knowledge and the technology to chart at least the broad paths we want the future to follow. No other generation in history has been so uniquely poised to exercise those uniquely human qualities, foresight and directed action. In the case of global warming we are in the arguably fortunate position of knowing it's here and probably will get worse, but also having the ability to slow it; we know that many species are in trouble and that only our concerted efforts will enable them, and thereby the ecosystems of which they are a part, to survive. The trick now, of course, is to actually use our foresight and abilities not only to dodge but also to deflect the bullets heading our way—including, perhaps especially, the ones aimed squarely at Earth's ecological heart.

Chapter 2

Behind Nature's Heartbeat

Give me land, lots of land, under starry skies above . . .
don't fence me in . . .
let me ride to the ridge where the West commences,
gaze upon the moon until I lose my senses,
can't look at hobbles and I can't stand fences . . .
don't fence me in.

—Gene Autry, from the song "Don't Fence Me In,"
written by Cole Porter and Robert Fletcher, 1934

[Ecosystems] are the basic units of nature on the face of the
Earth.

—Alfred G. Tansley, 1935[1]

IT WOULD be hard to find two more different
people than Gene Autry and Alfred Tansley. Autry was an old-time
country western singer and actor I watched perform when I was a little kid with a dripping sno-cone, as twilight began to cool the dusty,
sun-parched rodeo grounds at the Colorado State Fair. Tansley, on
the other hand, was a famous Oxford botantist and ecologist I first
learned about in a university classroom. They lived a continent, a
generation, and a culture apart.

Autry grew up in Texas and Oklahoma, coming of age in the
American West just before the Dust Bowl years. He worked as teleg-
rapher after high school and played his guitar, eventually parlaying

his talents first into radio fame, then movies and television. He had his first big hit in 1932, about the time Tansley was thinking hard about what an ecosystem was. Tansley, born and raised in London, was a product of Victorian times. After attending University College in London and Cambridge University, he took a post as lecturer in botany at Cambridge, then resigned that to broaden himself intellectually by studying psychology with Sigmund Freud. By the time Autry's singing and movie career was taking off, Tansley had become a professor of botany at Oxford University, where he was making major scientific contributions, not only in botany, but also in ecology and conservation biology—way ahead of his time.

As different as these two men were, there was a common denominator: each communicated something about nature. One came at it from an artistic perspective, celebrating the way that wide-open landscapes make us feel, a definition of nature that resonates with some people—no fences, solitude, and open spaces stretching as far as the eye can see. There are still places like that, though they are getting harder and harder to find. The other came at nature from science—identifying nature's building blocks and trying to figure out how they fit together. The difference in the ways the two men thought about nature illustrates two points.

First, although "nature" means different things to different people, it means *something* to most people. Toward one end of the scale is a more impressionistic view, toward the other end the focus is on the hard facts of nature, and there are infinite gradations in between. Second, the impressions we form of nature and the facts of ecosystems are inextricably intertwined: impressions of nature are feelings, but ecosystems are what evoke these feelings. As ecosystems change, so does the feel of a place, and thereby the human experience of nature. In the context of global warming, the relevant question is this: Will the changes we see in the coming decades, both in terms of how ecosystems work and the resulting conceptions of nature, fall outside the realm of all previous human experience?

Some would say that nature is already cooked. By altering Earth's atmosphere and taking over so much of the planet for the needs and wants of people, we've changed ecosystems everywhere, which could be (and has been) interpreted as the end of nature.[2] That view sets us (the bad guys) apart from ecology and nature (the good guys), a view not without philosophical and political merit. But that view steps around an important fact: ever since the first *Homo sapiens*—and even further back, *Homo neandertalensis*, *Homo erectus*, *Australopithecus*, and everything in between—first ate a plant, killed an animal, or was eaten by something more wily than ourselves, we have been part of, not apart from, nature and local and global ecosystems. Viewed from that perspective, we *are* Earth's ecology and we *are* nature, every bit as much as the standing crop of some ten to thirty million other species with whom we've been riding on the planet. What defines ecosystems and ultimately nature itself is how we and all those other species interact with each other and with those parts of the world that aren't alive, but which shape life: oceans, mountains, storms, and the like. In that view, nature hasn't "ended" just because we are changing the atmosphere, any more than it ended when cyanobacteria began to enrich the air with oxygen some 2.3 billion years ago (eventually making Earth habitable for animals like us). Nature, and the ecosystems which define it, are alive in this sense, but like most living things, they are moving targets, irrevocably changing from generation to generation.

Therein lies both a blessing and a curse. The blessing is that, even as an ecosystem evolves through time, it retains an ineffable but enduring character—an impression of nature—that hangs on no matter how much the specifics change. The curse is that there is no golden spike to mark which ecosystem, which point in nature, which point in time is the "right" point to be at. With gradual change and moving targets of "rightness," the death of an ecosystem and of nature can—from the human perspective—sneak up insidiously and silently, one little injury here, another there, until the heartbeat stops before we've even noticed something's wrong.

And that's the problem with global warming's impact on ecosystems. When we're talking about global warming, we're talking about climate. And when we're talking about climate, we're talking about ecosystems: Tansley actually invented the word *ecosystem* in 1935 to provide a name for the interactions between organisms and the "physical factors" of their environment, one of the prime "physical factors" being climate.[3] His definition has since morphed into many variants, but all of them basically regard an ecosystem to be "living organisms (plants, animals, and microorganisms) all interacting among themselves and with the environment in which they live (soil, climate, water, and light)."[4] Ecosystems come in all shapes and sizes. You can talk about a global ecosystem, which includes all the interacting organisms and environments on earth, or you can talk about the ecosystem of your stomach, which includes all the microbes that live there (the species), the food that goes in (the resources), and the acids (the climate) you generate to help those microbes digest the food.

The critical phrase is "interacting with the environment." Climate—by which we mean how hot or cold, how wet or dry, how long and variable the seasons, how frequent and intense the storms, and so on—is the most significant piece of the environment. Climate controls, or at least correlates with, nearly all other environmental variables; and it loops back to influence, in many cases actually determining, whether or not a particular organism can live in a particular place. Therefore it did not take biologists long to recognize some obvious correlations between how climate zones were distributed on Earth and how plants and animals were distributed.

The best-known correlations between organisms and climate are expressed as actual ecological "rules." For example, in 1833 Constantin Gloger noticed that birds in more humid and warmer areas tended to be darker in color than their counterparts in more arid regions; subsequently this was confirmed to be true for warm-blooded animals in general and became known as Gloger's Rule. (The difference in coloration probably has to do with camouflage in heavily vegetated versus lightly vegetated areas.) In 1847, Bergmann's Rule recognized that within warm-blooded species, animals get larger in cold climates, notably toward the poles. The underlying mechanism was thought to involve heat retention—larger bodies have a smaller surface-to-volume ratio, meaning that less metabolic heat is lost through the skin, all other things being equal. Allen's Rule, proposed in 1877, arises from similar metabolic considerations: it acknowledges that warm-blooded animals native to cold climates have shorter limbs than those native to warm climates.

Besides these rules that focus on how the morphology of animals correlates with climate, there are also many widely recognized relationships between distributions of species—biodiversity if you will—and climate patterns. For instance, the latitudinal (and elevational) gradient of species richness (i.e., how many species live in a given community) recognizes that, in general, more species live in the warm areas near the equator than live farther poleward, and at low elevations rather than high elevations. There is also a close correlation between the climatic characteristics of any place on Earth and the particular species that live there; thus as global warming changes the climate in a given region, so too will it alter which species constitute the ecosystems within that region.

Underlying such correlations between climate and distribution of organisms are causes that can be difficult to tease out. You have to consider basal metabolic rate, for example. Your basal metabolic rate is the amount of energy you expend while resting at room temperature. A high basal metabolic rate means you burn a lot of energy and have to eat a lot of calories just to stay alive, whereas a low basal metabolic rate means you can get by with eating less. If instead of resting at room temperature, you rest outside in the winter, your metabolic rate rises as you burn more calories to generate sufficient heat to keep you warm. This applies to all warm-blooded animals, namely mammals and birds. The link with climate is obvious: there is a certain temperature below which you simply can't eat enough to stay warm, so you die. That "certain temperature" is related to your basal metabolic rate—how efficient you are at generating and retaining heat from the calories you take in. Given this, there should in theory be a relationship between the coldest places certain animals can survive and their metabolic rates—and in fact there is. That is the basis of one of ecology's most recently discovered rules, Root's Rule (or the 2.5 Rule),[5] which recognizes that basal metabolic rate predicts the northernmost extent of many passerine bird species (probably most of the bird species you commonly see outside your window are passerines, a diverse group of perching birds that includes more than half of all bird species, for example, wrens, sparrows, jays, mockingbirds, cardinals, nuthatches, tanagers, thrushes, chickadees, and many others). The magic number is about 2.5—the northern-most range of the passerines Terry Root studied is where the energy needed to survive the winter is not more than 2.5 times the basal metabolic rate (measured in kilojoules per day).

Of course, winter temperatures, and any other climate variable you care to name, fluctuate from year to year. So a key part of figuring out the relationship between climate change and the fate of a given species (or, scaling up, a given ecosystem) is teasing out what scale of climate fluctuation causes lasting ecological change. Climate can, and does, change at many different scales of space and time. The spatial scales vary from as small as shifting patterns of shade on a single leaf, all the way up to the global gradient of warmer temperatures near the equator. The existence of spatial gradients means that even though we can specify a mean global temperature today for Earth as a whole, that doesn't change the fact that the mean temperature of Alaska is very different than the mean temperature of Florida. And with global warming, the mean temperature of Alaska may warm more than the mean temperature of Florida, meaning ecological effects vary spatially as well.

While spatial gradients are straightforward to think about, species and climate also interact over differing timescales, which can cloud our understanding of their relationships. In a time sense, climate is the average weather for many years. But how many years? That question is at the root of what is meant by timescales of climate change.

Think about climate change from a species point of view—that is, what happens over the entire life span of a species instead of the perspective we usually take, which is thinking about what happens over an average human life span. From a species point of view, if you are a mammal, your average life span (as a species) is somewhere between 1.7 and 2.5 million years. If you're a plant, reptile, or amphibian, the life span is likely somewhat longer; if you're a bird or a fish, perhaps a little shorter.[6] In order to have that long a life span, a species must be able to withstand (or, in an evolutionary sense, adapt to) the broad, slow shifts in climate that are natural as tracked over many millions of years, and also the more rapid fluctuations in climate that are nested within individual million-year time slices. Those more rapid fluctuations include cyclical changes over hundreds of thousands of years, back-and-forth drifts that take place over thousands of years, and changes that occur over hundreds of years or even just decades.

The climate changes that occur over millions of years are those that are driven by plate tectonics, sometimes called continental drift. For most of Earth's history the continents have been drifting around the globe, very slowly of course; presently the rate is between about 0.5 and 10 centimeters per year (0.2–4 inches), depending on which plate the continent is riding on. A half centimeter per year adds up to 10 kilometers (6 miles) over the life span of a typical species; at 10 centimeters per year, we're talking 200 kilometers (124 miles). Though slow, that amount of shifting around means that the shapes of continents and ocean basins are subtly changing; as continents bump into each other or are subducted beneath oceanic plates, they crumple such that mountains begin to build and plateaus are pushed up. These changes in turn affect the way ocean currents flow, and the way air currents flow around the globe—that is, climate. In effect, then, a species plays out its life span on a slowly changing climatic stage, at a timescale often called the tectonic scale (because it is driven by plate tectonics).

Usually climatic change at the tectonic timescale is no big deal. It is slow enough that species can generally shift around on the landscape (or seascape) as needed for their survival. Also, if selective pressures are changing as a result of tectonic-scale climate change, they are changing at a rate slow enough for evolution to keep up. Even some of the fastest tectonic-scale rates of climate change are not very dramatic by current global warming standards; for example, a rise in global temperature of about 3–4°C (5.4–7.2°F) over 1.5 million years.[7] In current business-as-usual scenarios, we will see about that same amount of global warming in just the next one hundred years.[8]

Those are pretty precise temperature estimates for millions of years ago. Where do they come from? The short answer is from an unlikely marriage between nuclear chemistry and paleontology, which paved the way for using ocean-dwelling creatures called foraminifera as paleothermometers. A typical foraminiferan, or "foram" for short, is composed of a single cell covered by a shell (also called a test), from which threadlike pieces of ectoplasm emerge. Picture a very tiny sphere (or cone or disk—they come in many varieties) for the shell, with holes through which strings of the gooey stuff are squeezing out, and you begin to get the idea. The entire organism is typically less than a millimeter in diameter (four hundreths of an inch), though some species grow up to several millimeters, and the largest one known is 20 centimeters (8 inches). It is the shells of the millimeter-sized (and smaller) ones that are important for temperature estimates, because such forams are abundant in the oceans, and when they die, their shells sink to the bottom and become fossilized in the mud.

Over the last several decades, samples of that mud—and the foram shells within it—have been brought up from the ocean bottoms in the form of cores drilled by oceanographic researchers. Those cores are cylinders about as thick as a grown man's fist and sometimes tens of meters long. Each one is a column of prehistory: by slicing them at regular intervals, the fossil forams that lived at successive slices of time can be compared—geologically youngest at top, oldest at bottom, back through thousands and millions of years.

By 1947, research voyages by scientists from Columbia University and elsewhere began to gear up, bringing back sediment cores from all the world's oceans. Paleontologists used the forams from those cores to figure out how old each successively deeper slice of mud was, as an aid to reconstructing the geological history of the ocean basins. But they also began to recognize a paleoclimatic signal. Certain species in the modern oceans lived only in waters of certain temperatures, so as those species came and went, visible as fossils in the cores, it indicated changes in water temperature through time. Eventually equations called transfer functions, which relate the foram species assemblages (that is, which particular species combined to form a given community) to sea surface temperatures, were worked out, allowing measures of temperature through time as assemblages of species were tracked down the core.[9] That was the paleontology part.

The nuclear chemistry part comes from Harold Urey, who made a discovery that revolutionized geology and climate science—and, when combined with the transfer function approach, ultimately provides a basis for showing us how out of the ordinary today's global warming really is. Urey found what amounts to a molecular paleothermometer in foram shells. While at Columbia University Urey had won the 1934 Nobel Prize in Chemistry for his discovery of a heavy isotope of hydrogen, deuterium, but left there to take a faculty post at the University of Chicago in 1945. During World War II he was Director of War Research, Atomic Bomb Project,[10] an experience that left him after the war "eager to do some new research on a problem that, as he put it, 'was not useful.'"[11] A "not useful" problem that interested him at the time was whether the dinosaurs died because they got too hot or too cold. To get at that, he needed a way to estimate earth's temperature over long expanses of geological time.[12, 13]

Urey reasoned that since he had developed equations that related isotope fractionation to temperature, and there were all those fossil foram shells sitting in cores stored in warehouses, if he could just identify the ratios of certain isotopes locked up in the fossils, then he could estimate what the temperature of the seawater had been when the forams were alive. He went back to Chicago and came up with a plan to apply newly refined techniques of mass spectrometry to the fossil shells. In spite of his Nobel prize work and his helping to develop the atomic bomb, he called extracting isotopic information from foram shells "the toughest chemical problem I ever faced."[14]

So he did what any smart professor does when facing a complicated task. He put a graduate student on it, in this case, Cesare Emiliani. Urey and Emiliani were building on knowledge that as forams precipitate their shells, they incorporate two isotopes of oxygen into them: a lighter one, oxygen-16, and a heavier one, oxygen-18, both of which come from the seawater in which they live. Urey had figured out that the ratio of oxygen-16 to oxygen-18 in the foram shells depended in a large part on the temperature of the water that the forams were living in. Emiliani took successively deeper foram samples from cores that had been recovered by previous oceanographic expeditions,[15] and he carefully measured the ratio of oxygen-16 to oxygen-18 in each sample. He then used Urey's equations to convert the ratios to paleotemperatures. From that painstaking work— remember there were no computers or even hand calculators back then—Emiliani finally demonstrated that regular fluctuations from cold to warm had taken place through the past 300,000 years.

It took decades of refinements by other scientists, including adjustments for factors other than ocean temperature that contributed to the oxygen-16 to oxygen-18 ratio, before the isotopic paleothermometer became as useful as it is today.[16] Nevertheless, what Emiliani demonstrated in 1955 was groundbreaking for climate science. Not only did he show that the paleothermometer worked in practice as well as in theory; his data also clearly illustrated that embedded within those long-term tectonic-scale climate changes caused by continental drift, there were more rapid fluctuations of climate that cycled between very cold times and very warm times.

Today we recognize that those cycles occur because of a more or less regular climatic pulse called the Milanković cycles, which over the past two million years have caused some 39 oscillations between very cold glacial times and warmer interglacial times. Within the last million years, each glacial-interglacial cycle has lasted about 100,000 years, with the cold times typically lasting much longer than the warm times. The Milanković cycles are so named because in 1941 a Serbian engineer and geophysicist, Milutin Milanković, published results of laborious calculations demonstrating that the sunshine energy that hits the top of the atmosphere—solar insolation—varied through time.[17] Milanković showed that differences in solar insolation through time arose from slight, more or less cyclical irregularities in the eccentricity, axial tilt, and precession of the Earth's orbit. (Eccentricity refers to the Earth's actual path as it orbits the sun, a path which varies from being nearly a circle to being more of an oval; axial tilt is how much the Earth tilts back and forth on its axis in a single plane; and precession is how much it wobbles, like a slowing-down top, around its axis).[18]

Because the three orbital cycles are fairly regular, it is possible to calculate how much insolation will strike any given latitude at any given time in the present, past, or future. That's what Milanković did. His calculations predicted that we should go through climate cycles that alternate between very cold times and reasonably warm times, so he suggested orbital variations as the principal mechanism behind the glacial-interglacial cycles. What Emiliani observed from his foram paleothermometers was consistent with what Milanković had suggested, but it took another twenty years before refinements in geological dating, in applying the transfer function and isotope pale-othermometer techniques to longer cores, and in statistical manipulations of the resulting time-series information made it clear that Milanković was right on the money. In 1976, the orbital variations were dubbed the "Pacemaker of the Ice Ages."[19]

That pacemaker is quite a bit faster than the tectonic-scale climate changes. The shift from a glacial to interglacial period, for example, amounts to a change of some 5°C (9°F) globally averaged over five thousand years. And embedded within each glacial or interglacial period, as well as within shifts between the two, are short-term climate fluctuations that heat things up or cool them down for anywhere from a few decades up to a few centuries. And nested within those, of course, are yearly, seasonal, and even daily fluctuations in weather.

What all this means from a species perspective is that many scales of climate change are in fact natural, from the slow tectonic scale, to the fast changes embedded within glacial and interglacial times, to the even more dramatic changes that characterize a switch from glacial to interglacial. So why worry about global warming, which is just one more scale of climate change? The problem is that global warming is essentially off the scale of normal in two ways: the rate at which this climate change is taking place, and how different the "new" climate is compared to what came before.

The rate of climate change is the amount of change (measured in degrees) divided by the number of years over which the change took place. If we take as an example the tectonic scale of climate change, we see that the fastest rates are around 4°C (7.2°F) per 1.5 million years, or about 0.000001°C per year. At the last major natural global warming event, the transition from the last glacial age to our present interglacial (the Milanković scale), the rate was about 5°C per 5,000 years, or about 0.001 °C per year. At yet a quicker timescale, the Medieval Warm Period, which as the name implies was a warm spell that commenced around 1,150 years ago and lasted 400 years, the rate was about 1 °C per 100 years, or 0.01 °C per year. Notice anything suspicious? The fewer the number of years over which we calculate the rate, the faster the rate appears. You can carry this right down to the difference between winter and summer, or day and night, which would give you tremendously high rates of temperature change. The reason rates appear faster when calculated over shorter time intervals is because short-term climate changes in one direction are typically counterbalanced by short-term changes in the other direction as you add more time—summer by winter, day by night, and so forth. So in order to figure out how fast current rates of global warming are compared to past "natural" rates, it is necessary to adjust mathematically for the varying time intervals over which the rates are measured.

When that is done, the rates are still scary. Using the Intergovernmental Panel on Climate Change (IPCC) projections for the future, the best-case scenario is that the rate of warming over the next hundred years will be 10 percent more than what we saw in the Medieval Warm Period, but the most likely scenario is that things will heat up from 100 percent to 300 percent faster. If the possibility of 10 percent–faster heating gives you any comfort, don't forget that it is equally as likely that the worst-case scenario will prevail—a warming rate of some 300 percent faster than the Medieval Warm Period. The expected rates are equally sobering if we compare them to standardized rates for the last glacial-interglacial transition, or any other natural global warming rate.[20]

Not only are we heating up way faster than normal, we started out relatively hot—remember we are in an interglacial swing of the Milanković cycles. Assuming even the lowest reasonable estimate (1.1 °C or 2 °F in the next century) for global warming, by 2050—you may live to witness it—Earth will be hotter than humans have ever seen it, that is, hotter than it has been in at least 160,000 years, which is the age of the oldest known *Homo sapiens* fossil. If we begin looking at the worst-case scenarios (heating of 4 °C to 6 °C or 7.2 °F to 10.8 °F), by 2100 Earth will be hotter than it has been in three million years. Three million years ago, not one species of mammal or bird that lives on Earth today was alive, as far as we know. Any way you look at it, by the time kids born today are grandparents, they will be living in a hothouse compared to the world in which people and many other animal species evolved.

It won't actually help that in the natural course of Milanković cycles we should be heading into an ice age in a few thousand years, because human-induced global warming has overridden the natural cool-down required for that to happen. For example, a key trigger to an ice age is that, as climate naturally cools, glaciers begin to grow. They reach a critical size at which they reflect so much heat (because light-colored ice is more reflective than dark-colored soil or vegetation) that they set up a natural feedback to cool Earth even more and thus grow even more. With global warming, glaciers are melting so fast all over the globe that within as little as fifteen years not even Glacier National Park will have any. Given that, the chances of setting up the natural feedback required to trigger an ice age are slim indeed.

Because we've interfered with such natural feedbacks, probably also off-scale is how long the "new" globally warmed climate will persist before reverting back to the "old" climate. Getting rid of greenhouse gases that have accumulated in the atmosphere is not a fast process—even if we could stop all greenhouse emissions today (not going to happen!), all else being equal, it would take centuries for the atmospheric composition to approach what was natural before the Industrial Revolution began. Even the best-case calculations, which assume major reductions in CO_2 emissions within the next 100 years, show global temperatures stabilizing at about 2°C (3.6°F) higher than normal, with anticipated worst cases being 4–6°C (7.2–10.8°F) higher than normal, or more. "Stabilizing" in this sense means global temperature staying more or less constant for at least hundreds, probably thousands of years. In short, as far as generations of humans are concerned, we probably never will revert back to the "old" climate. A hot Earth is here to stay, at least for as long as large numbers of people are on it.

That's why big changes in ecosystems are on the horizon. Ecosystems are not only the sum of the species within them—many of which will be affected individually by global warming—but the many ways those species interact with each other and with the environment. All those parts and interactions make ecosystems "complex systems"—essentially a bunch of different individual pieces (species, in the case of ecosystems) held together by some kind of network of interactions. The relationships between parts of the network are nonlinear, meaning that a change of a certain magnitude in one part can either greatly magnify or disappear as it travels through the network. Not all parts are equal—some parts may be redundant, meaning their removal may not have much of an effect, and some may be critical, meaning that their removal causes major disruptions. Complex systems are dynamic—they are always changing, but they tend not to change very fast for a couple of reasons. First, there are so many interacting parts that if you push at one part of the system, the push can often be absorbed in other parts. Second, complex systems are influenced by their past states—new innovation can only be built out of the pieces that are already in the system—and future states are influenced by the present state.

The good news is that all this means that complex systems are pretty robust and resilient. Unless something unusual happens, they are slow to change, and even when they are buffeted by events from outside the system they tend to return to the same stable state. Ecosystems are no exception, as we'll see in later chapters. The bad news is that when ecosystems (like other complex systems) do change, they tend to do so catastrophically and, for all practical purposes, irreversibly. That is because they tend to reach what are known as alternative stable states, and they shift rapidly from one to another because of threshold events.[21] Once a threshold is crossed, it becomes very difficult to return to a previous stable state, both because of the low likelihood of replicating previous conditions, and because another threshold has to be crossed to get back.

One way to envision thresholds and alternative stable states is with the oft-repeated analogy of a rowboat rocking on the waves. One stable state is upright; the alternative one is capsized. Whatever flips the boat is the threshold event. Threshold events can be caused by slow, accumulating change, such as having more and more people move to one side of the boat. Each addition of a person is a gradual change which has no effect on the stable state until you add one person too many—at which point you flip to the capsized state. Threshold events can also be fast changes of extraordinary magnitude—like a rogue wave. Ecosystems have evolved to rock back and forth on the normal waves of climate change—those at the tectonic, Milanković, and Medieval Warm Period scales, for example. Even so, every now and then a climatic threshold is crossed that flips local ecosystems into an alternative stable state.

The Sahara Desert gives us an example. From 10,000 years ago to around 5,500 years ago, the stable state was verdant, perennial vegetation with lots of wetlands. Then, within as little as several decades, that vegetation disappeared and the new stable state became the parched, bare Sahara we know today. The threshold was crossed because summertime solar insolation in the northern hemisphere has been steadily declining for 9,000 years, due to natural climatic variation caused by the Milanković cycles. Early on, high insolation drove strong summer monsoons into northern Africa, which irrigated the Sahara. Between 5,000 and 6,000 years ago, summer insolation dropped to a critical threshold, about 470 watts per square meter or 4.2 percent above modern values. Climate models show that below that insolation value, summer monsoons were not so readily generated, which in turn caused less vegetation cover in the Sahara, which in turn set up climatic feedbacks that further depressed the monsoons, which in turn meant virtually all vegetation was lost.[22] In effect, the ecosystem boat capsized.

With the off-scale global warming that is going on now, we can expect to see more of those ecological thresholds crossed. And they will be of both varieties: one too many people in the boat (as mean global temperature continues to rise gradually), and rogue waves (as global temperature rises abnormally fast and abnormally high, or as extreme weather events, like Hurricane Katrina, become more and more common). That means that on our watch we're moving into a world that will be all but unrecognizable compared to the one that Alfred Tansley studied, that Gene Autry sang about, and that many of us, maybe most, were born into.

On Our Watch

Depending on where you live, if you're a gardener, you may
actually live somewhat south of there.

—Joel M. Lerner, 2007[1]

WHEN I was at Kew Gardens one August day in
2001, it was misty, gray, and moist enough that occasionally I'd have
to wipe the condensed droplets off my glasses, but even so, the air was
warm and summer-soft. I strolled with my family through acres of
rolling, manicured green lawns tastefully intersected by splashes of
colorful flowers and well-placed, perfectly formed trees. On that day
Kew was the quintessential English garden, as it should have been,
given that it is situated ten kilometers southwest of London and that
its unabbreviated name is the Royal Botanic Gardens, Kew. It is, in
fact, exactly what all the world thinks an English garden should look
like. But in 2007, parts of Kew Gardens began to look like what you'd
expect to see in, say, southern France or Spain—a Mediterranean
landscape, with trees like Tuscan olives and cork oaks, and shrubs
like rosemary and lavender.

What Mediterranean plants have in common is an ability to
thrive in climates that are hot and dry in summer and that receive
their limited precipitation mostly as rain in the winter. The interesting thing about the new Mediterranean areas in Kew Gardens is that
they were not planted just as a novelty—they were installed to
demonstrate how the quintessential English garden is going to look

33

within the lifetime of most gardeners living in Britain today. That is, how gardens will grow in an English climate that is not only considerably warmer than today, but considerably drier as well, and where rain falls in a different season.

Replacing delphiniums and lupines with grapevines and citrus is a compelling way to visualize what otherwise may appear as dry statistics. If you trace weather patterns since 1659, when detailed records were first kept in England, you find that most of the years since 1989 were hotter than any that came before.[2] Over the last thirty years, the English spring (as defined by events such as leaves unfolding) has been arriving six days earlier and autumn (defined by events such as leaf coloring) has been arriving two days later each *decade*. This means that in the year 2000 the growing season was 24 days longer than in 1970. In the last decade and a half we have seen the longest thermal growing seasons, the most hot days per year, and the highest mean annual temperatures since record-keeping of such statistics began in 1770.

It is not only such indisputable observations that are changing the concept of English gardens, but also climatic models that indicate similar trends will continue over the next century. As interpreted in a report issued by the University of Reading Centre for Horticulture and Landscape, those models predict that: "By the 2080s a large part of southern England and South Wales will be 4°C (7.2°F) warmer in summer and 3–3.5°C (5.4–6.3°F) warmer in winter, while in northwest Scotland summers will be 3°C warmer and winters 2–2.5°C (3.6–4.5°F) warmer."[3] Goodbye, beech trees; hello, fantail palms. That's no joke.

Gardeners outside of England are also worrying about what to plant. By 2007, gardens at opposite ends of the world were reporting unusual events. In the Shanghai Botanic Garden, gardenias and sakuras bloomed in February, some 15 to 20 days earlier than normal. That was on the heels of a first-time-ever simultaneous bloom of chrysanthemums, orchids, and osmanthus a few months earlier, in November 2006. In New York, at the Brooklyn Botanic Gardens, cherry trees and Japanese apricot trees began to blossom three months earlier than normal (in January instead of March or April).

The New York Botanical Garden, instead of snow in January, had blooming snowdrops, witch hazels, and the "Spring's Promise" camellia, along with abnormally early flowering of more than 15 other species.[4]

Those New York records reflected a wider phenomenon in the United States. The U.S. Department of Agriculture has produced a gardener's bible of sorts, a "hardiness zone map" that in essence tells whether a plant you want to grow is suited to the climate zone (the zone being defined by combinations of temperature, moisture, frost-free days, and so on) in which you live. But now gardening experts have noticed that the map based on climate data from 1974 through 1986 is increasingly wrong; climate has actually changed since then. A more recent map, using climate data from 1990–2004, basically shifts the old USDA zones north by a zone or two, such that living in Maryland today is a lot like living in Virginia in 1970, from a plant's perspective—which is what Joel Lerner was talking about when he said you might live south of where you think you do.

It's one thing to notice changes in gardens that seem to correlate with historic global warming. After all, garden species, for the most part, are species that wouldn't be there anyway were it not for people deliberately planting them. But ecologists have very recently begun to worry as they notice similar, telling changes in "naturally occurring" species, that is, in the plants and animals that have found their way into or out of regions without the help of people. Geographic ranges are shifting, biological clocks are falling out of sync with respect to climate zones and some species are disappearing from places we think they ought to be. The list of species that seem affected by climate change, as judged by peer-reviewed scientific literature, is becoming disturbingly long, and it gets longer with each passing month. Species seem to be responding to climate change in unprecedented ways, though how they *can* respond is limited by the extent of human-caused habitat fragmentation, introduction of exotic competitors, and the sheer numbers of humans on the planet.

A little history clarifies just how fast ecosystems are changing, and how fast our knowledge about the extent of global warming's effect on species is growing. In the early 1980s, when as a graduate student I was first thinking about ecology and climate change, the big debates in our seminar rooms at the University of Washington were not *how* climate change might influence species, but *if* climate was any more important than competition and other interactions between species in controlling where a species might thrive. From my limited perspective as a student, the species-interaction side appeared to be winning. You were hard pressed to find an article in a mainline ecology journal suggesting that seemingly minor differences in climate were the driving force behind a species' success or failure in a given area.

Somewhere in the mid- to late-1980s, though, the tide began to shift as the evidence for global warming itself began to accumulate and as big-thinking paleoecologists like Tom Webb from Brown University coordinated the work of many individual scientists to gather vast sets of ecological, paleontological, geological, and climatological data from throughout the world.[5] When put together, those data from different scientific disciplines—fossil pollen, modern species distributions, modern climate patterns, climate models, and sedimentary information about lake levels, to name a few— made a convincing argument that plant species had in the past marched around the landscape to follow their preferred climate as it changed. In the case of plants, "marching" means that their seeds are dispersed into new areas by wind or animals; if the new area is favorable for growth, seedlings survive and thus the plant species adds to its geographic range.

Simultaneously, climatic models were lending credence to some previously speculative explanations about why certain mammal species that do not live together today coexisted in the same place some 10,000–15,000 years ago. For example, in the Appalachians the taiga vole (*Microtus xanthagnathus*) and the thirteen-lined ground squirrel (*Spermophilus tridecemlineatus*) are found contemporaneously in fossil deposits that date to around 14,000 years old. These little rodents do not live anywhere near each other today. The taiga vole, a fluffy, brown, short-tailed critter that would nestle into the palm of your hand, today lives only in northern Canada and

Alaska, where its favorite habitat is dense forests of black spruce. In contrast, the thirteen-lined ground squirrel, so named for the elaborate set of racing stripes down its back, today is found only in the southern parts of Alberta where taiga voles are absent, down the length of the Great Plains, and only as far east as lowland central Ohio. As a species, it favors grasslands. Because such past associations of species have no analogs in nature today, they were dubbed "no-analog assemblages." The explanation that paleontologists had come up with to explain no-analog assemblages was a climatic one, namely a less seasonal climate. "Seasonality" refers to the difference between summer and winter—the paleontologists were thinking that if winters were a little warmer than they are today, and summers were a little cooler, then those long-gone associations between species would make sense. Under those circumstances, southern or low-elevation species limited by severe winter cold could extend their range north and upward (which explained the fossils of thirteen-lined ground squirrels in the Appalachians), and northern species limited by summer warmth could extend their range south and to lower elevations (which explained the fossil taiga voles found alongside the thirteen-lined ground squirrels).[6] In fact, that sort of reduced seasonality is just what the climate models that were developed in the mid-1980s had predicted for the times and places that the no-analog species were found together. And the vegetation records developed by the palynologists were also consistent with the kinds of habitats in which the no-analog mammal species would be expected.

By the late 1980s, the convergence of these different kinds of information began to prompt some serious thinking about how global climate change might really affect individual species. Seemingly all of a sudden, in 1991 scientific papers pointing to the importance of global warming for individual species, for communities, and for ecosystems began to roll off the presses. Evidence for the effects of global warming on myriad species then began to gain momentum.

Here's what the numbers look like. In searches of the electronic database Web of Science, no papers that combine the key words "ecology" and "global warming" are listed before 1991.[7, 8] In 1991 and 1992, a total of 10 studies documenting or discussing the ecological effects of global warming were published. From 1993 through 1997, the rate of publication tripled, with 32 more experiments, observations, or discussions published during those five years. From 1998 to 2002, the pace accelerated—45 more papers in five years. And from 2003 through 2007, our published knowledge nearly doubled, with an additional 81 studies hitting the science journals.

If you search more broadly, still only within the Web of Science, by using different key words such as "ecology" and "climate change," the numbers are even more impressive—by my last count, 964 articles in respected scientific journals, with the first of those appearing in 1990.[9] Searches that look for effects of global warming on certain kinds of organisms give an indication of the breadth of life in which scientists are seeing responses: plants (as of 2007, 449 papers published, earliest in 1991), mammals (46 papers, earliest 1992), birds (73 papers, earliest 1992), reptiles (13 papers, earliest 1992), amphibians (11 papers, earliest 1995), fish (154 papers, earliest 1990), insects (40 papers, earliest 1992), and marine organisms (334 papers, earliest 1990).[10] In fact, by last count upwards of a thousand species—including plants, bugs, fish, amphibians, reptiles, birds, and mammals—seem to be showing responses to climate change.[11]

Even more telling than statistics on publications are the increasing numbers of species scientists are finding to have responded to global warming in recent years. Global-change ecologists have now compiled the individual examples by using a technique called meta-analysis.[12] Some indication of the emerging trends can be gleaned by considering two broad meta-analyses published in the same issue of the journal *Nature* in 2003: one by Terry Root and colleagues, the other by Camille Parmesan and Gary Yohe.[13] Using different approaches, both studies arrived at the same conclusion: global warming is already smudging ecosystems with its fingerprints.[14]

The Root collaborative study found 1,468 species that had exhibited some sort of biological shift over at least ten years through which trends in changing temperature had also occurred. Of the species they looked at, 81.1 percent (1,190 species) changed as one would predict from what was known about their physiology—for example, temperate-latitude species extending their geographic range toward the pole, or budding earlier in the spring, as temperature warmed. The changes were fast enough to discern in a human lifetime, especially from a bird's-eye view. The North American common murre (*Uria aalge*), for example, has been breeding on average 24 days earlier per decade for the past 25 years—two months earlier in 2000 than they were in 1975! The murres were one of 694 species that the Root collaborative study determined had shifted their spring phenologies at the same time climate was changing. (Phenology is the interaction between the yearly life cycle of a species and the yearly cycle of climate). Of those species, the significant shifts occurred in the spring, with breeding, budding, migrating, and so on taking place—on average for all species, 5.1 days earlier per decade over the last 50 years.

The Parmesan-Yohe analysis looked at a lot of the same data that the Root group did, but in a different way. Instead of only considering species that had shifted coincident with climate trends, they also considered examples that were matched with short-term climate cycles, and those in which changes did not seem to correspond with any climate event. Their logic was that publications might be biased toward reporting only results that demonstrated some sort of biological change through time, since often journals don't publish studies (if scientists even bother to write them up) for which the overall conclusion is "nothing happened." To guard against that bias, Parmesan and Yohe used only publications that reported on multiple species, and which included species for which "nothing happened" as well as species that changed in some attribute through time. Of the 893 species for which they found adequate information, some 51 percent either showed stable distributions through time or distributional fluctuations that neither supported nor refuted expectations of climate change. The remaining 434 species, however, showed clear range shifts that corresponded in time with climate shifts. Eighty percent of those shifted their ranges as one would predict from their physiology or other criteria given the nature of the climate changes—for a subset of 99 species of birds, butterflies, and alpine herbs these shifts were on average 6.1 kilometers (3.8

miles) per decade poleward or 6.1 meters (20 feet) upward in elevation. Like the Root study, the Parmesan-Yohe study also found overwhelming evidence for trends towards advancement of spring
phenology—62 percent of the 677 species they looked at demonstrated effects such as earlier spring breeding in frogs, nesting in
birds, flowering in plants, budding in trees, and the arrival of
migrant butterflies and birds.

What all this means is that if you are middle-aged and collected
butterflies as a kid, today you very possibly wouldn't find them in the
same fields, or in the same alpine meadows, as you did back then. If
you like to watch birds, you're seeing them in places you didn't use
to see them thirty or forty years ago, or not seeing them in places
and times of year where and when you expect them. And if pollen
makes you sneeze, your allergies are probably kicking in a little earlier in the year. If you think you've been noticing those things, you
haven't been alone. In fact, most of the observations included in the
meta-analyses come from sources like bird-watchers, butterfly collectors, and botanists—and so we know much more about the long-
term trends in those kinds of organisms than in others. Only a few
examples of mammal, reptile, amphibian, fish, or marine species
were included in these meta-analyses.[15] The right kind of data for
those organisms simply haven't been gathered in a systematic way
for long enough—there is, for example, no history of organized
"Christmas Mammal Counts," whereas the Audubon Christmas Bird
Count has been an annual bird-watcher event since at least 1900.
And whereas collecting butterflies and pinning them to a board has
long been looked upon as a favorable pastime for budding natural
historians, doing the same with, say, fish or mammals would raise
some eyebrows.

Even so, what we are beginning to learn about the little-sampled
kinds of species is paralleling the more extensive, more conclusive
plant-butterfly-bird stories. Take mammals. Given that one of the
big evolutionary breakthroughs of mammals was homeothermy, or
the ability to regulate body temperature, you might expect that
mammals would be very resilient to climate change. Yet, there are
signs that many of today's mammal species—among them the mar-

mots and polar bears mentioned in earlier chapters—are feeling the effects of the heat just as much as the birds and butterflies. Such effects are becoming apparent in subtle and not-so-subtle ways.

The subtle ways involve interactions between climate, vegetation, and reproductive success. A good example involves Donner, Blitzen, and Rudolph the Red-Nosed Reindeer—whether or not you believe in Santa Claus, reindeer are real. Also known as caribou, reindeer are the species *Rangifer tarandus*. They don't live exactly at the North Pole, but do roam the arctic tundra, and the northern forests of Alaska, Canada, Greenland, Russia, and Scandinavia. They have been studied for years because they play an important role in arctic ecosystems; they also are important economically and culturally for at least 20 ethnic groups of indigenous peoples, such as the Saami of Fennoscandia and the Tsaatan of Mongolia. Recently those studies have established a strong link between healthy reindeer populations and certain aspects of both winter and summer climate.[16]

Especially important is the amount and timing of winter precipitation—snow. Comparatively warm, snow-filled winters are bad for reindeer, decreasing body mass and male offspring, because more snow entails greater energetic drain in moving and less success in foraging. That is, the reindeer simply run out of steam as they plow through heavy snow, trying to find food.

Warm summers are also bad, for an entirely different reason: the bugs multiply and affect reindeer reproduction. You can appreciate this problem if you've ever walked around in Alaska, or another arctic or alpine region, in July without bug spray or at least a nice smelly cigar. With a 2–4°C (3.6–7.2°F) increase in summer temperature, increased harassment of reindeer by bugs like mosquitoes, warble flies (whose larvae travel around under the skin until they break through), and nasal botflies (which use the reindeers' nasal passages as nurseries for their larvae) leads to a 7 percent decrease in feeding and energy-expensive avoidance behaviors at a time when the animal is supposed to be building up fat reserves for the winter. Blood loss can be up to 125 g/day (4.5 ounces/day)—that's like sticking a needle into your arm and draining the blood until your measuring cup is a little over half full. Try that every day for a week and see how energetic you feel

afterward. No wonder, then, that summers of severe insects can be followed by increased reindeer mortality during the next winter, and
decreased pregnancy rates in the females that survive.[17]

The problem is that both winters and summers are getting warmer and wetter in the arctic, remarkably so. By 2080, winter temperatures are likely to rise between 2.5°C (4.5°F) and a whopping 14°C
(25.2°F) and summers from 4.0–7.5°C (7.2–15.5°F); winter precipitation will increase from 5–80 percent, and summer precipitation
from 10–20 percent. The reindeer are going to be getting it from both sides.

In the past, increased summer temperatures alone seemed enough
to diminish reindeer numbers in regions where we have the right
kind of information. During the last ice age, between 12,000 and
60,000 years ago, reindeer were common in southwestern France.
We know this both from the exquisite cave paintings left by prehistoric artists, and also from the hundreds of fossil bones the reindeer
left behind. When archaeologists Don Grayson and Françoise
Delpech have looked at those bones, they found an interesting
thing.[18] They matched the dated layers from which the bones came
with the paleoclimatic signals afforded by fossil pollen from other
sites in France, and they discovered that during the times when summers were coolest, reindeer bones were most abundant. The times
with warmer summers had fewer reindeer bones. And the reindeer
disappeared altogether when the climate warmed into its present
interglacial position, beginning around 12,000 years ago.

In some instances the climatic effects of global warming
on mammal species are not very subtle at all. The mammals just get
too hot. There is a furry little short-eared cousin of the rabbit called
a pika (*Ochotona princeps*), which you can't find anymore on some of
the mountaintops of the northwestern Basin and Range region of
northern Nevada and southern Oregon. In fact, 25 percent of the
populations of pikas throughout the Basin and Range have disappeared within the last century. We know this because mammalogists
recorded the presence of pikas on 25 of the Great Basin mountaintops in years ranging from 1898 to 1956; nobody bothered to check
again systematically until the mid-1990s, but by that time, six of
those early twentieth-century populations had gone extinct, and one

additional population was down to one individual. Their disappearance fits suspiciously with the timing of globally rising temperatures.
Pikas tend to die of heat stress if they are outside even briefly in what
we would consider fairly moderate temperatures, say around
25.5–29.4 °C (78–85 °F).[19] That's why they are only on the mountaintops in the Great Basin—as one goes upslope, the temperature cools
by approximately 2 °C (3.6 °F) per 305 meters (1,000 feet) of altitude,
so by going higher pikas can avoid the lethal warm temperatures of
the lowlands. In the last fifty years, though, those lethal temperatures
have been creeping upslope as the average temperature rises in the
Great Basin. The lower altitudinal limit of pikas on a given mountain
range creeps up correspondingly, until the pikas reach the very top of
the mountain. And when that gets too hot, they die. That this is
happening is suggested by matching the mountains on which populations have gone extinct with elevation and temperature. Pikas have
gone extinct mostly on the lower mountaintops (for a given latitude), and only on mountaintops that received 19.6 percent less
annual precipitation and at which daily maximum temperatures during June, July, and August are 7.7–10.2 percent higher as compared
to sites where pikas still live.[20]

Similar trends are showing up on the other side of the world, in
the Chinese Ili pika, *Ochotona iliensis*. That species shows how much
we don't know, and how fast we are losing what we do know—
Ochotona iliensis was only discovered in 1983, and described as a
species in 1986. Now global warming combined with other human
impacts seems to be causing it to disappear altogether.[21]

Being literally left to die at the top of mountaintops as climate
changes is a likely fate of many mammal species that tend to have
distributions restricted to highlands. That is indicated not only by
the pikas, but also by the past distributional changes of 25 other
species of shrews, squirrels, voles, jumping mice, and marmots analyzed by Rob Guralnick, a University of Colorado paleobiologist.[22]
Guralnick cut his academic teeth during the dot-com era, when he
developed one of the first natural history–oriented Web sites[23] (the
award-winning UCMP site) as a student back in the early 1990s. He
applied those computer skills to assess what chance mountaintop

mammals in the western U. S. stand against global warming as compared to flatlanders. By mining information in museum records, he
was able to tell how far north various species had moved their southern boundary during the last big global warming episode—the shift
from the last glacial into the present interglacial, compared to how
much they had changed their elevational range. He confirmed that
what we are seeing in the pikas today reflects the general response of
mountaintop mammals to global warming: first habitat fragmentation as the valleys heat up and populations withdraw to the higher
slopes, then extinction on the mountaintops that get too hot.[24]

Nowadays climate is warming much faster and starting out hotter
than was the case in the late Pleistocene, ensuring that species in
mountainous places will be affected. Climate-caused casualties of
such species are particularly troubling in today's world because it is in
mountainous places that many of our major nature reserves are confined. The affected species are not just rats, mice, and pikas. For
example, in southern California mountain ranges in the last sixty
years, thirty of the eighty mountaintop populations of bighorn sheep
have gone extinct. That correlates with documented climatic warming in the mountains and habitat fragmentation that prevented
sheep from dispersing across the lowlands to more favorable mountain ranges.[25] Nor does the loss of mountaintop species seem to be
restricted to mammals; the same has been documented for plants,
insect, and amphibian species as well.[26]

Just as troubling as the uphill movements of individual species are
the new interactions between species as they move upslope (or poleward) at different speeds. Some of those new interactions seem to be
bringing a chainsaw to whole branches of the evolutionary tree.
Recall that in the 2003 meta-analyses, amphibians were barely mentioned. Just three years later they became poster children for the dis-
astrous consequences of new species interactions that may result from
global warming. The victims, all extinct within the last two decades,
include at least 73 species of harlequin frogs (67 percent of the entire
genus *Atelopus*). Technically toads, harlequin frogs are so named
because their bright yellow or orange splotches are reminiscent of the
traditional court jester or "harlequin." They are, or at least were,

found near streams cascading through the tropical mountains of Central America, from Costa Rica, to Bolivia, to French Guiana. Like poison-dart frogs, their skin secretes a toxin, but they also have some other tricks. Males will develop functioning ovaries if their testicles are removed. Another victim in the same family (Bufonidae) has been the golden toad, *Bufo periglenes*, a dazzling bright-yellow frog first discovered by science in Costa Rica's Monte Verde cloud forest in 1966 and extinct by 1989.[27]

The killer is epidemic disease, caused by the pathogenic fungus *Batrachochytrium dendrobatidis*. As J. Alan Pounds, lead author of the 2006 study that discovered this troubling link, put it: "Disease is the bullet killing frogs, but climate change is pulling the trigger. Global warming is wreaking havoc on amphibians and will cause staggering losses of biodiversity if we don't do something first."[28, 29] All the more worrying is that these extinctions are occurring in so-called pristine areas, where the human hand is in theory light and which are supposed to be the places where species have the best chance of staying alive.

Batrachochytrium dendrobatidis is a chytrid fungus that works its toad-killing magic by infecting a toad's skin. Tiny little spherical zoosporangia infest the toad's skin cells (or in the case of tadpoles, the mouth), and then produce a microscopic tube that pokes out through the skin, eventually releasing mature zoospores so the cycle can start anew. It's not known exactly how this skin disease kills the toads—the fungus may give off a toxin, or reduce the respiration that takes place through amphibian skin. What is known is that once infected, frogs and toads die within 10 to 18 days.

It is also known that *B. dendrobatidus* thrives only under certain conditions—and it is those conditions that have been increasingly prevalent in the areas where the harlequin frogs have been going extinct. The fungus survives best where days are cool and nights are warm. Since 1977, the temperature gradients have been changing in the mid and higher elevations of the Central American mountains, such that warmer nighttime temperatures are creeping upslope and cloudier conditions are keeping daytime temperatures a little cooler than they used to be. It turns out that most harlequin frog extinctions have occurred at elevations where the minimum temperature has shifted toward the optimum for growth of the pathogen. As the climate has gotten better for the fungus, the pathogen has exploded to epidemic proportions in areas where it used to be either absent or marginal. Unfortunately for the harlequin frogs, the new zone of optimum climate for the pathogens now overlaps with the places they live—and where they are now dying in unprecedented numbers.

Similar kinds of range expansions have also been reported for pathogens that humans worry about. As of September 2007, the first cases of actual transmission of the so-called tropical infection chikungunya were reported in the Ravenna region of northern Italy. The problem is that northern Italy is not normally thought of as "tropical." Increased temperatures and humidity let a tropical disease spread, for the first time ever, out of the tropics. Chikungunya is not an illness you want. Its name comes from Swahili and means "that which bends up," because in addition to headache, achy muscles, and fever, arthritis-like symptoms in joints can cripple victims. There is no cure or vaccine.[30]

All of these observations—and many more like them—are causing ecologists to shift uncomfortably in their seats as they think about what is really happening. It would be one thing if these were isolated examples, but you see them everywhere you look. Even in the oceans, studies on organisms as diverse as squid, mussels and barnacles, plankton, those icons of marine biodiversity coral reefs, and whales and other marine megafauna are showing the same kinds of climatic impacts that seem to be rampant in the terrestrial realm, as warming affects water temperatures and currents.[31] The sum is frighteningly suggestive of global warming beginning to tip the balance of ecosystems already stressed by a myriad of other human impacts. At best, we seem to be witnessing wholesale changes in nearly every ecosystem on Earth. At worst, we may be witnessing the extinction of life as we've known it.

Chapter 4 ⌒

Witnessing Extinction

It's just a wasteland down there.

—Francis Chan, 2006[1]

THE NAME that stuck was "the dead zone," though it just as well could have been called "the killing fields." The underwater landscape looked like the refuse pile of some giant's crabfeed. The video images streaming from the submersible cameras showed nothing but the dull-brown seafloor littered with bleached, rotting crab claws, legs, and carapaces, in some places piled so deep you couldn't see the bottom at all. Nothing swam: the only movement was a light snow of pieces of the dead falling to the bottom. A huge sea star lay like a deflated garbage bag, its lifeless arms splayed in all directions as they began to rot. That was in 2006, at the bottom of Cape Perpetua, just off the coast of Newport, Oregon.[2] The dead zone stretched from there at least 120 kilometers (75 miles) up and down the Oregon Coast.

Five years earlier, the scene off Cape Perpetua was different. Orange and tan rockfish darted in and out of sea anemones that looked like cauliflowers on stalks, and nestled in the crevices between rocks were spiny, striped fish that looked like what you might see in an aquarium tank. Splashes of color were added by orange sea cucumbers, looking like single arms of a starfish with thorns. And the sea mud itself was alive with a vast quantities of marine worms.

The killer, ultimately, was a climate-driven oceanic process called upwelling. Upwelling is just what it sounds like. Shifting wind patterns, themselves ultimately related to climate dynamics, push the layer of water on the ocean's surface along the coast offshore. As the surface water is pushed away, colder and more nutrient-rich water from below wells up to replace it. The winds act a bit like an on-off switch—when the winds blow, upwelling is on, when they stop, it's off.[3]

Upwelling normally is a good thing—the influx of nutrients brought up from the deep triggers blooms of phytoplankton, which in turn become the fodder at the base of the food chain. Beginning in 2002, however, climate-driven wind patterns and ocean currents began to interact in a way that had not been seen previously, causing the upwelling off the Oregon coast to turn on and off in a way that led to a problem: oxygen-poor water started coming up from the deep, killing what was in its path.[4]

Since 2002, the winds have been particularly effective at driving intense upwelling; initially that fills the surface waters with nutrients coming up from depth. Those nutrients fuel phytoplankton, which bloom explosively. When the winds diminish, upwelling ceases, nutrients are quickly depleted, and all those phytoplankton that had been reproducing like crazy just a few days before die and fall to the bottom, where bacteria go to work decomposing them. Decomposition sucks oxygen out of the water—and so much decomposition goes on after those intense bursts of upwelling that oxygen levels near the ocean floor fall below that required to sustain life for fish and macro-invertebrates, a condition called hypoxia. A dead zone results when another upwelling event starts up, drawing those hypoxic waters up higher in the water column, into the shallower depths of species-rich areas like Cape Perpetua, where in some places the water has become not only hypoxic (low oxygen) periodically since 2002, but actually anoxic (without oxygen). Basically, those fatal episodes occur when offshore waters already low in oxygen because of the surface-to-depth mixing variations have been fueled with increased nutrients from cold subarctic influxes, while at the same time the wind patterns cause stronger upwelling. The fish may just swim away when they start to

gasp—nobody knows for sure what happens to them—but the invertebrates, like crabs, sea stars, sea anemones, and so on can't move fast
enough to avoid suffocation. Their lifeless bodies end up carpeting the
seafloor, as species all up and down the food chain die.

Dead zones were not unknown before the 2002 discovery off
Oregon—some thirty of them have been reported around the world,
in places like the Gulf of Mexico, the Black Sea, the Baltic Sea, and
Chesapeake Bay. Almost all of the other dead zones, though, are
dead because of pollution. In the Gulf of Mexico, for example, the
increased nutrients that lead to phytoplankton blooms and subsequent hypoxia come from fertilizers, animal wastes, sewage, and
eroding soil, all of which contribute an extra dose of nitrogen and
phosphorous to the Mississippi River before it discharges into the
Gulf. What makes the Oregon zone special is that it's dead not
because of pollution, but because of a climatic problem stemming
from global warming that nobody saw coming: not heat per se, but a
change in wind patterns, and ultimately ocean currents.[5] You have
to wonder: how many other surprises like that are out there waiting
for us?

We don't know of course. But what we do know from the Oregon
dead zone is that climate-induced killings over vast regions have now
been added to the otherwise long list of human impacts—pollution,
habitat destruction, habitat fragmentation, and so on—that can
destroy whole biological communities. The danger is that this new
kind of impact, when added to the other ones, will be the knockout
punch for the extinction of many species and even whole ecosystems.

Dead zones are just one example of how the knockout punch can
be delivered, and an alarming one at that since we tend to think of
the oceans as so vast that they can withstand the pressures of
humanity. But in fact many marine ecosystems are already teetering
on the brink. Nearly all of the marine megafauna—that is, big fish,
big mammals, and big turtles, as well as many aquatic birds and
invertebrates—have been pushed toward extinction by direct
human impacts like overfishing and indirect ones like habitat
destruction from pollution, trawling, and so on. That becomes all
too evident by looking at the numbers compiled from the IUCN

Red List, which classifies species as *extinct* (no reasonable doubt that the last individual is gone forever), *extinct in the wild* (no individuals remain in their natural wild habitat but some survive in captivity), *critically endangered* (at dire risk of extinction in the wild in the near future), *endangered* (high risk of extinction in the near future), *vulnerable* (high risk of extinction in the wild in the medium-term future), *near threatened* (may soon move into the vulnerable or worse categories), and *lower risk* or *least concern* (not in immediate danger of near-term or medium-term extinction if appropriate conservation measures are ensured).

In the marine realm, of the 170 bony fish species for which the IUCN Red List has adequate data to evaluate, 72 percent are at best in the vulnerable category (and some of those are in the endangered, critically endangered, or extinct category—the same holds for the rest of the groups I'll mention). Sharks are in trouble too—of 370 species with adequate data, 32 percent are vulnerable to extinction or worse. Of the eight marine reptile species (mostly turtles) with adequate data, 88 percent are at best vulnerable. Marine mammals: of 90 species, 38 percent vulnerable or worse. Birds: 345 marine species, 30 percent vulnerable or worse.[6] These endangerments, remember, are what we have before we even add potential effects of global warming.

From a more tangible perspective, that means that you have already missed your chance to see recently extinct species like the Japanese sea lion and you better look fast if you want to see critically endangered animals like the Yangtze river dolphin (which may already be extinct), or vulnerable ones like several kinds of fur seals and most of the big whales. And it means that as one fishery and then another nears collapse, like those for cod, haddock, bigeye tuna, and southern bluefin tuna, you pay more at the store, if you can get it at all.

But even more disturbing, it means that the oceans now largely lack the abundant big fish and mammals that should be in the upper regions of the food chain. By some estimates, as many as 90 percent of the world's large fish have been fished out.[7] Mega-mammals such as eastern gray whales, commonly considered to be a success story in conservation, exist at population sizes that appear to be only 28–56 percent of their historical abundance (based on analyzing their genetic variability), and what seems to be holding them at those low levels now are unfavorable climatic conditions in their northern feeding grounds.[8, 9] Those sorts of changes in size and population density profoundly change ecological dynamics, and ultimately ecosystems themselves.

In the North Pacific, there used to be killer whales at the top, sea otters and sheepshead at the middle, and sea cows near the bottom of the food chain. Now, sea otters are so sparse as to be on the endangered list, sheepshead are vulnerable, and Stellar's sea cows are extinct. In the Atlantic, sea mink and cod used to be at the top; today, sea mink are extinct and and cod populations are decimated ("vulnerable" in Red List terms). As a result, those species lower on the food chain grow in abundance—to the extent that sea urchins, no longer held in check by the predators whose numbers we've depleted, wipe out entire kelp forests, which is to say, entire ecosystems.[10]

In estuaries, the effects of breaking links in the food chain are even more evident. Jeremy Jackson, a tall, ponytailed marine biologist at the University of California at San Diego, has a phrase that captures the situation perfectly: "the rise of slime."[11] Prior to human impacts on estuaries, the top link of the food chain consisted of numerous large predators—whales, seals, sharks, and in some estuaries crocodiles. They ate whatever they wanted if they could catch it, including a whole second tier of abundant, but smaller, less voracious predators—various birds, predatory fish, turtles, and some invertebrates. The middle links were composed of vast numbers of grazers—many fish species, sea cows, and invertebrates, and also filter feeders such as oysters (which as a happy coincidence kept the water clean, just like your swimming pool filter). At the base of the food chain the predominant species were benthic algae and sea grass. As people hit the middle links hard through overfishing practices and with land-based habitat alteration that increased sediment and nutrient loads to the estuaries, the grazers and filter-feeders (especially species like oysters) were depleted to the point where top predators could no longer be supported. At the base of the food chain, phytoplankton, previously kept in check by the grazers and filter-feeders, proliferated, their blooms aided by the increased nutrient loads from land-based runoff.[12] *Phytoplankton* is a fancy word for algae and bacteria, which, if you squish them between your thumb and forefinger, you realize are slime. Hence Jackson's accurate catch-phrase, made all the more accurate by what generally takes over the middle links of the food chain: jellyfish of various sorts—so much so that some (former) shrimp fishing grounds are now jellyfish fisheries. The top links of the food chain simply disappear.

The rise of slime would be a problem without climate change, but it thrives particularly in warmer waters. And it is more than unsightly, turning water cloudy shades of green, yellow, brown, and red. It can be downright unhealthy. The myriad problems were effectively summarized by *Los Angeles Times* reporter Kenneth Wiess:

> In Australia, fishermen noticed the fireweed around the time much of Moreton Bay started turning a dirty, tea-water brown after every rain. . . . When fishermen touched it, their skin broke out in searing welts. Their lips blistered and peeled. Their eyes burned and swelled shut. . . . Off the coast of Sweden each summer, blooms of cyanobacteria turn the Baltic Sea into a stinking, yellow-brown slush that locals call "rhubarb soup." Dead fish bob in the surf. If people get too close, their eyes burn and they have trouble breathing. On the southern coast of Maui in the Hawaiian Islands, high tide leaves piles of green-brown algae that smell so foul condominium owners have hired a tractor driver to scrape them off the beach every morning. On Florida's Gulf Coast, residents complain that harmful algae blooms have become bigger, more frequent and longer lasting. Toxins from these red tides have killed hundreds of sea mammals and caused emergency rooms to fill up with coastal residents suffering respiratory distress. North of Venice, Italy, a sticky mixture of algae and bacteria collects on the Adriatic Sea in spring and summer. This white mucus washes ashore, fouling beaches, or congeals into submerged blobs, some bigger than a person. Along the Spanish coast, jellyfish

swarm so thick that nets are strung to protect swimmers from their sting.[13]

Coral reefs also are feeling the double whammy of "traditional" human impacts (pollution, overfishing, and so on) followed by global warming. A healthy coral reef has a food web that includes lots of birds, sharks, monk seals, and sometimes crocodiles at the top. In the middle are predatory invertebrates and predatory fish, who eat the myriad species of grazing invertebrates and grazing fish. The grazing fish and invertebrates are joined by sea cows and sea turtles, and the entire herbivorous cohort keeps sea grasses, algae, and sponges at bay.[14, 15] Healthy coral ecosystems are remarkable not only for their beauty—as anyone who has ever snorkeled or scuba-dived through one can attest—but also as the chief reservoirs of biodiversity in the ocean. As reef biologist Nancy Knowlton puts it, they are the "rainforests of the sea," supporting somewhere between one and nine million species within their complex food webs.[16] Coral reefs are, in fact, among the most productive and diverse environments on Earth. They are also among the first to show how global warming can tip the balance toward wholesale loss of entire ecosystems.

When ocean temperatures rose 0.5–1°C (0.9–1.8°F) above normal summertime maximums in the Indian Ocean in 1998, 80 percent of the corals there turned from their normal rainbow of colors to white (called bleaching), and 20 percent of the reefs died.[17] That is a big swath of death and destruction across a seascape that is equivalent in size to all of North America. To help people appreciate the magnitude, Jeremy Jackson likened that single coral-killing event to all the leaves falling off 80 percent of the trees in North America on one summer night. One month later, 20 percent of those trees are dead. You would probably notice.[18]

The reason coral reefs are so affected by slight temperature rises is because the reef-building organisms—several species of colonial cnidarians—are symbionts, which is to say, they help algae, and algae helps them. The hard, sharp parts of coral reefs that skin your leg when you accidently brush against them are in fact secretions of calcium carbonate that form around billions of living, soft, tiny saclike

coral polyps. Inside each polyp is a single-celled alga called zooxanthellae. The zooxanthellae photosynthesize and thereby provide oxygen, fix carbon compounds, and give nutrients to the coral polyps. In
return, the coral polyps supply the zooxanthellae with a protected
environment in which to live and also the carbon dioxide needed for
photosynthesis. All works smoothly—until it gets too warm, at
which point the zooxanthellae die, photosynthesis stops, and the
coral polyps bleach white, since it is the zooxanthellae that give
corals their color. With death of the zooxanthellae comes death of
the polyp, and with death of the polyp, there is no more secretion of
new calcium carbonate. The reef structure itself then becomes brittle
and breaks down into rubble.

At the time, the Indian Ocean bleaching catastrophe was the
culmination of successively more and more bleached corals in more
and more oceans that had been taking place since the seas started to
warm up in the 1980s. With each summer that temperature spiked
above its normal maximum, more corals in more parts of the ocean
were affected, rising from bleaching in only one reef province in
1980, to bleaching in six provinces by 1987, to ten in 1998.[19] (A reef
province is a geographic area that shares common reef species in a
certain part of a certain ocean.) That, of course, has been happening
on top of the many other stressors that cause coral reefs to die, which
range from overfishing the species that keep coral-smothering algae
and voracious polyp-eaters (like the crown-of-thorns starfish) in
check, to pollution that clogs feeding mechanisms and causes disease.
Coral reefs continue to disappear worldwide, and those that remain
are irrevocably different in species composition, structure, and diversity from the way coral reefs had previously maintained themselves
for hundreds of thousands of years.[20]

These stories from the ocean point to a frightening trajectory of
widespread extinction as global warming delivers a coup de grâce to
already stressed ecosystems. The picture is no rosier if we look on
land—despite an arguably heightened conservation ethic for the
landscapes people actually see and inhabit. A major problem on land
is collatoral extinction from habitat fragmentation, an inevitable by-
product of one of the few straightforward laws of ecology: bigger

pieces of real estate support more species. This is called the species-area relationship, which in mathematical terms states that the number of species increases in a very predictable way as the sampling radius gets bigger and bigger, or $S = cA^z$, where S is the number of species, A is area, and c and z are constants. Intuitively, the species-area relationship is a no-brainer: of course you will find more species if you conduct a census across, say, ten kilometers rather than across only one kilometer. What makes it very powerful is how tight the mathematical relationship actually is. Using that relationship, you can predict how many species you will find in a given area of whatever size you choose in a given kind of landscape and biogeographic province. You can also flip the species-area relationship around, so to speak, and use it to predict how many species you might lose if you reduce the size of the real estate that contains suitable habitat.

A cooperative effort by 19 scientists did just that for land-based species and published the results in the journal *Nature* in 2004.[21] The scientists used state-of-the-art climate modeling techniques to track how climate zones are expected to shift given minimum, average, and maximum projections of global warming by the year 2050—just about the time kids born today hit their early forties. They calculated how much those shifting climate zones would either reduce or enlarge the available habitat for a wide variety of species (1,103 in all) of mammals (112 species), birds (238 species), frogs (23 species), reptiles (44 species), butterflies (69 species), other invertebrates (10 species), and plants (607 species). Then they used the species-area equations to determine how many species might be expected to be lost as a result of shrinking habitat—remember, this is just shrinking habitat due to global warming, not habitat lost to bulldozers. In the neutral tone typical of scientific writing, they noted simply that somewhere between "15–37 percent of species in our sample of regions and taxa will be 'committed to extinction.'"[22] That was only for their mid-range model of climatic warming—if the higher estimates of global warming prove closer to the truth, the number of species "committed to extinction" rises to somewhere between 21 and 52 percent. Here's another way to express the same thing. Look around you. Kill half of what you see. Or if you're feeling generous, just kill about a quarter of what you see. That's what we could be talking about.

This dire scenario is not so far-fetched if you take a look at what we've done in just the past few centuries, even before current rates of global warming became a problem. Exact numbers of historic extinctions are hard to come by, in part because species are going extinct before we even discover them, but we do know this: from the year 1600 to 2001, approximately 490 animal species and 580 plant species were wiped off the face of the Earth, nearly all of them from impacts such as concerted hunting or destruction of habitat. Extinction, of course, is the fate of all species over the long course of time: it is estimated that more than 99 percent of all species that have ever lived on Earth are extinct. That means there is a normal background rate at which species are always going extinct. Cause for concern arises when extinction rates elevate far above that background rate. That this is happening today is indicated by comparing the background extinction rate with the current rate. That far-from-simple comparison has been made by Helen Regan and her colleagues.[23] They first figured out what the "normal" (that is to say, non–human caused) extinction rate was for the kinds of organisms that have a rich fossil record—marine invertebrate animals whose 550-million-year history has been well documented by paleontologists, as well as mammals, which are represented by abundant fossils through the time they have been abundant on Earth, approximately 65 million years. By counting up the numbers of species that disappear at given slices of geologic time, and standardizing that against the numbers of species known for that time, extinction rates for each time slice can be calculated, and then an average, or background, extinction rate computed for all time slices. That background extinction rate for marine invertebrates turned out to be 0.25 extinctions per million years; for mammals, it is 0.40 extinctions per million years. That provides a context for interpreting how severe, for example, the mammal extinctions that have taken place since the year 1600 really are. Sixty mammal species have gone extinct in those 400 years, out of 4,327 known mammal species on Earth. Using the extinction-rate equations, and then taking into account uncertainties inherent in

comparing fossil data with more recent historically recorded information, produces a startling result. Over the past 400 years, the extinction rate for mammals appears to be between 17 percent and 377
percent faster than normal.

Now, add to that already-existing extinction pressure the kinds of
changes that global warming is causing in species all over the world. If
you think about the examples of how global warming affects species
that we've seen in this chapter and earlier ones, you realize that the
changes sort into five broad categories: where species are found, how
many of their individuals are on the landscape, how individuals look,
how they interact with the yearly cycle of seasons, and even, in some
cases, what is their genetic makeup. Biologists have a word for each
one of those kinds of adjustments. Respectively, they are called
changes in geographic range, abundance, phenotype, phenology, and
genotype. Taken as a whole, how those attributes of species are changing suggest that global warming is going to—possibly already is—
accelerate extinction even more, both on land and in the sea.

Since we tend to regard what we've experienced in our lifetime as
normal, and we're right in the midst of species crashing all around us,
it's sometimes hard to see just how much trouble we're really heading
for. There is a way, however, to get some perspective: by looking
backward to the last time climate-induced ecological changes and
human impacts intersected, some ten millennia ago. Back then, just
as now, species were trying to move as global warming was affecting
their geographic ranges, abundance, phenology, phenotype, and
genotype, just as humans were rapidly increasing their footprint on
Earth. The result, as we'll see in the next chapter, was less than
encouraging: the biggest extinction event in millions of years. Especially hard hit were species that, as is frequently the case today, had
no place else to go.

Chapter 5 ⌒

No Place to Run To

[The] extinction [of the giant Irish elk] may be traced to late
glacial changes in climate.

—Stephen Jay Gould, 1974[1]

ABOUT 16 kilometers (ten miles) south of Grafton
Street in downtown Dublin, halfway to a little place called Ennis-
kerry, was what we used to call the Elk Tombstone. It was big rock on
the edge of Ballybetagh Bog, probably dropped there by glaciers, on
which paleoecologists had chiseled in rough letters: "ELK 1934."[2]
They were referring to Irish elk, scientifically known as *Megaloceros
giganteus*,[3] magnificent beasts, standing nearly two meters at the
shoulder (over six feet), with antlers that would reach from the head-
lights of your neighbor's SUV to its taillights (a tip-to-tip span of
some four meters or thirteen feet). When I asked the owner of the
place if I could go out there and look for some, he replied "Why sure,"
in a classic Irish brogue. "They come down to water there nearly
every night." That wasn't quite the answer I expected, because Irish
elk have been extinct in Ireland for more than 12,500 years. My
interest was in finding out whether climate had anything to do with
it—a speculation that had come and gone in the scientific literature
for centuries, but which had never been been critically examined.

Irish elk were just one of the casualties that occurred the only
other time that Earth ran the natural experiment of rapidly growing

the numbers of people on the planet at the same time the globe warmed by some 5°C (9°F).[4] The elk went extinct along with two-thirds of all the largest animals on the planet in a geologically short span of time that, depending on where you were in the world, started around 50,000 years ago and mostly ended around 11,500 years ago. That was near the end of the Pleistocene as the glaciers of the last ice age were melting. Earth had never seen anything quite like it. There had been previous warming events from glacial to interglacial times—recall the Milanković cycles described in Chapter 2—but there had never been a glacial-interglacial transition at a time when significant numbers of people were distributed over most of the Earth's surface. And never had there been a period when so many large mammals are known to have vanished forever within such a short interval of time.[5] What happened back then shows that the ecological responses to global warming we've seen in previous chapters are serious indeed, providing a retrospective look that illustrates just how climate-induced ecological changes—for example, in phenology, geographic range limits, and phenotype—can play out to an end game of extinction, sometimes in unexpected ways.

The Irish elk, like the other animals that went extinct near the end of the Pleistocene, are called megafauna because they were so dramatically large. By definition, megafauna are animals that weigh more than about 44 kilograms (or 100 pounds). Although the smallest megafauna are only about the size of a small sheep, the largest are elephant- to giraffe-sized. Fifty thousand years ago, there were at least 150 genera (and each genus can have more than one species) of terrestrial mammals that fit that discription. By 9,000 years ago, two-thirds of them were extinct.

We know this from finding their bones in hidden graveyards—fossil deposits that are often discovered accidentally when a backhoe hits a huge bone in the midst of excavating for a housing development, when a road grader is clearing a ditch, when a stream erodes away its bank, or when a spelunker stumbles on a skeleton in a cave. Such lucky accidents, along with concerted searches by paleontologists and archaeologists, have turned up thousands of bones of big, dead animals. Nearly all of them are from species that had made it through much of the Pleistocene, including some of those Milankovič-scale climate changes that were similar in magnitude to the one that heralded the switch from the last glacial to our present interglacial. But by about 50,000 years ago, extinction pulses began to show up, first in Australia, then in Eurasia and northernmost North America, and finally in central North America and South America.

In Australia, the kinds of animals that died included oversized kangaroos, wombats the size of prize hogs, and a giant marsupial that looked like a wombat on steroids, *Diprotodon*, so big you would need a step stool to climb onto its back (though you probably wouldn't have wanted to). Besides Irish elk, Eurasia lost grass-eating woolly mammoths, leaf- and bush-eating mastodons, and woolly rhinos, which unlike their African cousins were covered in long hair and had their nasal horns flattened and oriented to act as snow sweepers. North America also lost species like mammoths and mastodons, along with giant bison that had horn-spans wider than NBA basketball players are tall, short-faced bears that were bigger than a modern record grizzly, saber-toothed cats, and ground sloths that could stand on their hind legs and easily munch the plants hanging off of your second-story balcony. The death toll in South America also included a wide spectrum of large sloths, along with car-sized glyptodonts covered with bony armor, and litopterns, strange-looking animals which at first glance you might think resembled a horse until you noticed their camel-like necks and short, elephant-like trunks.

In the 1960s, a University of Arizona scientist, Paul Martin, started thinking hard about why so many species seemed to go extinct at the last glacial-interglacial transition when they had apparently survived earlier ones.[6] His entry into the world of extinct animals was through the back door, so to speak. At the time Martin's research used palynology (the study of fossil pollen) to try to unlock the secrets of past vegetational changes. The problem was, he worked in the desert Southwest, where the lakes from which palynologists usually get their fossils are notably scarce. So Martin came up with a novel approach: he extracted the pollen from the fossilized dung he found of Pleistocene animals, notably giant ground sloths. (There are six genera of giant ground sloths that went extinct in North America.) Preserved in caves and rock shelters courtesy of the dry Arizona climate, the dung is not really fossilized at all. It is simply clumps of, well, dried-out dung, about the size of those miniature footballs that third-graders like to throw around, and about the same shape except that one or both ends are flattened. The tip-off that it went through an animal's digestive tract is that it is full of bits of plants, all cut to the same size by the teeth of whatever chewed the plants up. Martin noticed that many of the plants he was finding in the 11,000- to 30,000-year-old dung still grew in parts of the Arizona desert today, so it didn't seem likely that disappearing food sources led to the sloths' extinction. And that got him to thinking about what did.

After compiling the information that was known in the 1960s on the other animals that went extinct throughout the world, Martin thought he noticed an intriguing pattern: the timing and intensity of extinction seemed to correspond with the first entry of Homo sapiens into areas where the big animals had lived without humans for thousands of years. In areas where humans and big animals had evolved together (Africa) or where humans dispersed early on (Eurasia), extinctions were not very pronounced. But wherever humans seemed to suddenly appear on continents (North America, South America, and Australia) or islands that had previously been free of them, extinction seemed to follow. Martin used that timing and other arguments to make the case that hunters—even at the low population sizes of the late Pleistocene—killed large animals so frequently and efficiently that the megafauna were hunted to extinction, an event he called "overkill." The extreme version of the overkill hypothesis, which postulated the killing of massive numbers of megafauna in as little as a few hundred years, became known as blitzkrieg.

Could hunters using stone tools really slaughter so many animals? Martin's idea set the stage for forty years of sometimes fierce debate that to some extent still goes on today. On the con side are statements such as this: "In North America, archaeologists and paleontologists whose work focuses on the late Pleistocene routinely reject Martin's position for two prime reasons: there is virtually no evidence that supports [the theory of overkill], and there is a remarkably broad set of evidence that strongly suggests that it is wrong."[7] On the pro side, we hear statements like: "To the extent that [those who argue against overkill] attempt to substantiate their opinions with actual evidence, they provide outmoded data and interpretations and ignore or deliberately omit the most recent chronological, archaeo-logical, and climatic data."[8]

That debate was hot in the mid-1980s, when we used that Elk Tombstone to decide where to dig for Irish elk at Ballybetagh. The "we" included Mick and Pat, two undergraduates from Trinity College; digging involved laying out a grid of a few meters on a side, carefully shoveling down through the peat into the bone-bearing clay layer below, and mapping the important sedimentary features and fossils as we went down. It also involved a heavy-duty water pump, which each morning, and periodically during the day, we used to empty shin-deep water out of the ever-deepening hole—we were digging in a bog, after all.

From radiocarbon dating, we knew that the geologically youngest Irish elk specimens at Ballybetagh were some 12,500 years old,[9] and the oldest ones were around 14,000 years old. They were found only in the upper half of a distinctive, tan-colored clay layer, which was beneath the peat that formed the surface of the bog. That meant that the elk lived near the end of a time that paleoecologists called the Alleröd, a relatively warm time (still cooler than today) toward the end of the last glacial, when Ballybetah Bog was not a bog at all, but was instead a lake, with shores hosting lots of grasses, shrubs, and birch trees, just the nutritional stuff that Irish elk needed to eat in order for the males to grow their huge antlers and the females to grow babies. We knew about that ancient vegetation from bits of plants that are fossilized in the mud, and also from tiny fossil pollen grains. Right on top of the Alleröd sediments was a sterile gray gravel, which signaled the final icy cold snap of the last glacial, a time called the Younger Dryas.[10] Temperatures plummeted in that period and glaciers once again grew in Ireland for a few hundred years; at Ballybetagh, from at least 12,500 to 11,900 years ago. During that time it became too cold for the nutritious grasses, shrubs, and birch trees that had previously grown around Ballybetagh; instead they were replaced by dwarf willow and arctic-alpine herbs and shrubs. The cold snap destroyed the Irish elk's habitat—at least 1,600 years before any archaeological evidence of human arrival on the island.[11]

It was global warming at the time that, counterintuitively, caused the Younger Dryas cold snap—illustrating that warming the planet has some very big, sometimes unexpected effects. As the world was passing from the cold part of a Milanković cycle into a warm part— that's what caused the change from the last ice age into our present interglacial—summers became warmer and warmer in northern regions where there were extensive ice sheets. That caused so much glacial ice to melt that the North Atlantic received an influx of fresh water, which in turn caused rerouting of ocean currents—with the ultimate effect of cooling places like Ireland and the rest of northern Europe.[12] That cooling was fast (coming on in as little as a few tens of years) and intense (as much as a few degrees Celsius); after a few centuries of the fresh water mixing with salty water normal ocean currents were restored, ending the brief regional cold spell.[13]

In recording that anomolous response to global warming in northern Europe, Ballybetagh was no different from many other Irish peat bogs where Irish elk bones had been found,[14] usually in the course of local farmers using L-shaped shovels called "slanes" to dig out bricks of peat—in Irish parlance "turf"—that they would stack to dry. It was those bricks of turf burning in fireplaces and stoves that gave Dublin its own magical, welcoming smell on winter mornings, not quite like wood smoke, not quite like tobacco smoke—and, of course, as that peat burned it was releasing into the atmosphere CO_2 that had been sequestered in the bogs for thousands of years. In cutting those bricks, farmers would occassionally push their shovels through the base of the peat, through the Younger Dryas gravel, and into the Alleröd clay below. Every now and then, just as as the shovel passed into the clay, they would hear a resounding "clunk," which they soon learned to recognize as the sound of the shovel smacking an Irish elk fossil. This happened often enough that by the late 1800s a burgeoning industry in selling Irish elk bones began to blossom, leading entrepeneurs to bypass the shovel initially and instead use a long, thin pole to push through the peat. Where the pole stopped with a clunk, they dug.

Some of the skeleton hunters were particularly industrious—among their leftovers are piles of Irish elk bones that eventually ended up in a dark, unheated warehouse in a dicey part of Dublin, an annex of the Irish National Museum of Natural History to which I was led by Nigel Monaghan, the curator of paleontology there. Like a macabre spare parts shop, the humeri were in one pile, the femora in another, the vertebrae in a third, skulls were arranged on their own set of shelves, and so on—in short, a paleo-paradise. Many of these leftovers were from Ballybetagh bog. This, combined with the primary field evidence we were digging out of the bog, was just the stuff that was needed in order to crack the question of what happened to Irish elk when that Younger Dryas cold snap hit. Instead of just dusty old specimens hidden in the back room of the museum, those Irish elk fossils became a story written in bone of how a species actually responded to global warming—at the same time offering a glimpse into our own ecological future.

The story that those bones and their entombing sediments told was that global warming is fully capable of causing extinction as the timing of the seasons becomes mismatched to the yearly biological cycle of a species—that is, as phenology changes, to use the terminology introduced in the last chapter. Likewise, the Ballybetagh bones told us that preceding extinction, you can expect changes in how a species looks, or phenotypic changes as climate influences nutrition and other factors that affect growth and development. That became apparent by measuring the Irish elk skulls and antlers. Were those Ballybetagh animals, which were dying just when the climate was changing from the good Alleröd times to the much colder Younger Dryas times, any different from the "average" Irish elk that had lived in Ireland over the previous couple of thousand years, when all the paleo-vegetation and lake-sediment indicators said times were good for the animals?[15] That was easy enough to find out by comparing the measurements of the Ballybetagh bones to other Irish elk fossils that came from throughout Ireland, from sediments that spanned the entire last half of the Alleröd times from 14,000 to 12,500 years ago.

Armed with calipers, tape measure, and an extra lamp, and bundled up against the Dublin winter (it was cold in that dark warehouse), I began began measuring: lengths of skulls, heights of antler burrs, circumferences of basal antlers, so on. The first thing that became obvious was that the Ballybetagh skulls were very small. The length of the skull is a reasonable predictor of overall body size—the fact that we had small skulls meant that the Ballybetagh animals were phenotypically different from the average Irish elk of the previous millennium or so. Instead of growing up big, the Ballybetagh elk had grown up small. Typically, small adult size reflects some combination of marginal nutrition or disease during fetal or postnatal growth—during those critical toddler and teenage years, those Ballybetagh elk were apparently not getting enough to eat to allow them to grow as big as they might have.

The second thing that became apparent was that even accounting for the small size of the Ballybetagh elk, their antlers were abnormally small.[16] Whereas adult body size reflects conditions over all the years the animal is growing, antler size reflects conditions only during the year before the animal's death. Remember that antlers are shed and regrown yearly. There is a balance between how much of the caloric and mineral intake goes into building body fat and how much is available for building antlers. Although antlers are genetically hardwired to take their portion of that nutritional input for their growth, their ultimate size in any year (all other things being equal) varies according to how good the spring and summer period is nutritionally—in good years, big antlers, in bad years, small antlers.[17] Therefore those animals that were dying at Ballybetagh were dying after spending a previous spring and summer without quite enough to eat.

The smaller elk and smaller-than-normal antler size (even when taking the small bodies into account) reflected an underlying mismatch between the yearly rhythm of an Irish elk's life and the changes in seasons. That is, phenology killed them. For male Irish elk (females don't have antlers), the annual growth and shedding of antlers (as we know from studying living deer) was genetically hard-wired to day length, such that shedding occured in early spring, growth of a new set began almost immediately, and then the new antlers grew rapidly such that they were fully formed within three to five months.[18] The result was that the males had to deposit 45 kilo-grams (100 pounds) of calcium phosphate on their heads within at most 150 days. If you do the math, you realize that you would literally have been able to watch those antlers grow. That is a tremendous energy drain,[19] which would have taken place at exactly the same time that male Irish elk had to build up their fat reserves for the rest of the year. Those fat reserves for the entire year have to be banked in spring and summer, because the rut (or mating season) begins in the fall, a time when the males have only one thing on their mind, and it is not eating. After the rut, when the hormones subside and their heads clear, the male elk find that they are facing a long win-ter, that they are getting skinny and hungry, that there is not much to eat, and that what forage is available is no longer very nutritious.

The females too face the problem of a caloric deficit in the win-ter, but for different reasons than the males. Rather than growing antlers in the summer, females are nursing babies—trying to feed both themselves and their calves while they add fat reserves. During the winter, just when times are toughest, they are growing a new organ quite different from the antlers of males—a placenta (rather like growing a new internal organ the size of your liver), which has the purpose of nourishing the other energy drain they are growing, a fetal Irish elk. That direct cost of pregnancy and, after that, nursing, means female Irish elk may well have had a yearly energy bill that was even higher than that of the males.[20]

It all works out if there is abundant vegetation available for long enough in the spring, when the new shoots are maximally nutritious, and if plants stay nutritious long enough into the summer. If the plant-growing season is too short, however, the yearly energy budget for Irish elk—a balance between putting on fat in the spring and summer and using it up in the fall and winter—tips in the wrong direction. In that case, the number of animals that die during the late winter lean times begins to outpace the number born in the spring and surviving to reproduce. If that goes on for too many years, extinction results.

It was that kind of accelerated winterkill that those too-small skulls and antlers had recorded for the Ballybetagh elk. In effect, global warming had triggered a shortening of the plant-growing season and threw it out of phase with the Irish elk's yearly life cycle, causing nutrition to suffer, which in turn stunted growth and antler size.[21] Eventually the nutritional deficit reached the point at which even those small elk with relatively small antlers were having trouble: deaths began to outweigh births, and population sizes began to dwindle, until finally, some 12,500 years ago, Ireland's last Irish elk died.[22]

From looking at Irish elk outside of Ireland, another relevant point became very clear: had Ireland's Irish elk been able disperse to other areas as climate was changing unfavorably there, they could have survived. But Ireland is an island (though a big one), so they had no place to run to. That illustrates the problem with fencing in a species (in this case by the North Atlantic Ocean) that is experiencing climate change. Scale that up, and there is an obvious parallel to what is happening globally today: rapid global warming is hitting many species that are, for all practical purposes, "fenced" into relatively small islands of suitable habitat separated by vast swaths of human-altered landscape.

Roaming free on the the European mainland, Irish elk demonstrated their capacity to persist through changing climate, both from warm to cold and cold to warm, by simply moving—until too many people blocked their way. Before 24,000 years ago, during a relatively warm time in the last glacial stage, Irish elk were widespread, with the northern part of their range extending into Ireland, Great Britain, and Denmark; the western border following the coast of France; the southern edge running through northern Spain, northern Italy, Austria, the northern shore of the Black Sea, and Azerbaijan; and the eastern edge along Russia's Volga and Kama Rivers. When Europe got much colder with attendant vegetation changes, Irish elk moved—between 24,000 and 15,400 years ago they virtually vanished from western Europe, their range contracting exclusively into the eastern, Russian portion of their former range. As northern European habitats once again warmed and Russian habitats degraded (from the elk's perspective) during Alleröd times, Irish elk shifted their distribution back north and east, out of central Russia and into northern Germany, Denmark, Britain, and especially Ireland. And later, as the Younger Dryas was bringing death to the last Irish elk in Ireland and also culling other northern European populations, the species range once again shifted, this time shrinking to a tiny area in the foothills of the Urals of southwestern Siberia, where it hung on as climate warmed in earnest, finally flickering out some 7,650 years ago, well past the Younger Dryas and into the present interglacial.[23] The final flicker seems to correspond in time with climatically induced vegetational changes that pushed Irish elk down from the Ural foothills onto the Siberian plain, where by that time armed bands of Mesolithic hunters were waiting to finish them off.[24] For Irish elk, extinction was finally complete, with climate having taken them out in some places, and people finishing them off in others.

The double whammy of global warming and more direct human interference—not necessarily in that order—now seems to have been important in the worldwide decimation of the megafauna that Paul Martin had first noticed when he set the stage for the subsequent argument over the relative importance of overkill and climate change in the megafauna die-off. It is hard to discount that humans had major impacts when you look at the chronology of extinction; after 40 years of scrutiny, Martin's original observations about timing have been refined and remain a strong argument that humans contributed to the killing. In Australia, many extinctions followed the first landing of *Homo sapiens*. In Eurasia, extinctions followed the entry and expansion of *Homo sapiens* populations (as opposed to the long-present *Homo neandertalensis*). In North and South America, extinction came hot on the heels of humans who migrated across the Bering Land Bridge from Eurasia. And on islands, extinctions invariably followed the first contact by people.

But those late-Pleistocene humans clearly did not kill everything by themselves, even in some cases when we know they were exerting heavy hunting pressure; examples of extensively hunted megafauna species that did not go extinct include bison in North America and reindeer in Europe. And as we saw with Irish elk, there are some places where species went extinct without significant (or any) human presence on the landscape. Similar examples include asses (hemionid horses) and short-faced bears in the Yukon, where the extinctions happened just as climate was changing unfavorably for the affected species (from warmer conditions within the last glacial to full-on glacial times). This had already occurred by 24,800 years ago, long before humans arrived in the region. In Alaska and the Yukon, another kind of stocky-bodied Eurasian horse (called caballoid horses) survived after the asses died out, only to decrease in body size (indicating probable nutritional problems as climate changed the quality of their forage, just as we saw for Irish elk) before humans arrived. The fossil evidence indicates that caballoid horses finally went locally extinct about 14,700 thousand years ago, either slightly before or just as humans first showed up in the area.

These sorts of observations suggest a one-two punch in the global context—one punch being direct human impacts, the other being global climate change and especially global warming—with the intensity and timing of each punch varying continent by continent. Australia started things out with just the first punch—human impacts. People arrived there some 50,000 years ago. Within the ensuing 20,000 years, 88 percent of the 16 megamammals that had inhabited Australia prior to human arrival were extinct. The extinctions occurred even in the absence of any unusual climate changes, and species that died had lasted through glacial-interglacial transitions that came before humans inserted themselves into the ecosystem. Evidence of widespread fires and lack of any kill sites suggests that most of the extinctions were caused by indirect human impacts. Some scientists argue that the Australian extinctions were very sudden,[25] but the fact that the most recent dates on extinct fauna range from older than 50,000 to as little as 32,000 years suggests the dwindling may have been spread out over thousands of years.[26]

In Eurasia, the human punch was a quick staggering jab followed by two hard hits of climate change. There *Homo neandertalensis* had long coexisted with megafauna, without any apparent megafaunal extinctions. The new human punch came with entry and expansion of populations of *Homo sapiens*, with their arguably more sophisticated stone-tool technologies. Even so, it was only during times of climate change, when species were trying to follow the shifting of their preferred climate (as we saw with mainland Europe Irish elk) but people got in the way, that extinction occurred. Eventually 36 percent of 25 megafauna genera bit the dust, in two separate pulses. The first extinction pulse took out straight-tusked elephants and hippos between 48,500 and 23,500 thousand years ago, roughly when *H. sapiens* entered the region and at the same time climate conditions went from a warm to a cold spell in the last ice age. The rest of the extinctions in Eurasia clustered around the Pleistocene-Holocene global warming event, beginning nearly 14,000 years ago, by which time *H. sapiens* were distributed widely across the continent for the first time and numbers of people were rapidly increasing.[27]

Perhaps most telling is that extinction was most severe where both punches—human impacts and climate change—were simultaneous and powerful, as in central North America.[28] There, the first bands of Clovis-culture hunters, so named because their distinctive bloodletting spearpoints were first found near Clovis, New Mexico, arrived nearly 13,000 years ago. They were the dominant North American people for the next 200 years.[29] Their arrival and heydey coincides almost exactly with the dramatic climatic changes that heralded the end of the ice age in North America.[30] In all, 34 genera died out (72 percent of the continent's megafauna), with the last appearance of 15 of them securely dated to between 13,500 and 11,500 years ago. Those 34 genera included every species above the 1,000-kg size class, more than 50 percent of the species in the 32-kg to 1,000-kg size classes, and 20 percent of those between 10 kilograms and 32 kilograms.[31]

Now the whole world seems on the brink of receiving a similar kind of one-two punch that hit North America some ten millennia ago, but the punches are very much stronger. One can't help but get the uneasy feeling that the same kind of thing that happened in the late Pleistocene is happening again. Today's human population densities and impacts make the end-Pleistocene population expansion look like kid stuff, the speed at which Earth is warming is faster, and we are starting out already warm instead of in a glacial time. When late-Pleistocene human impacts coincided with global warming it was bad enough; by wiping most of the large, land-based species off the face of the Earth, the ecological pulse of the planet was changed forever. At the rate we're going today, we almost certainly are changing that ecological pulse again—this time, far outside the bounds of past fluctuations.

PART TWO

Normal for Nature

Chapter 6 ～

California Dreaming

At this point I wish to emphasize what I believe will ultimately prove to be the greatest purpose of our museum. This value will not, however, be realized until the lapse of many years, possibly a century, assuming that our material is safely preserved. And this is that the student of the future will have access to the original record of faunal conditions in California and the West, wherever we now work.

—Joseph Grinnell, 1910[1]

ANNIE ALEXANDER drove a hard bargain. Born in 1867, she came of age in a time when women didn't yet have the right to vote, and certainly weren't expected to traipse around the deserts of Nevada with a gun or spend their days digging up fossils in the hot sun. Yet it was those kinds of activities that caught her fancy and led her to propose on October 28, 1907, a new natural history museum at the University of California at Berkeley, though with some stipulations:

> Should the University of California within the next six months erect a galvanized iron building furnished with electric light, heat, and janitor's services and turn it over to my entire control as a Museum of Natural History for the next seven years, I will guarantee the expenditure of $7,000 yearly during that time for field and research work relating exclusively to mammals, birds, and reptiles of the west coast, with

the understanding that the University of California would be
in no way responsible for the management of the funds for
carrying out the work, or selection of collectors. . . .[2]

In short, she wanted a building complete with maintenance, and
control over the hiring and expenditures her money would pay for.[3]
And she wanted Joseph Grinnell as her museum director. The
university accepted, and the Museum of Vertebrate Zoology was
born.

Joseph Grinnell, starting out as a "cock-sure" and "fresh" young
zoologist, eventually became one of the giants of ecology.[4] A talented
field biologist—part of his upbringing took place on Chief Red
Cloud's Sioux Reservation in the 1880s—he was the first to explicitly define an "ecological niche" and, in 1917, to point out how inti-
mately the distribution of species is related to climatic conditions.[5, 6]
He also readily saw how important it was to document the geography
of species in his era, so that future generations would have a baseline
for assessing how human impacts had changed nature. He and
Alexander decided to build their museum around that ambitious
concept. One of the places they targeted was John Muir's playground,
the Yosemite region.

Although Muir and Grinnell had crossed paths in Sitka, Alaska,
in 1896, and Alexander's wider social circle included him, Muir was
almost a generation ahead of the other two in his accomplishments.[7]
Like Grinnell and Alexander, Muir was thinking about the future,
but not in quite the same way. His dream was to actually keep what
was in Yosemite from changing, and he spearheaded the establishment of Yosemite National Park to help do so. One hundred years
later, scientists are still using the fruits of Alexander's and Grinnell's
dreams to see if Muir's dream came true—and to determine the likelihood that both Muir's dream and his park will disappear into thin
air because of global warming.

Therein lies a major value of nature preserves like Yosemite,
whether or not they are designated as parks. They are the places
where the human touch on the planet is among the lightest. Therefore we can use historic and fossil records from such places to moni-

tor Earth's pulse through hundreds, thousands, even millions of years, and thereby get a sense of whether the changes we've seen in the past few decades are unusual in the bigger scheme of things. Today in Yosemite, it's the century-long historic record that's informative, just as Grinnell, Alexander, and Muir envisioned.

A hundred years ago must have been a heady time for the three California naturalists. Muir had convinced Congress to approve Yosemite and Sequoia as national parks in 1890, and in 1892 he had launched the Sierra Club. National parks were still a new and exciting idea. After Yellowstone, Yosemite and Sequoia and were the second and third national parks established in the United States (not counting one that was decommissioned) and the fourth and fifth in the entire world.[8] By 1900, one additional park had been set aside (Mt. Rainier in Washington, 1899), and Muir was hard at work, pressing for the creation of more such reserves. He saw the writing on the wall—California, and the whole American West, was changing before his eyes:

> Only thirty years ago, the great Central Valley of California, five hundred miles long and fifty miles wide, was one bed of golden and purple flowers. Now it is ploughed and pastured out of existence, gone forever—scarce a memory of it left in fence corners and along the bluffs of the streams. . . . [In] . . . the Sierra . . . the noble forests . . . are sadly hacked and trampled, notwithstanding the ruggedness of the topography—all excepting those of the parks guarded by a few soldiers.[9]

As Muir was penning those words, Annie Alexander was starting down the road that would lead to her lasting scientific legacy. She had a passion for the outdoors which, in 1900, was being kindled to a fever pitch as she listened to John C. Merriam's paleontology lectures at the University of California at Berkeley and spent nights under the stars and days armed with "pick and collecting sack" on paleontology expeditions. Heiress to the C & H Sugar fortune, she began funding Merriam's research and by 1901 was funding her own expeditions as well, beginning with a months-long trip to collect fossil vertebrates at remote Fossil Lake, Oregon. With that, the die was cast: besides discovering fossils, she discovered that she liked the intimate connection with nature she experienced through fieldwork, and the feeling that comes from making contributions to science through ensuring the specimens that she and others collected would be properly cared for, studied, and reported. That led her to be not only a lifelong benefactress of the University of California at Berkeley, but also a hands-on scientific participant in much of the work and infrastructure she funded, including establishment of the Museum of Paleontology and Museum of Vertebrate Zoology on the Berkeley campus.

It was the Museum of Vertebrate Zoology (MVZ) that Alexander set up first. Her interest in zoology had been developing alongside her passion for paleontology. An African hunting safari with her father in 1904 was the signal event, in what was for her a wonderful but tragic firsthand experience of remote, wild places. The wonder came from seeing nature raw with her father: herds of giraffes, lions roaring in the night, and "every morning the sunrise over miles of tall grass laden with dew. . . . We have made every day count. I doubt if there are two more delighted people in this country than Papa and I."[10] The tragedy came with death: First, a former classmate of her father's, Thomas Gulick, died after becoming ill early in the trip. Then, as she and her father admired Victoria Falls, a boulder dislodged from the cliff, crashed down, and crushed her father's foot. Alexander stood by helplessly as he slowly died after his leg was amputated under primitive conditions.

In the aftermath of such tragedy, Annie Alexander realized that she wanted to make a difference doing something she loved: "I felt I had to do something to divert my mind and absorb my interest and the idea of making collections of west coast fauna as a nucleus for study gradually took shape in my mind."[11] That, and a specimen-collecting trip to Alaska that further honed her interest in natural history, eventually led her to seek out Joseph Grinnell.

Alexander didn't meet Grinnell for another three years. But they had unwittingly been traversing the same intellectual and physical landscapes. While Alexander was getting her first formal exposure to natural history at Berkeley, she had no idea Grinnell was living on the other side of San Francisco Bay. In 1900, in his own words, he had just returned "from a year and a half of adventure in Alaska, [and] it was finally decided that I could be trusted to attend a real university; and in the middle of the spring semester of 1900 I reached Stanford [to begin a zoology graduate program], with certain personal handicaps which must have been distressingly outstanding."[12] Ironically, after surviving a good portion of the years 1896–1899 in Alaska's wild backcountry, where he had amassed an impressive collection of birds and other vertebrates, Grinnell came down with a severe case of typhoid fever in Palo Alto, which sent him back home to Pasadena in 1903. Grinnell settled in to teach ornithology at what was then Throop Polytechnic University (now California Institute of Technology), and it was there that Annie Alexander sought him out in 1907.

She had recently returned from her first trip to Alaska and was putting together a second expedition with the express purpose of collecting mammals and birds of scientific value. She contacted Grinnell in the hope that he knew the whereabouts of one of his ornithology students, Joseph Dixon, who had been recommended to her. That conversation evolved into a longer one. Alexander discovered not only how much Grinnell had already sampled and cataloged the vertebrate fauna of Alaska, but also how well his qualities matched what she was looking for in a director of the museum she wanted to establish at Berkeley. He had a keen knowledge of natural history, a scientific acumen, and perhaps more experience than anyone at the time in collecting, documenting, and preserving the skins and skeletons of Western vertebrates; what's more, he knew how to inspire people to work together. For his part, Grinnell discovered that Alexander was an astute planner, a remarkable natural historian in her own right, and a consummate field biologist. The upshot was that Alexander took Grinnell's student Dixon on the expedition, but it was Grinnell himself who was her real find. Upon her return, she invited Grinnell not only to examine the materials of the Alaskan expedition, but also to direct the new museum she was setting up. Grinnell agreed and on April Fools Day, 1908, he started as director.[13]

Like John Muir, Annie Alexander and Joseph Grinnell recognized that they were watching the West vanish. Whereas Muir's response was to protect big parcels of land, Alexander's and Grinnell's was to save samples of the species that were disappearing, and to accurately document where those species thrived in the absence of human impacts. The "samples" were the skins and skeletons of dead animals, carefully preserved, labeled, and intended to be kept essentially forever in the new museum that Alexander commissioned. The skins and skeletons were cross-referenced to accurate descriptions of the places and habitats in which the animals—now museum specimens— had lived. Grinnell came up with a scheme to observe and sample animals systematically in the wild using a series of transects that ran more or less east-west across various parts of the state of California, capturing and observing animals from the lowest to the highest elevations. One of the transects ran right through John Muir's new Yosemite National Park.

With that project, the separate visions of Muir, Alexander, and Grinnell came together to give us exactly what we need today: a way to see firsthand how global warming has been affecting a biologically rich area, in this case one of the world's most famous nature preserves. Muir, in effect, had delineated a museum of nature—a relatively undisturbed parcel of land where, he hoped, Earth's processes could unfold more or less as they would undisturbed by the heavy hand of humans.[14] Alexander built the museum to hold the "voucher specimens" that now tell us what species should be in Yosemite if climatic and other conditions had remained more or less unchanged over the past century. And Grinnell spearheaded the science that makes those skins and skeletons, collected so long ago, of inestimable value today.

In a series of Yosemite expeditions that spanned the years 1914 to 1920, Grinnell and his teams put in 957 "man-days," or the equivalent of one person working every day of the year for three years without a break.[15] They collected 4,354 vertebrate specimens, all of them now sitting in drawers in the museum, and each catalogued as to habitat and other relevant information recorded in some 2,000 pages of field notes. Grinnell and his colleagues published this impressive compilation of ecological data in 1924 in a treatise entitled "Animal Life of the Yosemite."[16]

Today, those thousands of specimens and thousands of pages of notes have a lot of eyes focused on them—two of which are Jim Patton's. Although he'd deny it, Patton is the modern equivalent of Grinnell when it comes to collecting and studying rats. No-nonsense, straight shooter, competent, wry: those are the words that come to mind when you look him in the eyes. After some three decades building his own legacy at the Museum of Vertabrate Zoology (including a stint acting as MVZ director), Patton nominally retired. If retirement to some people means putting your feet up and taking it easy, in Patton's case it means putting on his boots to focus on the field work he loves—and that's trapping rats.

Which was a lucky thing for current MVZ director Craig Moritz, when in 2002 he hatched a plan with others at the MVZ and Yosemite's scientists to figure out whether global warming and other human impacts had already changed the park's ecosystem. What he needed was somebody who, like Grinnell, had a lot of savvy about the habits of animals in the wild, who wrote up his results as prodigiously as he collected, and who was a charismatic leader; a person who, in addition, would look at it as a privilege to live out of a tent and work 14- to 16-hour days in the middle of nowhere, on a schedule that called for going out after dinner and setting trap lines until dark, then getting up before dawn to check the traps, spending the intervening hours writing minute details about all the animals that were collected, and then, when necessary, skinning and stuffing mice. Patton was his man.

Patton is three generations removed from Grinnell; Moritz four generations; and the younger scientists on the project five. Only now are they bringing to fruition what Grinnell had started so many years ago: they're going back to the same places in Yosemite where Grinnell had made his observations to see if the same species are still there. Around the MVZ, they call it the "Grinnell Resurvey Project."

The field crews knew that a couple of species—like grizzly bears—were absent from the park not because of climate, but because people had killed them or otherwise driven them out long ago.[17] What they hadn't counted on was the changes they saw in many of the small critters. "I was dumbfounded," Patton said, when he peered into one of the Sherman traps in Lyell Canyon.[18] A Sherman trap is a rectangular aluminum box about as wide and tall as a pint-sized milk carton but twice as long; it has a spring-loaded door at one end, and at the other you stick some peanut butter and oats. When a rodent scurries in for a free midnight snack, *snap*—the trapdoor shuts. Sherman traps are nice because if you want you can let the animals go after you see what they are. Patton's surprise that morning in Lyell Canyon was to find, staring back at him when he carefully pushed open the trap's door, the bulgy black eyes and big ears of a piñon mouse, otherwise known as *Peromyscus truei*.

Piñon mice are called that because they typically are found where piñon trees grow. Or junipers. Or other kinds of plants that grow in hot, dry places. The reason Patton was dumbfounded was that the piñon mouse he caught was at 3,100 meters (10,200 feet), where there were alpine forests and meadows and where it was supposed to be too cold for piñon mice, as it had been in 1915 when Grinnell was out there. Grinnell's crews didn't find them above 2,133 meters (7,000 feet), and only on the drier, warmer, east side of the Sierra. Neither were piñon mice now occurring as low on the slopes as they had in Grinnell's time: Patton's crews discovered that their lower boundary appeared to be some 305 meters (1,000 feet) higher today than it had been a century earlier. Like the pikas mentioned in Chapter 3, the piñon mice apparently are marching upslope.

They are not the only ones. At a California State Government conference on climate change held in 2006, Chris Conroy, a curatorial associate at the MVZ and key participant in the Grinnell Resurvey Project, summarized what he, Patton, Moritz, and the rest of the team were discovering about how Yosemite's fauna had changed since Grinnell's time, and found that a pattern was emerging.[19] That pattern became even more evident by 2008, when the team's results were published in the journal *Science*.[20] Key findings in respect to climate were in the small mammals, like the piñon mouse, primarily because they are the best sampled and not directly affected by other human activities like hunting.

In Grinnell's time, the small mammal fauna of the Yosemite region—the park and the area outside the park covered in his trapping transect—included 56 species.[21] The good news is that nearly all of those species are still found in the park or immediate envi-rons—in that respect, John Muir's dream of preserving the species and their habitats is still intact. The bad news, though, is that many of those species have changed where they live in the park, in a way that indicates some may be on the way out.

Both Grinnell's survey and the current resurvey showed that not all of the small-mammal species are everywhere in the park: at any one place, only between 6 and 20 of them are common. That reflects the diversity of Yosemite's habitats, ranging in elevation from about 1,200 meters (4,000 feet) in Yosemite Valley to over 3,900 meters (more than 13,000 feet) at places like Mount Lyell. The species tend to sort out more or less by elevation, according to the climate and resultant vegetation that tends to follow the altitudinal gradient, with hotter, drier habitats down low, and moister, cooler habitats up high, as one would expect.

At any given elevation, the Grinnell team is finding that notice-able changes in the mammal fauna are afoot. At every one of the 16 localities sampled by 2006, there were some species that were only there in Grinnell's time, and others that are new arrivals today. The percentages of missing taxa or new arrivals vary by locality, but in general, between one-third and one-half of the species present in a given place today seem to be different from the ones that were there 90 years ago. That is a lot of faunal turnover in a short time.

The disturbing part is that the turnover of species is not random, as you might expect if species were simply expanding and contracting their ranges as they do year to year in response to normal fluctuations in weather, food supply, and so on. Instead, the changes point toward ecological adjustment due to warming temperatures, often—but not always—disadvantageous to the species. As of 2008 at least 28 of the small mammal species had been well-enough sampled to determine whether they are in the same place that they were in Grinnell's time, or whether significant changes in distribution have taken place. Of those 28, half have moved in directions that would be expected if global warming were displacing them.[22]

Take, for example, species characteristic of the lowlands, like the piñon mice mentioned earlier. Other lowlanders in Yosemite include the California pocket mouse (*Chaetodipus californicus*), the California ground squirrel (*Spermophilus beechyi*), the California vole (*Microtus californicus*), the western harvest mouse (*Reithrodontomys megalotis*), and the dusky-footed wood rat (*Neotoma macrotis*). At least four of these six lowlanders (piñon mice, California pocket mouse, California vole, western harvest mouse) have extended their ranges on average about 502 meters (1,647 feet) upward. It's still not certain whether some of those range extensions are due mainly to climate or to vegetation changes associated with forest fires, but the pattern is suggestive of a climatic cause. In the bigger picture, these species have geographic ranges that are the most southerly of the Yosemite fauna, extending all the way down into Baja California. To the north, none except the western harvest mouse make it very far past the Oregon-Washington border. That kind of overall distribution indicates that such species do perfectly well in some pretty hot places, but do not survive where winter temperatures get too cold.

Today, winter temperatures in Yosemite Valley are about 4°C (~7°F) warmer than they were in Grinnell's time.[23] While this is only a single climate station in a topographically diverse region, its climate record becomes very interesting when you compare the amount of warming to what's called the "lapse rate." The lapse rate is a meteorological term which simply means that as you go higher in elevation, the air cools off at a more or less regular rate, namely, for every 305 meters (1,000 feet) you go up, temperature cools by about 2°C (3.6°F). The math is pretty simple: put together the lapse rate with the amount of warming the park has experienced, and you see that the winter temperatures those lowland species are feeling today at a given location may be just about the same as what their counterparts were feeling some 600 meters (around 2,000 feet) lower 90 years ago. If this is true, then over the past 90 years, these small-sized species characteristic of the lowlands have been rapidly expanding to fill their available climate space; as the critical winter temperature values that limited their overall distribution migrate upward in elevation, they seem to be following right behind. For such species, global warming in Yosemite may actually be good news as it expands the habitable space available to them.

Not all species are so lucky. Some of the species whose overall geographic ranges are mostly confined to upper-elevation or northerly locations, where summer temperatures never get very warm, are literally being squeezed out of the park. In Yosemite such species include pikas (*Ochotona princeps*), golden-mantled ground squirrels (*Spermophilus lateralis*), Belding's ground squirrels (*Spermophilus beldingi*), alpine chipmunks (*Tamias alpinus*), long-tailed voles (*Microtus longicaudus*), and water shrews (*Sorex palustris*). On average these species have lost the lower 418 meters (1,371 feet) of their geographic range as compared to where Grinnell found them.

Even harder-hit species are the bushy-tailed wood rats (*Neotoma cinerea*) and Allen's chipmunks (*Tamias senex*). In Grinnell's time, bushy-tailed wood rats and Allen's chipmunks were two fairly common "northern species" that could be found through much of the altitudinal extent of the park; they were found through some 1,300 or more meters (4,300 feet). Today, they have become rare and are confined to a narrow zone of just 100 meters (328 feet) centering on about 2,450 meters elevation (8,000 feet). Western jumping mice (*Zapus princeps*) represent another "northern" species that has been losing both the bottom and top of its range, which contracted 159 and 64 meters (522 and 210 feet), respectively, since Grinnell's time.[24] These three species have the majority of their geographic range to the north of Yosemite, with their southern and elevational limits related to warm summer temperatures. When you consider that today summer temperatures in Yosemite Valley are 6°C (~11°F) hotter than they were 90 years ago,[25] it is not surprising that species whose geographic range is limited by high summer temperatures are being squeezed out.

What is particularly troubling is that species apparently limited by high temperatures are losing the tops of their elevational range as well as the bottom. Given what we know about lapse rates, you would expect both the bottom and top of the elevational range to migrate upward at approximately the same rate, at least until you run out of mountaintop. Two things conspire against that, though. First, mountains are much wider at the base than they are at the top. That means that, for any given range of elevation, there will be less area on the mountain at higher elevations compared to lower ones. For any species in the act of moving upslope, that means absolutely fewer available habitats into which individuals can disperse, which in turn, means lower population sizes. If population sizes cannot grow to a critical level, the species cannot persist.

Second, and perhaps especially pernicious for species limited by hot summer temperatures, is that the actual temperature you experience on the ground at high elevations is higher than what you experience at lower elevations. You know this if you've ever hiked around without a hat at 3,000 meters (10,000 feet) or so. Less air, less filtering of solar radiation, more sunburn, more dehydration. At ground level itself, where the small mammals live, this effect is even more pronounced. Studies of the actual, on-the-ground temperature experienced by ground squirrels has demonstrated that in the summer it's a lot hotter for them at elevations above 3,000 meters (10,000 feet) than a thousand or so meters lower.[26] The lesson is that animals limited by hot summer temperatures don't have a lot of options in the face of global warming: high temperatures squeeze them from the lower elevations, but they can't move very far uphill because the upper slopes are effectively too hot for them as well.

The resurvey team has looked into other explanations for the species range-changes they've observed, and in most cases have been able to discount potential causes other than climate change. For example, photographs taken 90 years ago show that vegetation zones have not changed substantially at the elevations where the biggest changes in species distributions have occurred. Nor have direct impacts by people disturbed the backcountry to an extent that could explain the observed species readjustments.

But the Grinnell team did find a couple of surprises that are hard to explain from climate change alone: a typically northerly distributed species, the montane shrew (*Sorex monticolus*) has shifted its lower elevational boundary downward 1,000 meters (3,280 feet). Also unclear is what is driving pronounced range contraction in a critically endangered kangaroo rat, *Dipodomys heermanni*, which since Grinnell's time has lost the bottom 63 meters (207 feet) and top 293 meters (961 feet) from its elevational range. Kangaroo rats typically are desert animals, so would be expected to do well with global warming in Yosemite. Whatever their cause, such shifts hint at altered ecological dynamics.[27]

That we can't predict every species response is also illustrated by those species the Grinnell team found that seem relatively unaffected by the temperature changes in Yosemite so far.[28] Three of them are northern species; their occurrence in Yosemite is near the southern boundaries of their respective species' ranges in the California Sierra. A fourth unaffected species occurs only in a narrow elevational band in the Sierra. These all seem like prime candidates for showing elevational range retractions in Yosemite, yet they have not.

Other unaffected species are those that have geographically wide distributions outside of Yosemite, indicating their tolerance to a wide variety of climatic conditions. Examples include the deer mouse (*Peromyscus maniculatus*) and the brush mouse (*P. boylii*). Where Grinnell found them, the Grinnell Resurvey team found them.

The Grinnell Resurvey Project, like global warming itself, is still a work in progress. But already it is teaching some important lessons about how global warming has hit Yosemite and is changing the ecology of the park. First, the climate-induced community changes in mammal fauna are taking place in "real time"—that is, the species ranges are changing just about as fast as climate is. So as climatic conditions continue to change in the park, we can expect the communities to diverge farther and farther from those that were there when Muir pushed for the park and Grinnell trapped in it. Second, if current trends continue, as seems likely given climatic forecasts, we can expect to lose some once-widespread, common species by virtue of losing the climate that supports them in the park. They won't be back once they go. And third, along with changes that can reasonably be attributed to climate change, there may be unexpected effects on species—such as the unexplained expansion the Grinnell team saw for the montane shrew—that contribute to the overall ecological change.

That is the sobering part of the story—but there is still a silver lining, at least for the time being. All but perhaps two of the small-mammal species that were there in Grinnell's and John Muir's time are still somewhere in the park.[29] That means that in a broad sense, Yosemite's ecological integrity is still largely intact, if we define ecological integrity as maintaining the species that interacted within the boundaries of the park when it was established. It is also still intact if we define ecological integrity as the potential for continued interaction of the natural complement of species—a more appropriate definition given that we know that habitats and communities within ecosystems typically expand and contract through longer courses of time (recall the discussion in Chapter 2). The optimistic view is that John Muir, were he walking through the park today, could breathe a sigh of relief that it has fared as well as it has—especially considering the crowds of people who use the park, and the obvious signs of their use, such as pavement and campgrounds. From the ecological perspective, the assemblages of species may be rearranged into communities somewhat different than they were 100 years ago, but nevertheless they are still in the park and have the potential to continue to rearrange themselves as particular habitats ebb and flow.

Looked at in that light, Yosemite's pulse may be flickering some, but it is still strong. John Muir's dream is still alive. The danger is that the climate trends of the past decades will not only continue but will intensify, which in turn will push those climate-sensitive species now teetering on the brink of extinction in the park over the edge. At a minimum, that means the loss of three species (Allen's chipmunks, bushy-tailed wood rats, and possibly western jumping mice) already seemingly on the way out. Others, like the six "northern species" the Grinnell resurveyers documented marching upslope, almost certainly will follow, and after that, several other species whose current distributions seem like they ought to retract if things get hot enough, but which haven't yet been affected. Put that in the context of how much change there has otherwise been in Yosemite's ecosystem since Muir's time, and it becomes clear that if current climate-driven ecological trajectories continue, over the next couple of decades global warming alone could cause more loss of species in Yosemite, and bigger changes in its ecosystems, than did the pressures on the park introduced by settling, agriculturalization, and the urbanization of California over the past 100 years. In short, John Muir's dream, which we've been able to keep alive for a century despite an increase in California's population to nearly 37 million people, could be snuffed out.

In some ways, we stand at the same crossroads today that John Muir, Annie Alexander, and Joseph Grinnell saw themselves at a century ago—where ecological changes are outpacing those of previous generations. What made those three great, and what gives their lives a lasting legacy, was their ability to look into the future and to do something that would help shape that future for the common good. Each contributed—Muir with political activism, Alexander with business savvy, and Grinnell with scientific acumen. Their combined legacy was even greater than their individual ones: together, they gave us not only a piece of nature to save, but a way to know if we're actually saving it. Today, in a warming world that Muir, Grinnell, and Alexander never anticipated, we're facing the same kind of choice about nature that they did: let it go, or dare to shape its future.

Chapter 7 ⟿

Disturbance in Yellowstone

If we are dealing with a system profoundly affected by changes external to it, and continually confronted by the unexpected, the constancy of its behavior becomes less important than the persistence of the relationships.

—C. S. Holling, 1973[1]

In 1872, the United States government established Yellowstone National Park as the world's first legislated effort at nature conservation. As a result, the park now forms the core of what is arguably the largest intact natural ecosystem in temperate parts of the world—Greater Yellowstone, covering 73,000 square kilometers (18,000,000 acres) across a broad swath of wild and magnificent country in northwestern Wyoming, eastern Idaho, and southern Montana.[2] You can get farther from a road there than anywhere else in the contiguous lower 48 states, and that's so far that getting there on horseback still takes a few days. A day and a half into one of those backcountry trips, my horse stiffened and stopped dead in his tracks, snorted and laid his ears back, then skittered around, kicking up dust from the trail. I was startled out of my reverie, and like the horse, I knew what it was before I saw it. I had been unconciously taking in the smell of warm pine needles; all of a sudden, another scent was in the air—one that triggers ancient instincts and raises the hair on the back of your neck: the musky odor of a grizzly bear. Like most such encounters, the meeting proceeded peacefully enough, with the bear seemingly about as surprised to see us as we were to see him, and both of us giving each other the proper amount of respect and going on our way. These kinds of Yellowstone encounters can't help but give you the feeling that the place may not have changed that much since 1872, and even before. Grizzly bears and other wild species like elk, moose, bison, mountain lions, and dozens more seem to be a normal part of life there, doing what they have always done.

In fact, that feeling is backed up by hard data[3]—the kind of data that helps us realize just how serious the 100-year trajectory of climate change we've seen so far for Yosemite and elsewhere really is. Scientists have actually used fossils and other information to track Yellowstone's ecological pulse through much longer, the past three thousand years, and importantly, through a past warming event called the Medieval Warm Period. That begins to be a long enough span to recognize whether today's climate changes are affecting the park—and by inference, other ecosystems—in particularly disturbing ways. Monitoring an ecosystem over three thousand years is no easy task, though; the right place, the right kind of information, and the right kind of people seldom come together at the right time. Luckily, they did in Yellowstone.

In the summer of 1988, the same summer that the Senate Committee on Energy and Natural Resources was holding hearings on global climate change on Capitol Hill, Yellowstone Park was burning. From a distance, it looked like dirty thunderheads billowing out of the park. In the heat of it on the ground, the first thing you saw was a rolling, swelling, ugly gray cloud rising out of the next drainage as the fire climbed up the ridge between you and it. Then the lodgepole pines exploded in flame, like so many match heads, as the fire crested the ridgeline. Flaming bits of tree trunk and branches caught the hot wind, an advance guard of incendiary bombs. John Varley, Chief of the Division of Research in Yellowstone at the time, recalls: "It smelled awful. It smelled like being in the middle of a bonfire. You could taste it in your food and in your sleep, and you had the feeling that you always needed a shower."[4]

If you close your eyes when you talk to Varley, who headed up the research office in Yellowstone for 23 years, you could easily imagine you're talking to the old-time movie actor Jimmy Stewart, with his not-quite-slow, almost gravelly drawl. You get the sense that every-thing you're hearing is a discovery. One of the researchers he had out in the field that summer was Liz Hadly, who was trying to figure out what Yellowstone was like a few thousand years before the U.S. gov-ernment decided to protect it. What Hadly and Varley had in mind was, in effect, to establish the natural baseline for fauna in Yellow-stone, so that it would be possible to assess which vertebrate species were native, and which had been noticeably influenced by human impacts since the park was designated.

During that summer of 1988, Hadly and her crew crouched in Lamar Cave, dressed in their bright-yellow, flame-retardant Nomex firefighter shirts as smoke was filling the air. They were frantically bagging up the fossils they had been carefully extracting from the cave over the past weeks and getting them ready to be flown out by a firefighting helicopter—a "helitack evacuation," in smokejumper's jargon. The fires were getting too close and word had come down to get out fast. Usually, they hiked seven kilometers (a little over four miles) out of the backcountry with the bags of rocks on their backs, but with fires burning all around, that had become too risky—for the fossils at least, which filled the helicopter's weight capacity. For this last hike out, the researchers ended up shortcutting the usual round-about route by fording the waist-deep Lamar River, hurrying through the surreal, smoke-filled, ember-spitting landscape. They, and their hard-won spoils from a season's worth of work, were headed back to Hadly's home in Gardiner, Montana.

That, too, ended in evacuation. When the fires began encroach-ing on Gardiner and residents were urged to load up their irreplace-able goods and leave, Hadly filled her car with the fossils and got out of town. Today, the fossils reside in fireproof, climate-controlled museum cases in Hadly's lab at Stanford University, where she and her students have been analyzing them to understand how Yellow-stone's vertebrate species have (or have not) persisted in their eco-logical relationships in the face of both climate changes and direct human impacts.

"Analyzing," loosely translated, means "years of painstaking work." In the case of figuring out what happened over three millennia in Yellowstone, that work began in Lamar Cave, three years before the helitack evacuation. When you duck from the sunshine into the perpetual shade of the cave, you're greeted not only by refreshingly cooler air on a hot summer day, but also by what Hadly calls the smell of the past—it's sweet and pungent at the same time, a little on the strong side, but not unpleasant. In fact it's wood rat urine, in this case the pee of *Neotoma cinerea*, the bushy-tailed wood rat. It stains the rock walls black, creating a shiny curtain called amberat. Two good things about amberat: it is a natural preservative, and it means that wood rats have been living in the place for years, in some cases thousands of years.

You may know wood rats by their other common name, packrats, so called because they have the habit of collecting odd objects they find lying around and bringing them back to their nests. That habit is a very lucky one for people who study the past—among the favorite items for wood rats to collect are bones, and even better, bones encased in the pellets that owls, hawks, and other raptors regurgitate or that wolves, coyotes, and other mammalian carnivores defecate. Usually, those bird and mammal predators range up to a few miles from their homes to find small animals to eat, and roost or den near the places that bushy-tailed wood rats frequent, that is, crevices, rock shelters, and caves found along cliffs. Raptors, especially, occupy the same roosting areas generation after generation, and each generation regurgitates its share of bone-packed pellets that fall to the base of the cliff below the nest.

In lucky instances like Lamar Cave, generation after generation of the bushy-tailed wood rats that call a particular crevice home sneak out at night, grab a few pellets, and decorate their nests with them. The same furtive rats also grab small bones of larger animals that happen to die near the cave entrance—a hoof here, a molar there, sometimes a finger or toe. The net effect is that the bones, plants, and other things the rats collect build up into a pile of junk called a midden, which under the right conditions, like the dry air and constant temperatures found in some caves, is protected from decay. Through their collection, generation after generation, of raptor pellets, carnivore scat, and carcass parts, bushy-tailed wood rats are even better than scientists at sampling the fauna that lives in a given area. Discrete layers in the middens each represent a snapshot in time. Each snapshot can record more than 90 percent of the mammal species present within a 5–15 kilometer radius of the midden, and accurately reflect the relative abundance of the small ones like various rodent, rabbit, and insectivore species.[5] In ideal settings, those snapshots accumulate one on top of the other over thousands of years[6]—and that is what happened at Lamar Cave. When Hadly's trowel finally scraped against the bedrock floor of the cave, some 2.5 meters (8 feet) below the bone-littered surface she had first troweled off nine years earlier, she was looking at the Yellowstone of 2,860 radiocarbon years ago, plus or minus 70 years.

That was the oldest of 18 radiocarbon dates she had obtained, each of them from a discrete part of the ancient midden. When assembled in chronological order and calibrated to calendar years, the radiocarbon dates identified five slices of time, the most recent one sampling species that lived back to 300 years ago, then samples from, respectively, about 300–600 years ago, 600–1,200 years, 1,200–1,900 years, and finally the oldest time-slice sampling species that lived between about 1,900 and 3,500 years ago.[7]

Time is generally an abstract concept. In Lamar Cave, it became something you could touch. Each one of those temporal snapshots was in reality composed of layers of bones, dirt, plants, and yes, wood rat feces. Essentially each spoonful of each layer was scraped off with a trowel. With each scrape, bigger bones were recorded and collected, and everything else was bagged, hauled to the river, and washed through screens, off of which tens of thousands of bones were picked and identified. With that, the Yellowstone that was there some 3,200 years before the park was set aside came alive. And importantly, so did the Yellowstone that was there at time slices centered on about 150, 450, 900, and 1,600 years ago. Stacking those snapshots one on top of the other and flipping through them began to give something akin to the jerky animation you get by flipping through a series of cartoon sketches—in this case, the playback was of how the park's ecosystem had changed through three millennia. And it told something very interesting.

From the viewpoint of C. S. Holling's ideas about "persistence of relationships"—Holling is an eminent ecologist at University of Florida who authored the famous paper on ecological disturbance quoted in this chapter's epigraph—the park had not changed very much through those 3,200 years, and by the year 2000, it still hadn't. Despite being surrounded by human impacts like logging, agriculture, and settlements that make the boundary of Yellowstone National Park visible from outer space, the park still has 39 of the 40 mammal species that it had 3,200 years ago.[8] That includes the big predators, grizzly bears (*Ursus arctos*) and wolves (*Canis lupus*), for example, and the big prey they eat, such as wapiti elk (*Cervus elaphus*), moose (*Alces alces*), bison (*Bison bison*), and bighorn sheep (*Ovis canadensis*). The bones from Lamar Cave showed for sure that at various times between 300 and 1,700 years ago, wolves and grizzlies had frequented the same rangeland where elk were calving, just as they do today. That the elk had been calving nearby, not just passing through, was shown by a jaw of a baby elk, easily recognizable by its small size, paper-thin jawbone, and partially erupted baby teeth. The calf was so young it could not have traveled far before it died and decomposed near the cave, where the jaw eventually was preserved after a wood rat dragged it into a midden.

Calving time is mealtime for the big predators. Usually it happens in the spring, right when the bears are coming out of hibernation and feeling a bit hungry. Hadly describes coming across one of those calving grounds early one morning, just as new grass was greening between the melting patches of snow, and hearing the panicked bleating of a herd of female elk—short, high-pitched notes in rapid succession. Their terror came from watching a grizzly bear tearing one of their calves to pieces. An hour or so later not much was left. And in recent years, it's not uncommon for park visitors to see wolves feeding at an elk carcass, with coyotes hanging back to wait for the leftovers and ravens circling overhead awaiting their turn, interactions that the Lamar Cave bones imply have been going on for thousands of years.

Those kinds of ecological interactions were temporarily interrupted in Yellowstone by human intervention. By the 1930s, all the wolves had been shot out, and up until the late 1960s grizzlies enjoyed feasts at garbage dumps that had bleachers around them so that tourists could watch.[9] But, just as people had caused these particular changes, people were able to fix them. Beginning in 1970, the garbage dumps were closed, and bears eventually started to hunt and forage on their own again. Wolves were reintroduced in 1994–95—but not until after a decade of heated political debate, in which the Lamar Cave finds helped to demonstrate that wolves were, in fact, native to the park long before it was a park.[10]

The wolf eradication, then reintroduction, gave some insights into what happens to ecosystems when you tinker with populations of large carnivores. Since wolves were set free from their reintroduction cages in 1994 and they resumed their place in the large-carnivore niche, the ecosystem has returned to a state where coyotes have fallen slightly in number.[11] With fewer coyotes to compete with, life is better for foxes, which have become more abundant. The wolves cull more elk than the coyotes were able to, and do so year-round. As a result, more food is available for species that depend on carrion to feed them during the lean late-fall, winter, and early spring months, species such as ravens (*Corvus corax*), bald eagles (*Haliaeetus leucocephalus*), golden eagles (*Aquila chrysaetos*), magpies (*Pica pica*), grizzly bears (*Ursus arctos*), and black bears (*Ursus americanus*). Putting wolves back into the ecosystem actually appears to be buffering such species against the variations in winterkill that are being introduced by recent climate changes in the park.[12] Moreover, aspen and willow are regenerating in areas where bigger elk populations had kept them pruned during the missing-wolf years.[13]

Those fixes—making grizzlies wild again and bringing back wolves—were by no means easy, as John Varley can attest, but they meant that Yellowstone's ecosystem once again was operating as Lamar Cave showed it had done hundreds and thousands of years ago. Lamar Cave also showed how the Greater Yellowstone ecosystem responded to what was the most significant global warming event, prior to the current one, in the past 3,200 years. The Medieval Warm Period, mentioned briefly in Chapter 2, saw the globe warm by 1°C (1.8°F) over 100 years, beginning near 1,150 years ago.[14] The globally warm times lasted for about 400 years and made possible such events as the Viking colonizations of Greenland.[15]

To figure out whether or not the Medieval Warm Period affected ecosystems in Yellowstone, a record of climate change independent of the Lamar Cave bones was needed. That's where Yellowstone's fire history came into the picture. About the time Hadly was digging bones out of Lamar Cave, Grant Meyer was digging charcoal out of gully walls. He was working out how often fires had burned in Yellowstone over the past thousands of years. Meyer knew that when a fire burns off the vegetation in mountainous topography such as Yellowstone, abnormally large volumes of sediment erode off the hill slopes and end up in the streams, where eventually the sediment settles out in distinctive layers. Meyer's approach was to find and map those distinctive layers buried in ancient stream deposits, radiocarbon-date the enclosed charcoal and other organic debris, and use that to work out when in the past forest fires had ignited on a regular basis.

By tracking the fire history preserved in the stream deposits, Meyer also tracked the climate history. In order for forest fires to ignite frequently, the climate has to be right—that is to say, hot and dry during the summer, just like it was during those fires of 1988. His fire and climate data implied that starting about 3,500 years ago, Yellowstone's climate was wet, then from about 2,700 to 1,900 years ago it was warm with variable moisture and increased fire frequency, then precipitation increased again with fewer fires from 1,900 to 1,200 years ago. From 1,200 to 700 years ago, Meyer discovered a very warm, dry time with high fire frequency in Yellowstone: the Medieval Warm Period.[16]

Hadly matched up her faunal sequences with Meyer's alluvial sequences and saw a couple of interesting things. First, the main response of environmentally sensitive species was to either decrease or increase their relative abundance—that is, how many of their individuals were running around the landscape—according to the prevailing climate of the time. For example, in the warm times like the Medieval Warm Period, there were more ground squirrels (*Spermophilus*) than voles (*Microtus*). Ground squirrels typically occupy the most arid microhabitats of a given landscape, whereas voles live in the relatively well-watered grassy areas. In warmer, drier times, a bigger percentage of the landscape is covered by the dry microhabitats, hence more ground squirrels, and in wetter times, well-watered grasslands expand, hence more voles. But despite such climatic shifts into, then out of the Medieval Warm Period, and the resulting changes in population sizes in the respective species, both kinds of microhabitats remained, and so did the species that occupied them.[17]

The same sort of thing held for the habitats of all 40 of the mammal species in the Lamar Cave record. Despite changes in relative abundance, every one of them made it through both the earlier, more minor climatic fluctuations, and at least 39 of them through the more intense warming of the Medieval Warm Period. Even species that were rare in the ecosystem made it through: the prairie vole (at least in the earlier changes in climate), jumping mouse, and pika, for example. That suggests that mountain ecosystems such as those in Yellowstone maintain their species interactions—the species stay put—in the face of naturally occurring climate changes. In ecological parlance, they are persistent in the face of such perturbations.

Studies that compare the Yellowstone faunal data with similar sorts of data from other mountain ecosystems make the point even more strongly: there are core assemblages of mammals—including rare species—that seem to stick together in mountain ecosystems. A small proportion of other species may come and go, but those core species are very resistant to the natural climatic perturbations that occur on the timescales of tens, hundreds, and thousands of years. Think of each of those species as an occupant of an ecological niche and it becomes evident there are certain sets of ecological niches that stick together even in the face of these naturally occurring climate changes. Again in ecological parlance, the ecosystem itself has inertia, meaning that it takes a lot to push it out of its usual condition.[18]

Those findings drive home the point that the climate-related changes we are seeing today, even in common species, are truly out of the ordinary. The changes in relative abundance in themselves are not too disturbing—the Lamar Cave record shows that those fall within the range of normal fluctuation so far. What is disturbing is that formerly common and persistent species are disappearing from where they used to be (as in those range retractions in Yosemite described in the preceding chapter), which means their ecological niches are shriveling up and disappearing. What happens when an ecological niche shrinks too much during a climate change is illustrated by the only mammal that Yellowstone lacks today, compared to what was there over most of the past 3,200 years.

It's an insignificant little beast in most people's eyes, a mouse-sized, short-tailed fuzzball called a prairie vole, or *Microtus ochrogaster*. But prairie voles have achieved a notoriety of sorts because of what their genes tell us about monogamy. There is a wonderful illustration in a 2004 *Nature* paper by Miranda Lim and colleagues in which two prairie voles are huddled together. Right next to that is another picture, which shows the brains of prairie voles lighting up as a certain chemical receptor, vasopressin, activates, indicating that a companion is likable.[19] The Lim team transferred the prairie-vole gene that stimulates vasopressin into another species of vole that is not monogamous, the meadow vole (*Microtus pennsyvanicus*). With that single alteration, non-monogomous meadow voles had their brains light up too, and they became more likely to stay with just one partner, suggesting a genetic contribution to fidelity.

Today the closest prairie voles to Yellowstone are about 50 miles (80 kilometers) to the north, in tall-grass prairies. Studies on living voles have shown that within those tall-grass prairies, their population densities vary with available moisture, more voles being found in moister places. But it can't be too moist or meadow voles (those polygamous ones) replace the prairie voles. That sort of information suggests that when prairie voles were present in Yellowstone, there were areas of denser grasslands than there are today.[20]

The Lamar Cave fossils indicate that prairie voles lasted in Yellowstone almost continuously, though individuals were scarce in the populations (which biologists term "occurring in low abundance") for 2,300 years, beginning 2,900 years ago. By the end of the Medieval Warm Period, prairie voles were gone. In Yellowstone, combining Meyer's alluvial chronology with fossil pollen records indicates that the Medieval Warm Period and the prairie vole's disappearance line up almost exactly with the time that grass cover—

the habitat needed by prairie voles—was sparsest in the 3,500-year history.[21] Climate returned to cool, moist conditions from 600 to 300 years ago, but for most of that time, there are no prairie vole fossils. Two teeth (maybe from the same individual) were found in a layer that probably dates to between 300 and 80 years ago.[22] Prairie vole presence at that time would mean that it took at least 300 years for them to make their way back into the park after climate once again returned to pre–Medieval Warm Period conditions. But it seems that after the Medieval Warm Period they still have not been able to re-establish themselves as a lasting part of the Yellowstone ecosystem.

In that there may be a lesson for other places that are being affected by climate change today. Unlike the case of species that we pluck from ecosystems and then reintroduce intentionally—like wolves—there may be no going back for a species whose habitat is eliminated when climate changes. Even if climate returns to pre-change conditions, there is no guarantee that all the habitats that were there before the climate change will return.

How does the amount and rate of the global heat-up during the Medieval Warm Period compare to what is coming down the road for Yellowstone in the next century? As noted in Chapter 2, there seems little doubt that the rate of warming is faster now than it was during the Medieval Warm Period—in the best case, 10 percent faster, in the worst case, maybe up to 500 percent faster. As for magnitude: in the year 2000, we attained roughly the global temperature that prevailed during the Medieval Warm Period, and by now we're about 0.4°C (0.7°F) warmer than that.[23] It doesn't sound like much. But for the ecosystem in Yellowstone, it may be a lot, at least as judged from some of its species' recent responses.

Living alongside all those mammals during the Medieval Warm Period were four amphibian species: the blotched tiger salamander (*Ambystoma tigrinum melanostictum*), the boreal chorus frog (*Pseudacaris triseriata maculata*), the Colombia spotted frog (*Rana lutieventris*, formerly *Rana pretiosa*) and the boreal toad (*Bufo boreas boreas*). The tiger salamander has bones distinctive enough to trace its fossil history through the Lamar Cave deposits. Like all the mammal species (except the prairie vole), the tiger salamander was in the

Lamar Cave region before, during, and after the Medieval Warm Period. Like the warmth-loving mammals, tiger salamanders increased in abundance during the Medieval Warm Period. They also did something else, something only an amphibian can pull off. They metamorphosed faster during the Medieval Warm Period.[24] Tiger salamanders have the ability to either remain in an advanced tadpole stage, ultimately reaching sexual maturity without ever leaving the water, or to metamorphose into full-blown, land-dwelling salamanders that lose the tadpole tail. You can tell whether they were in the tadpole-like, sexually mature (or paedomorphic) stage or whether they had fully metamorphosed by looking at their vertebrae.[25] In the Lamar Cave layers deposited during the Medieval Warm Period, the vertebrae indicate that as ponds shrank, metamorphosis was triggered in more than usual numbers of salamanders. Life seemed good for salamanders during that warm time—there were more of them, and a higher percentage of them were going through the normal sequence of tadpole-through-adult life-history stages.

Ponds are shrinking in Yellowstone again, but now so much that it has become detrimental to amphibians. This time, rather than increasing in number and metamorphosing earlier, salamanders are dying. So are chorus frogs and spotted frogs. In the latest attempt to compare Yellowstone's present ecology to its past, Hadly and one of her graduate students, Sarah McMenamin, compared a census of amphibians and ponds taken in 2006, 2007, and 2008 with a similar census taken in 1992 and 1993, and then analyzed climate trends in Yellowstone over the past 60 years.[26] They came up with some disturbing results.

Looking back from 2007, there has been no hotter consecutive stretch of 15 years in Yellowstone for at least the last 60 years (which is how far back consistent climate records have been kept in the park). The park's local trend is consistent with the global trend, in which 12 of the hottest 15 years ever recorded fell between 1995 and 2007 and nine of the hottest ten were since 1997 (the hottest was in 2005, and 2007 and 1998 tied for the second-hottest). On top of the warming trend is a trend for less and less precipitation in Yellowstone over the past six decades. Hotter temperatures and less precipitation combine to cause more-frequent and more-severe droughts—and that is what has been happening in the park. In the last seven years (2001–2007), Yellowstone has experienced the worst droughts ever recorded there. McMenamin saw the results of all those hot, dry years when she went out armed with camera, notebook, and collecting gear in 2006 to find the ponds that had been censused 13 years earlier. The pictures she took were of lots of dried mud flats where there should have been ponds, and of dead, mud-encrusted salamanders around the edges of some of the ponds that were left.

After compiling their data, the researchers found that 8 of the 46 ponds that were hydrologically active in 1992–93 were dry in 2008 (a relatively wet year), and nearly half were dry in 2006 and 2007 (dry years). In the 1992–93 surveys, amphibians were found in 43 of the ponds; but in the 2006–2008 surveys, amphibians were found in only 21 ponds. And in those ponds, there were on average fewer species of amphibians than there had been 13 years earlier.[27] The stark statistics showed that three out of four of the amphibian species in Yellowstone are in decline. This is in the nature reserve where species have been protected longer than anywhere else. The decline is tied to global warming that just slightly exceeds what Yellowstone's ecosystem as a whole—and at least one of those amphibian species—had sailed through without much problem in the Medieval Warm Period. We seem to be witnessing, right now, more-drastic climate-induced ecological responses than Yellowstone has seen in 3,200 years.

That puts us in a unique place in ecological history. In the past three millennia, the role of climatic change in structuring the Yellowstone ecosystem has been to work from the bottom up, so to speak, tweaking the "little" things: little in the sense of mostly affecting plants and small animals, and "little" in the sense of changing the abundance of a moisture-loving species here or a dry-habitat species there. In the past 150 years, people started hitting Yellowstone species hard from the top down, directly influencing the big animals at the top of the food chain—first killing wolves and taming bears to eat garbage, and then fixing those mistakes. Now we are at the stage of trying to hold things steady at the top while global warming kicks the foundation out from below.

If you roll back the clock to those wolf-killing and bear-feeding days in Yellowstone, it's hard to fault people. They were just trying to do what seemed right at the time. The world seemed big, and it just didn't seem possible that we'd reach the state we're at today, where local problems have global causes and global consequences, where eradicating a species out of a park can wipe it off the face of the earth. We shot those wolves and fed those bears, partly because we didn't know any better. With global warming today, we don't have that excuse. As we've seen from the numerous examples discussed in previous chapters (and we'll see more in the pages that follow), the Yellowstone story is but one of many in the saga of how we are changing the global ecosystem. All of those examples add up to tell us that our generation is riding a wave of ecological change bigger than humanity has ever seen, because we're doing something we didn't even know we could do a century ago—changing Earth's baseline climate. That puts us in a fundamentally different position than we were in just a few decades ago, when our goal was to kill or tame everything that got in our way. It also puts Earth's species in a fundamentally different position than they have been in perhaps ever—including during the only other time they saw climate change anywhere near as quick and dramatic as is happening today. That was during the Pleistocene ice ages, which began some two and half million years ago.

Chapter 8 ⌒

Mountain Time in Colorado

The synergistic, or combined, effects of habitat fragmentation
and climate change represent one of the most potentially serious
global change problems.

—Terry L. Root and Stephen H. Schneider, 2002[1]

"COLORADO SPRINGS, Co.—'Old Mose,' said to be
the biggest grizzly in the Rockies, that has terrorized the country for
almost forty years and eaten up two men and hundreds of cattle, is
dead at last," ran the story in the *New York Times* on May 6, 1904.
Old Mose was one of the last grizzly bears to amble around South
Park, Colorado, a Mongolian steppe–like place about three and a half
hours southwest of Denver (if there is no traffic). It's not really a
park, but the early trappers called it one, because they saw vast herds
of bison, elk, and other animals there, reminiscent of game preserves,
and the name stuck. The air is thin there, and clear, with the low
places 2,750 meters (9,000 feet) above sea level, the high country
more than 4,260 meters (14,000 feet), and the vistas are still as wide
as the ones Old Mose must have witnessed. In some of my more pen-
sive moments, I've tried to imagine the last thing he saw; to read the
historical accounts, it was thirty of J. W. Anthony's bear-hunting
dogs, snarling, snapping, surrounding him in a frenzy as he took six
bullets from a 30-40 rifle. Today, all that's left of the bear—representative of grizzlies throughout Colorado—is his hide, bones, and skull.
The skull stares vacantly across the shelves of similarly bleached

bones in a climate-controlled room in the University of California Museum of Vertebrate Zoology (MVZ), and Old Mose now goes by the name of specimen number MVZ 113385.

At the time, killing Old Mose seemed like the right thing to do. Besides lots of livestock, he had killed at least three people and mauled others, following his own instincts on what was right. But, from an ecological point of view, the demise of Old Mose was momentous—no more were grizzlies at the top of the food chain, where they had been in that ecosystem for thousands of years.

Not far from where Old Mose was killed is a cave called Porcupine Cave, which he might have holed up in sometimes. Other bears did, leaving their fossilized remains along with those of more than a hundred other kinds of animals. Just as the fossil bones in Lamar Cave tell us about the past in Yellowstone, those from Porcupine Cave tell us how an ecosystem in the Colorado Rocky Mountains reacted to ancient climatic changes. But the story held in Porcupine Cave differs from that in Yellowstone in two important respects: first, it is about animals that lived not just a few hundred to a few thousand years ago, but about animals that interacted closer to a million years ago, long before humans ever made it to North America. Second, the Porcupine Cave bones tell us how ecosystems responded to global warming that was severe enough to shift the world from glacial times to interglacial times.

The amount of warming from a glacial to an interglacial time is analagous to what we expect with today's global warming, about 5°C (9°F). The rate of change, however, is much faster today; with glacial-interglacial transitions, the warming unfolded over millennia, whereas today, equivalent warming is taking place in just a century or so. With that difference in mind, looking at the kinds of faunal changes that accompanied glacial-interglacial transitions in Porcupine Cave offers an important perspective on ecological response to global warming. For one thing, the perspective is considerably longer than what we can get from places like Yellowstone and Yosemite; for another, it is about as good as you can get for understanding "natural" ecosystem response to climate change, in that there were no people to interfere with how the animals were reacting. Put that together with the kinds of things that happened to Old Mose after people got into the act, and we have the recipe for answering some key questions: how global warming that isn't caused by humans affects ecosystems, how (or if) that differs from what warming is causing now, and importantly, how ecologically serious the synergy of nonclimatic human pressures combined with today's global warming really is. In 1986, I set out to collect the fossils and related information that would help address those kinds of questions.

The previous year Don Rasmussen and I had bounced down the 65 kilometers (40 miles) of dirt road that leads to Porcupine Cave, gritty dust filtering into every crevice of his old red Toyota 4Runner and coating us and everything else inside with the same shade of brown. Our enthusiasm was just as thick as the dust as we fishtailed in and out of the ruts and through the washboards, Don talking animatedly about his latest great find. He's a geologist, the kind who finds oil in places where others might not think to look, and he's also a vertebrate paleontologist, the kind who has a special talent for finding important fossils. As he tells it, that comes from growing up in eastern Montana's dinosaur country, a place that in certain people is guaranteed to inspire respect for wide-open spaces and curiosity about nature—in his case geology and fossils, mainly.

What Don didn't say, though it was clear enough after I spent some time with him, was that whatever was in that childhood also inspired an abiding work ethic and seemingly boundless physical stamina. We were headed to the middle of nowhere, where we were going to hike to an abandoned mine tunnel in the rarefied air you find at 2,900 meters (9,500 feet) in the Rockies, then drop into a crack in the bedrock and enter a natural cave. There we would crawl around on our bellies all day in the pitch dark—with headlamps, of course, so that Don could show me the fossils that he and his son Larry had discovered there when they were exploring one weekend. For them, exploring meant something akin to what went on in the stories I used to hear about my coal-miner grandfather—taking a shovel and crowbar into an underground passage where you can't even stand up straight, and moving rock and dirt, hunched over or flat on your belly, all day long. In the course of that adventure with his dad, Larry noticed something that probably hundreds of spelunkers before them had missed—tiny bones littering parts of the cave floor.

Don was bringing me back to assess whether those bones might tell us anything new about the Ice Age animals of the high Rocky Mountains. The sky was gunmetal gray and a cold wind was starting to blow as we ducked beneath the 125-year-old mine timbers that kept the mountain from crashing down on our heads. The smell of the past—wood rat urine—was particularly strong; the reason why became obvious as we worked our way back into the darkness, moving slowly at first to let our eyes adjust. At the far end of the old tunnel, we dropped into the natural cave by balancing on a rickety ladder that was three parts wood and two parts rusty wire. In the 1870s, this must have been a scene of major disappointment, as the miners' picks suddenly crashed through the rock into the black void, dashing their hopes of following a silver- or gold-bearing seam in the limestone (technically, dolomite) to the mother lode. They had inadvertently found their way into a cave that had been sealed for hundreds of thousands of years.

But from our point of view, they *had* hit the mother lode, or at least put the promise of it within our grasp. Lying there as Exhibit A for both the wood-rat smell and for how bones got into the cave was a jumble of twigs, plants, raptor pellets, and coyote scat—a wood-rat midden. The pellets and scat were chock-full of little rodent, rabbit, and insectivore bones, and were lying right next to bleached white ribs. Later we would find a dead wood rat in that very midden. Farther back in the cave, a half-century-old tobacco can would verify that wood rats had no trouble hauling their treasures into parts of the cave that were sealed from humans, just as they had for thousands of years—actually, hundreds of thousands of years—before the miners opened up the cave for the first time. That tobacco can had been left outside the cave by two cowboys in 1939—we know that because they left a note in it—after they shook the last flecks of tobacco into the lunchtime cigarettes they were rolling.[2]

In science, if you're lucky, there are moments when you know without a doubt that you're looking at something big, when the thrill of discovery sends the adrenaline coursing through your veins.

As we knelt there at the base of the last thirty-foot vertical shaft we had just dropped down, we were graced with one of those moments. Our world was silent, utterly dark except for what materialized in the beam of our headlamps—a flash of gray cave wall here, sparkle of gypsum there, the tan, scuffed, soft leather of well-worn work gloves against the orange-yellow dirt. As we carefully sifted the top inch or so of the flourlike cave floor through our fingers, our world focused even more: lying there in our hands, spotlit by our head-lamps and starkly contrasted against the dirt-stained gloves, were small jaws, leg bones, even parts of skulls, all a muted yellowy-white and clinking like bone china. They were fossils, and there were hundreds, thousands of them.

And that was just the beginning. When we crawled out of the cave that day, snow was blowing, but that did little to cool our excite-ment. We knew that Porcupine Cave was the kind of place we needed to answer the questions we had in mind. What we didn't know was that we were in for fifteen years of hard work: the cave would turn out to hold more than 26 distinct deposits of abundant fossils, and require the efforts of four major scientific institutions, more than two dozen scientists, and hundreds of volunteers.[3] Impor-tantly, the fossils that were recovered represented many different ages in the geological past, ranging through nearly a million years of the Pleistocene.

The Pleistocene began about 1.8 million years ago when the Earth cooled to the point at which glaciers grew over most of the northern hemisphere and enlarged in the southern continents. The glaciers then melted, grew again, melted, grew again, and so on, through some 39 cycles or so, driven largely by the Milanković orbital variations explained in Chapter 2. The glaciers last retreated about 11,500 years ago, marking not only the end of the Pleistocene, but also the beginning of the interglacial time in which we now live.

At Porcupine Cave, some of the fossils came from animals that had lived during glacial times, others from animals that had lived during interglacials, and in some places, the interglacial-age deposits were stacked right on top of the glacial age ones. Because the fossils were collected by wood rats, and augmented by carnivores who dragged their prey into the cave and also sometimes died there, there was a reliable sample of which species (and to some extent, the abundance of individuals within each species) were present during the cold times as compared to the warm times. With that information, it becomes possible to assess the kinds of ecological changes stimulated by those "natural" global warming events.

But it's never as easy as it sounds. Before we could determine how climate had affected the mountain fauna, we needed to find a way to date those fossils reliably. When we came out of the cave on that snowy day in 1985, we were pretty sure that our sample bags held fossils of animals that lived between 10,000 and 50,000 years ago. We were wrong, as we learned when we tried to radiocarbon some of the bones, and found that they no longer had enough organic material—collagen, in the case of bones—to yield a radiocarbon date at all. That, and the "clink-clink" we got when tapping them together, as opposed to a softer-sounding "clunk-clunk," should have been a tip-off. The bones were actually much older than the age range for which radiocarbon-dating is reliable, which goes back to about 50,000 years. That finally became evident when we sat down with museum collections and began to identify the rodent teeth we had collected. We discovered that what we had brought out that day were jawbones of species which elsewhere had only been found in deposits that were hundreds of thousands of years old.

That realization, like most aha! moments in science, ultimately was possible because of the work of past giants—ultimately, in this case, William Smith, the "Father of English Geology." Smith was a surveyor by trade, eventually turned mapmaker, who traipsed about the English countryside in the 1790s and early 1800s, surveying for mining companies and landowners. He began to notice that everywhere he went, layers of rock were stacked one on top of the other in a predictable pattern. He also noticed that each layer of rock contained a predictable assemblage of fossils (of marine invertebrates, in the case of the rocks he worked with), each successively higher assemblage being a bit different from the one just below it. What he didn't know, though it later became evident with the work of Darwin and others, was that he was seeing the results of evolution. The distinct assemblages of fossil species were there because each layer of rock sampled a different interval of time. Through time, new species evolve and old species go extinct, such that each time slice has its own characteristic combination of species. Those combinations were what Smith was noticing, and he and later geologists used them to define the geological timescale as we basically now know it. So if you can identify the species, you can usually place yourself in geological time.

The same principal has long been applied to telling time with fossil mammal teeth—but at a much more resolved timescale. In the case of the Pleistocene, the timetable was built primarily from the teeth of voles, through three decades of work by Charles Repenning. "Rep" was tall and slim, sported a neatly trimmed Clark Gable mustache that matched his gray-white hair, and looked incomplete without a cigarette dangling from his mouth or pinched between his fingers. I say "was" because of the sad twist of fate that, after surviving heavy combat and internment in a prisoner-of-war camp during World War II, he was murdered for his fossils—matchboxes full of vole teeth, though the thieves were undoubtedly hoping for far more—and the war memorabilia he kept in his home.

Like William Smith, Repenning developed his own geological timetable by carefully assembling all the information about which fossil voles were found where, using a variety of information to assess the age of the deposits in which each fossil was found, and then arranging the whole mess in a series of tables and charts that showed where and when each species had lived. Later those charts were refined, as Rep's cigarettes filled the room with a thick blue smoke while he argued principles of geologic dating with then-graduate student Chris Bell, whose job it was to make sense of the voles from Porcupine Cave.[4] The end result was a biochronology—a fairly detailed recognition of the maximum temporal ranges of each fossil and modern vole species—that resolved geological time to chunks of thousands of years, rather than the millions that Smith's scheme had recognized nearly two centuries before.

By matching our species to Rep's and Bell's charts, it looked like we were sampling faunas that were between 700,000 and 1 million years old. We were in the Pleistocene, all right, but not the late Pleistocene. We were sampling faunas that lived long before humans ever got into North America—in fact, long before *Homo sapiens* had even evolved—ideal for our purposes, since we could then be sure that the faunal changes we were seeing were not influenced at all by people, and were indicative of the "natural" response to global warming.

Nailing down exactly which parts of the middle Pleistocene's many possible glacial-interglacial transitions we were sampling required pulling out a paleo-compass. One of the constants we rely on as humans today is true north. But at various times during the Earth's past, the magnetic poles flip-flopped such that what now looks like north to a compass needle would look like south. What causes this flip-flop of Earth's magnetic field is not fully understood; it may be related to storms in the molten, iron-rich core of the Earth. Whatever the cause, the effect is fortunate for determining geological age, because it makes possible a geologic dating technique called magnetostratigraphy.

Magnetostratigraphy works on a couple of basic principles. First, most rocks contain magnetic mineral grains, and as the rocks form, the mineral grains align themselves like billions of microscopic compass needles, all pointing toward what is north at the time. So a record of Earth's changing magnetic field is actually locked in the rocks. Second, the flip-flops of the Earth's magnetic field do not happen at regular intervals; they are more or less random, so that you might go for a long period of time (say, hundreds of thousands of years) with a magnetic field that is like today's (called a "normal interval"), which gives way to a short period of time (thousands of years) in which the magnetic field is reversed, then a medium-long interval in which it is normal again, and so on.

If you envision a column of rocks, then, with the geologically oldest at the bottom and youngest at the top, and color black all the rocks that record a normal magnetic interval, and white all the rocks with a reversed magnetic polarity, you would end up with something like a bar code—a sequence of black and white bands distinctive from all others by the pattern of variably thick black and white stripes. In your local supermarket, each distinctive bar code can be tied to a particular product and price; in the case of magnetostratigraphy, each distinctive bar code can, at least in ideal cases, be tied to a certain interval of time.[5]

Deep inside Porcupine Cave, those microscopic compass needles were locked in the fossilized wood rat middens, clay deposits, and in the flowstone that was interspersed with the bone deposits. The trick in seeing which way the ancient needles point is to get them back to a paleomagnetics laboratory without disturbing their orientation—not so hard with the solid flowstone but a delicate task given the softer sediments we were working in. The process starts by cleaning off a small section of the wall of the excavation with plastic tools—metal is usually a bad idea when magnetism is involved. Then you carve at the wall until you have sculpted a tiny block of the sediment, just a little bigger than a sugar cube, that is still tenuously attached, and you hold your breath as you gently press a little plastic box over the sediment cube. Carefully, carefully, you use a very accurate compass to record the orientation of one of the faces, so that the cube can be oriented properly when it is demagnetized (the process by which you uncover the ancient compass direction) back in the lab. If all goes well, you break the sediment cube away from the wall and your sample is in the box and ready for the magnetometer. If you are unlucky, you either destroy the sediment cube as you press the box on, or all the sediment falls out of the box as you try to free it from the wall, in which case you swear and start over. In those cases where the cube-and-box technique just won't work, the tricks of the trade include encasing a football-sized chunk of the sediment in plaster and impregnating it with epoxy, or using special rectangular piston corers to extract a small block of the precious dirt.

Scientists who specialize in magnetostratigraphy are facetiously called paleomagicians, and they worked their magic in a few different places in Porcupine Cave.[6] One key place was at the bottom of that thirty-foot shaft where Don and I had first sampled fossils, a room in the cave that came to be known as the Pit. By the time the paleomag work was underway in the late 1980s, the surface on which we had knelt in the Pit on that cold day in 1985 was gone—instead, there was a hole about the size of two graves lined up side by side, about 2.5 meters (8 feet) deep. Each garden-trowel of dirt had been bagged, labeled, and hauled out of the cave to be screened for fossils. In the walls of the excavation, the Pit's history was starkly displayed in distinctive layers—the loose, flourlike dust that Don and I had sifted through our fingers at the top, and below that, alternating irregular horizontal bands of dark clay pellets interbedded with flowstone and compacted remains of wood rat nests.

Those different layers told us about the different climates that had been outside the cave during times past: the dry dust meant hot, dry times, the clay layers cold, moist times, and the flowstone warm, moist times. As our eyes followed the layers from the geologically oldest ones at the bottom to the youngest at the top, we were looking at a glacial time, then an interglacial, a glacial, a relatively cool interglacial, another glacial, and finally, recorded by the loose, flourlike dust at the top, a hot, dry interglacial.

The paleomagicians pieced together bits of a magnetic bar code from those layers, which, when combined with the biochronology, gave just the dating information we needed.[7] The topmost glacial-interglacial transition recorded in the Pit was in the neighborhood of 800,000 years old. As it turned out, that neighborhood was a good one to be in, because it's where one of the Pleistocene's most dramatic global warming events took place.[8]

Thirteen thousand fossil specimens later, we were finally there. If you consider that processing each specimen—which includes cleaning, identifying, and curating it into a museum collection—takes, on average, about one hour, this means that eight person-years later, we finally had some answers as to how those natural global warming events had affected the fauna.[9] All told, 127 species had left their bones in Porcupine Cave.[10] Of those, 44 species of mammals told a story about what had happened as cool, moist glacial times swung into hot, dry interglacial times, in a world unaffected by humans.

The biggest surprise was what those species told us about how ecological communities react to global warming. There has long been some controversy among ecologists about whether communities—that is, groups of interacting species—are more or less stable through time, in the sense that most of the species stick together during times of environmental change, or whether the communities are more or less random assemblages of species that just happen to end up in the same place as each responds to environmental conditions independently. The stability model is called the Clementsian community concept, after ecologist Frederic Clements.[11] In 1936 he argued that, left to its own devices, vegetation reaches what he called a climax stage, and that in a given kind of environment (prairie, for example, or redwood forest), similar sets of species would always end up together in the climax communities. In contrast, another ecologist, Henry Gleason, had built a case for "individualistic" species-response more than a decade earlier, arguing that "every species of plant is a law unto itself, the distribution of which in space depends on its individual peculiarities of migration and environmental requirements."[12] Thus, the random-assemblage idea became known as the Gleasonian community concept.

In the context of global warming, these concepts take on considerable importance. If the world is Clementsian, in the best case we could see whole communities migrating toward the poles or to higher elevations as the world warms, and in the worst case, we could see whole communities disappear in a geological heartbeat. If the world is Gleasonian, we would expect to see reshuffling of species across the landscape, with the extreme outcome being that the natural communities of tomorrow will be virtually unrecognizable by today's standards.

The mammalian fossils in Porcupine Cave indicate that Clements versus Gleason is not necessarily an either-or proposition; the world is both Clementsian *and* Gleasonian in the way communities respond to natural global warming events. The Clementsian aspect became clear after we saw which genera of mammals were most common in the latest glacial period represented in the deposits, and comparing those to the genera that were common in succeeding times: first the succeeding interglacials, then two hundred years ago (before European humans affected the fauna much), and finally to the situation today. Amazingly, there was not much difference. In the old glacials, in the old interglacials, in the historic part of our present interglacial, and in the present, the most common small mammals are voles (especially genus *Microtus*), ground squirrels (*Spermophilus*), wood rats (*Neotoma*), gophers (*Thomomys*), marmots (*Marmota*), and various rabbits (represented by several genera). The kinds of small animals that are abundant on the landscape in this region today are also the ones that were most abundant some 800,000 years ago (Taxonomically, this similarity was at the generic and subfamilial levels.). Further pointing to some sort of community cohesiveness was that the rank-order abundance of genera (and in the case of voles, of subfamilies) was not much affected even by major climatic transitions from glacial to interglacial times.

Clements may have been on to something—these communities were looking pretty stable in the way they were held together. In fact, other studies have now shown that this general community cohesiveness among mammals has prevailed for the Rocky Mountain West since Porcupine Cave time to the present, and also in coral communities in the ocean.[13]

But stability isn't the whole story—the Gleasonian world is in the details of what happens at the species level. Many species did respond individualistically, as Gleason envisioned. Tracing fauna from the topmost glacial at Porcupine Cave into the warmer 800,000-year-old interglacial beneath, we saw the kinds of changes that have been pointed out in previous chapters. For example, during the interglacial, the relative abundance of individuals belonging to warmth-loving species (like ground squirrels and sagebrush voles) increased at the expense of individuals belonging to cold-tolerant species (such as bog lemmings and other voles), and at least one moisture-sensitive species (pocket gophers of the genus *Thomomys*) retracted its range from the Porcupine Cave area altogether.

But two other species that also retracted their ranges out of the area, the Mexican wood rat (*Neotoma mexicana*), and southern plains wood rat (*N. micropus*), shouldn't have, at least by the logic of what we think we know about their habitat requirements. They do fine in even hotter, drier places than Porcupine Cave probably was during that mid-Pleistocene interglacial. And particularly noteworthy, and different from any examples in previous chapters, is that we also saw three species go extinct as the glacial gave way to the interglacial at Porcupine Cave: voles known as the Virginia mimomys (*Mimomys virginianus*), the Pliocene vole (*Allophaiomys pliocaenicus*), and Gryci's vole (*Phenacomys gryci*). These species had been on Earth for at least a million years previously and had made it through earlier, milder glacial-interglacial transitions. This one, just a little more intense, was apparently enough to do them in.

What all of these species that went extinct or were locally exterminated at the glacial-interglacial transition had in common was that they existed in low population sizes throughout the times they were present in the Porcupine Cave record. This highlights the fact that global warming, even the milder, nonanthropogenic version, can wipe out species if they already occur in low abundances; thus such species today are at particular risk. But interestingly, in the absence of humans, that particular climatic risk seems to act strongest and most directly on only the smallest herbivores.

This became evident when we divided the species into categories by their relative body size (mouse size to rat size, or beaver size, or bigger) and by their trophic level, or place in the food web (e.g., herbivore, omnivore, or carnivore), a kind of a shorthand way of delineating ecological niches.[14] Sorting species in these ways showed that the prehuman climate change recorded at Porcupine Cave decreased diversity only in the small herbivore category, when the combined species count for rodents and rabbits fell from 29 to 24 species.[15] Those 24 species seem to reflect the interglacial norm—there are 24 species in this size and trophic category today as well. Climate change by itself did not seem to affect the number of species very much at all in other trophic and size categories. The numbers of species in each category—small, medium, and large carnivores and omnivores, and medium and large herbivores—is about the same for both the mid-Pleistocene glacial and the present interglacial prior to European human influence.

Interestingly, even though the numbers of species in each size and trophic category remained similar, the actual species that filled each category changed a bit through time—usually because ecologically similar species from nearby moved in. This suggests that what remains constant is not quite what Clements had envisioned. It is not the particular species themselves in communities that vary little (for example, a particular species of ground squirrel), it is the ecological niches that species fill (the ground squirrel niche itself, which is connected to other niches by what that ground squirrel eats and what eats it). What the size-trophic category analysis at Porcupine Cave actually tells us, then, is that the ecological niches and the relationships among them in that ecosystem remained remarkably constant for some 800,000 years—up until 200 years ago.

But not today. The ecological structure of the area has changed more since European settlers arrived in the Porcupine Cave region 200 years ago than that structure had changed in the previous 800,000 years, and that brings us back to Old Mose and what happened to animals like the grizzly. The trophic-size analysis showed that species counts of large and medium-sized carnivores and omnivores fell only in the last 200 years, when people shot or trapped out all the grizzly bears, wolves, lynx, and wolverines, and decimated the prey-base of black-footed ferrets. We're not replacing those carnivores and omnivores with anything other than us. That, of course, seems to be repeated just about anywhere you look on Earth: where humans move in, the first species to go are typically those big carnivores, either by our deliberate efforts or as indirect effects of removing their prey or fragmenting their range.

All that shines a harsh light on the ecological warning signs of today's global warming. First, Porcupine Cave teaches us that when global warming on the order of 5°C (9°F) is played out over a longer time than the tens of years we've observed so far, or the few hundreds of years of the Medieval Warm Period in Yellowstone, it's not just going to be a matter of changing the numbers of individual critters on the landscape as their habitats shrink in area or become modified. Instead, we can expect reductions in numbers of species and even extinctions in the lower size and trophic categories. That is what we now know effectively happens at much slower rates of temperature change than today's rate of global warming. Second, today it's not just global warming cutting at the lower size and trophic levels that we have to worry about. Other human impacts are slicing away at the highest trophic and size classes as well. Not only that, today's abnormally fast, severe global warming itself is causing populations of some of the largest mammals to dwindle—polar bears in the arctic, bighorn sheep in the California Sierra Mountains (as we've seen from earlier chapters) and many of Africa's big animals (as we'll see in the next chapter). It's like putting nature in a vise. As we squeeze, we are inexorably metamorphosing the ecological relationships and the ways ecosystems work that have been in place for upward of hundreds of thousands of years—to put it in human terms, for time immemorial.

Chapter 9 ⤳

Africa on the Edge

> Africa suffered no obvious pulse or burst of extinctions of
> megafauna to match those in near time on other landmasses. . . .
> Large-animal extinctions . . . were relatively few and episodic,
> not only in near time . . . but over the last several million years.
>
> —Paul Martin, 2005[1]

Andrew is a Bushman. He lives in the Kalahari
Desert along the border between South Africa and Botswana, an area
partly encompassed by Kgalagadi Transfrontier Park. A small, wiry
man with a thousand-watt smile, he has incredibly sharp, twinkling
eyes. He speaks no English, but as he began teaching us about the
world he grew up in, our lack of a common language didn't really
matter. It was all hands-on training anyway. Earlier in the morning,
crouching in his khaki cargo shorts and bush shirt, he had shown us
which roots to suck a few drops of precious water from, and which
ones hosted the chrysomelid beetle larvae used to poison arrows that
some Bushmen (a vanishing number) still use for hunting big game
in the traditional way. Now it was time to take a break under a thorny
acacia tree, the only shade in sight. With pantomime in which by
now we had become perfectly fluent, he explained how you don't just
plop yourself down under a tree in this ecosystem. First you approach
warily, looking for lion or leopard tracks, to make sure you do not surprise any local man-eaters that also had the idea of a good rest. Then

you cautiously scan any places that the big cats might be nestled behind, taking particular care to look for any bits of fresh carcass on the ground, which might signal that lions are somewhere around, even if not in sight. Then you look very carefully into the trees, to be sure that part of a leopard's meal is not dangling above you, or worse, the leopard. Finally, assuring yourself that the place is safe, you sit down in the shade. At which point, Andrew jumped up as if he'd sat on a hot poker, grabbed his butt, and fell over in mock-death, illustrating that you don't want to forget to check for highly poisonous puff adders.

On another day, in South Africa's Kruger National Park, some 800 kilometers (500 miles) east of the Kalahari, we piled into 4-wheel-drives just as twilight fell to look for nocturnal wildlife and feast at a back-country barbecue that was being laid out for members of the professional conference which had brought us there.[2] As in most African parks, you're not allowed out of the vehicle—there are too many things waiting to eat you. There was, for example, the story of the guide who walked behind the truck to take a leak and was dragged off by a lion. Those kinds of stories, and the green eye-shine of big carnivores that flash back at you as the truck lights sweep across the bush, tend to make you appreciate your limitations. Just after our spotlights passed over a leopard curled up at the base of a tree, we drove through a gate in a tall chain-link fence, incongruous in the middle of a dark night in the South African bush. Also incongruous were the rows of tables with dazzling white linen tablecloths, silver cutlery, and wine glasses glinting in the light from the fires over which white-coated African cooks were searing huge slabs of meat. A haven of civilization in the middle of the wild. Five-year-old Clara, however, was nervous. "Um, Mama," she said, as she tugged on her mother's shirt, hesitant to interrupt whatever conversation was going on. "Um, Mama, there's a hyena looking at me." That got the attention of the group. Fifteen meters (or yards) away, a hyena had locked its eyes onto Clara with the intensity that only a predator looking at a meal can show. For us, an adrenaline-spiked moment. For the African cooks, no big deal—they waved big sticks, shouted until the hyena ran off, and moved their rifles a little closer to where they were working. We suddenly realized that the gate we had driven through was just for show: except for few meters of chain link extending on each side of the gate, there was no fence. We were out there in the middle of the night tearing through our meat with all the other carnivores.

Such is life in an ecosystem that has probably changed less than any other since the Pleistocene. Nobody knows what protected Africa from the worst of the fatal combination of humans and climate change that, by 11,500 years ago, decimated the rest of the world's large animals—species like mammoths, mastodons, Irish elk, ground sloths, and giant armadillos. What we do know is that Africa still has most of its megafauna.[3] Ironically, the usual explanation is that humans and large animals evolved together in this ecosystem, and early on they worked things out to keep nature in balance. That balance, at least as quantified by the number of native species in each size class, seems to have been changing in recent years. Many of Africa's largest animals are now in danger of disappearing. That would mean an end to the last vestiges of the world's megafauna, and to what are apparently the last vestiges of naturally structured mammal communities.

Of the remaining African megafauna (animals of more than 44 kilograms or 100 pounds), the following numbers of species are classified by the IUCN as vulnerable, endangered, critically endangered, or extinct in the wild: four of the six perissodactyl species (zebras and rhinos) and one more that is near threatened; two out of the five carnivore species (lions and cheetahs); nearly 40 percent (19 of 49) of the artiodactyl species (antelopes, sheep, bovids, pigs, giraffes); all of the primates (gorillas and chimpanzees); and the only remaining proboscideans on the continent (the elephants *Loxodonta africana* and *L. cyclotis*).[4] It has long been recognized that direct human actions such as habitat destruction and hunting are the chief causes of the recent decline in all these species. Those impacts also take their toll in more subtle ways.

Take, for example, Africa's elephants. Not only has poaching of elephants for their tusks and conversion of their natural habitat into land uses that better support humans reduced their numbers, it is also apparently driving them crazy. Literally. In a perfect world, elephants live together in extended family and social groups, and they can expect to live about 70 years. The little ones, who mostly stay within 4.5 meters (15 feet) of their mothers until they are about eight years old, are raised by not only their mother, but also by their grandmothers, their aunts, and friends of the family. Eventually the young female elephants are integrated into a complicated matriarchal network, where they learn how to fit into the social hierarchy, and meanwhile the young males run off with all-male groups, where they learn what is acceptable and unacceptable elephant behavior, what lines can never be crossed without consequences. In that undisturbed world, there is a lot of communication, both vocal and tactile, and there is mourning and what can only be called funerals. When an elephant dies, survivors hold vigil over the body for about a week. They bury it with earth and brush, and for years continue to revisit the bones, touching them with their trunks in greeting, as if they were still alive. If all that seems a lot like human behavior, it is.[5]

Now imagine going into a family, gunning down the grandparents and parents, and maybe mutilating them too—in the case of elephants, cutting off their tusks, for example—as the youngsters watched. Or maybe just kidnapping the youngster and throwing it into a prison with only kidnap victims like itself for company. If those were humans, you'd know what to expect of those youngsters: a lot of psychological problems, manifesting in part as violent, erratic behaviors. So too with elephants today—in some African parks, elephants are actually raping and killing rhinos from something akin to post–traumatic stress syndrome. And, their aggression toward humans has markedly increased over the past couple of decades. As Charles Siebert, who researched this problem for the *New York Times*, put it: "All across Africa, India, and parts of Southeast Asia, from within and around whatever patches and corridors of their natural habitat remain, elephants have been striking out, destroying villages and crops, attacking and killing human beings."[6] What we're seeing is not only a dwindling of the number of elephants, but also the eradication of, for lack of better words, elephant culture.

Those are the kinds of costs hidden behind direct the human

pressures we've traditionally thought about. What is now just becoming apparent is the effect of throwing today's global warming on top of the rest—namely, to further imperil many already endangered megafauna, and to add to the endangered list a large proportion of species which now exist in reasonable numbers in many African parks, but which, if current trends continue, will soon be in trouble.

Kruger National Park provides an illustrative example. When I was there in 2001, besides watching endangered elephants, lions, and cheetahs, our group marveled at the grace and beauty of the more common animals, such as kudu (*Tragelaphus strepsiceros*), waterbuck (*Kobus elipsiprimnus*), eland (*Tragelaphus oryx*), even warthogs (*Phacochoerus africanus*), and we kept our eyes open for the more elusive roan antelope (*Hippotragus equinus*), sable antelope (*H. niger*), and tsessebe (*Damaliscus lunatus*). Except for the warthog, otherwise known as Pumba of *Lion King* fame, all of these animals are large cloven-hoofed ungulates, with horns that twist in intricate patterns and coats of varying shades of brown to gray to almost black, depending on the species. They are, in a sense, a hallmark of Africa, with related species extending back in time millions of years. It's hard to imagine a Kruger Park without them. But their populations have declined in Kruger over the past 40 years, and at least three of them seem to be on the way out. What they share is vulnerability to the effects of global warming. They also share a rating by IUCN criteria of being species at low risk for extinction—meaning that species not otherwise in trouble seem to be getting into trouble as a result of global warming, at least in parks where they have long been an integral part of the ecosystems we have sought to preserve.

In 2003, Joseph Ogutu and Norman Owen-Smith, two biologists who have spent a good part of their careers studying the large mammals of Africa, pulled together the numbers from wildlife censuses that had been conducted between 1977 and 1996 by flying over Kruger in fixed-wing aircraft and helicopters.[7] Ogutu and Owen-Smith were interested in those numbers because researchers elsewhere had noticed a correlation between the population dynamics of many kinds of organisms across the globe and the North Atlantic Oscillation (NAO) or El Niño-Southern Oscillation (ENSO), ocean currents that ultimately influence the precipitation in the northern and southern hemispheres, respectively. In Kruger, Ogutu and Owen-Smith were trying to see if the more or less cyclical fluctuation between El Niño and La Niña in the central tropical Pacific also correlated with year-to-year precipitation variations and with the waxing and waning of the wild megamammals in the park—that is, whether climate was influencing those species. What they found was a climate correlation, but not the one they expected.

El Niño is the name given to months or years when the tropical central Pacific is warm. During El Niño times, warm, nutrient-poor tropical waters sneak down the western coast of South America, replacing the normally cold, nutrient-rich waters of the Humboldt Current. Because this phenomenon typically first becomes apparent sometime around Christmas, the warm condition took on the name El Niño, the little boy, in reference to the arrival of the Christ child. The flip-side condition, when a strong, cold Humboldt Current extends along the coast of northern Peru, is accordingly called La Niña. In South Africa, the main effect of strong El Niño conditions is reduced rainfall in the normally wet months from October to March.

When Ogutu and Owen-Smith pulled together the climate data from some twenty stations in and around the park, they found, as expected, that there was a clear El Niño influence: lower seasonal and annual rainfall. But the fluctuations in numbers of each mega-herbivore species did not track the fluctuations in rainfall. Instead, all seven species mentioned above began to decline dramatically around 1988, uncorrelated with either the oscillations between El Niño and La Niña, or with mean annual or wet-season rainfall. When two other climate indices were fitted into the statistical models, though, the declines began to make sense: the animals began to fall off in number just at the time when rainfall during the dry season (April to September) was abnormally low while global and local temperatures began to increase. That combination effectively shortened the growing season for plants, reduced the amount of forage during the critical months when every drop of rain counted, and offset even the wet-season precipitation gains of the La Niña years. There simply was less and less water to sustain adequate green forage during the dry season, and the animals couldn't move outside the park to find the green vegetation they needed. As a result, by 1995 there were only 25 free-ranging roan antelope left in Kruger, 550 sable antelope, and 250 tsessebe, down from highs in the mid-1980s of about 500, 2,300, and 1,200 animals, respectively.[8] Ogutu and Owen-Smith calculated that should those warming, dry-season drying trends occur from late 2002 onwards, Kruger will lack roan antelope altogether by 2016—less than a decade from now. Sable antelope and tsessebe may fall to perhaps 285 and 70 animals, respectively.[9]

They may have been overly optimistic. If IPCC and other climate models are right, the coming climate in Kruger could well be even worse for sable antelope, tsessebe, and other herbivores than it has been during the warming and drying trend of the past few decades. Compare the numbers. The local rise in temperature over the years the megaherbivores declined, from 1988 to 1995, was about 0.4°C (0.7°F), the decrease in annual precipitation was about seven millimeters (0.28 inches), and the decrease in dry-season rainfall was about ten millimeters (0.39 inches). IPCC scenarios suggest that the local temperature in Kruger will rise another 2.5–5°C (4.5–9°F) by the decade of 2090 (relative to the period 1980–1999), considerably more than the temperature change associated with the decline of the seven species that Ogutu and Owen-Smith saw in the 1990s. In addition, IPCC models suggest that dry-season rainfall will be as much as 10–20 percent less in the decade 2090 as compared to the time covered by Ogutu and Owen-Smith's study.[10] Other models suggest that dry-season rainfall will be even less than that by the 2020s.[11] Any way you look at it, the warming and drying that caused megaherbivores to decline in Kruger in the late twentieth century was mild compared to what's likely to be coming. If present trends continue, look for a Kruger Park without roan antelope, sable antelope, or tsessebe in less than two decades and with reduced numbers of kudu, waterbuck, eland, and warthogs.

Also, look for a Kruger that loses a wide spectrum of smaller-bodied species as well, and one that potentially has new species move in. A research team lead by Barend F. N. Erasmus from the

University of Pretoria modeled how 179 species of animals would respond to the 2°C (3.6°F) temperature increase that is slated to occur in South Africa when CO_2 in the atmosphere doubles, which could happen as early as 2050.[12] Their sample included 34 bird, 19 mammal, 50 reptile, 19 butterfly, and 57 other invertebrate species. For each species, they determined the statistical relationship between its present distribution and prevailing climate. Then they used climate models to see what the climate would be like over southern Africa when CO_2 concentrations doubled. Finally, for each pixel on the computer map, they compared the modeled climate with the climate required by each of the species. If there was a match, the species was considered to inhabit that pixel. If there was no match, the species was deleted from it. That process allowed them to estimate how the geographic ranges of each of the 179 species would respond to the predicted climate change. In the simulation those 179 species did not fare all that well. Seventy-eight percent of them showed contraction of their geographic ranges. The researchers summed it up by saying: "Predictions suggest that the flagship Kruger National Park conservation area may lose up to 66 percent of the species included in this analysis." And that's by climate change only—that doesn't take into account any land transformation that will undoubtedly occur as the human population of South Africa continues to grow at 1.9 percent per year.[13]

Another analysis, similar in concept but focusing on a wide variety of mammals distributed throughout Africa, makes it clear that we are not just talking about the loss of a few species. We're talking about loss of many species, and major dislocations of those that survive. An international team headed by Wilfried Thuiller from the Université Joseph Fourier in France assessed how likely African parks are to continue to conserve the species within them. Their results suggest the answer in just two words: not very. The Thuiller analyses statistically related the occurrence of 277 large- and medium-sized mammalian species with certain climate parameters, then used climate models to assess which areas would be able to maintain each species as climate warms.[14]

Their models indicated that by 2050, 10–15 percent of the mammalian species they studied will be by IUCN standards critically endangered or extinct, and by 2080, approximately 25–40 percent will be. That's just due to global warming—the models held land use constant for the future, almost certainly an optimistic projection, as at least some of the suitable habitat for many species that is now present outside the parks will probably be transformed by human use in coming decades as the human population increases. The predicted endangerment of so many species that are not presently endangered comes from estimates of the degree to which global warming will reduce the area of climatically suitable habitats throughout Africa. With reduced habitat, animal population numbers fall, and with reduced numbers of animals comes increased risk of extinction.

At the geographic scale of individual parks, the changes in species promise to be even more dramatic. In Kruger, for example, of the 87 mammal species there today, 20 are projected to disappear by 2080 in the worst-case scenario model (and "only" 13 in the best case). The model also predicts that global warming will produce climates suitable for 20 new species in Kruger. "New species" are those now in Africa but not in Kruger, where the climate is presently unsuitable. Those new species will be the ones that can stand really hot, dry dry-seasons. If those species can actually get there, the net number of mammal species in 2080 could be about the same in the park as today, but a large proportion of them (minimally about one-quarter of the analyzed species) will hold different roles in the community—small-bodied herbivores moving in while large herbivores and large carnivores drop out, for example. Consequently, the ecological interactions within those communities—the operation of the ecosystem itself—will be substantially different. This balancing of species numbers assumes dispersal corridors connecting the islands of suitable habitat, which is not the case today.

In the Kalahari, which contains the Kgalagadi Transfrontier Park, the situation is even more dire. By 2080, both the best- and worst-case scenarios predict that the park's climate will be unsuitable for 39 of the 45 studied mammal species that live there now. It will gain suitable climate for only eight to ten new species, for a net loss of 29–31 species (two-thirds of the studied species). If the "new species" can't move into the area, the Kalahari could be left with only six species of large and medium-sized mammals. That means that by global warming alone—even discounting increased direct human impacts that are virtually certain—the African ecosystem to which Andrew introduced us could virtually disappear in 65 years or less. The ecological interactions that have been robust enough to persist through the first appearance of the human species some 160,000 years ago, through the largely human-caused extinctions of megafauna everywhere else on Earth, and even through the dramatic ways people have changed the landscape over the last century, may finally be lost forever.

The flickering out of familiar species associations—especially those that have lasted as long as those in Africa—heralds more than the end of familiar species in national parks and elsewhere. It also signals the flickering out of familiar conservation philosophies. Keeping or restoring "biotic associations" as they were when the park was first set up may become simply impossible. If a place has the wrong climate to support a species, the "old" biotic associations can't be preserved in any recognizable form. Managing for biodiversity runs into a brick wall if there are no natural dispersal corridors by which species can track their needed climate to adjust their biogeographic range. Even conserving individual species will become more and more difficult as the climate they need disappears in the only places they now exist.

In short, global warming elevates the stakes for ecosystem conservation. While once the endgame was to keep certain places from changing too much or to restore them to some past condition, we now have to worry about how to keep whole ecosystems from disappearing, as places like Kruger and the Kalahari illustrate on land, and places like coral reefs and dead zones illustrate in the sea. Gone will be not just the species in such places, but the actual ecological niches the species occupied, and the interactions between species that fill those niches. Keeping nature healthy in that world will be a Herculean effort, one that will play out on an ever-shifting field, where some patches of land are taken away by bulldozers, backhoes, and plows, and many of the patches they miss are taken away by climate change.

It's not abstract: at stake are all the ecosystems the world considers as crown jewels, places like Kruger, the Kalahari, Yosemite, Yellowstone, and many others I haven't discussed, in rain forests, Patagonia, tundra, the Arctic, the Antarctic, coastal areas, coral reefs—name your favorite. What makes all those places so special is that they still reflect, to varying degrees, the intricate trial and error of nature, the millions upon millions of chance events that accumulated over hundreds of thousands, ultimately millions of years, to build them into the living, breathing places we love. These are "the last best places," as far as relatively undisturbed ecosystems go, but in each place, holes are beginning to show up in the ecological fabric. Business-as-usual global warming will not only strip away many of the species that now remain in such ecosystems, but also stretch them past the point where they can bounce back, so altering them in composition and function that we will barely recognize them. In effect, whole ecological legacies are in danger of being erased—along with nature's actual capacity to continue its trial-and-error method of ecosystem construction, maintenance, and restoration.

PART THREE

Uncharted Terrain

Chapter 10 ⌒

Disappearing Act

This is the assembly of life that took a billion years to evolve. It has eaten the storms—folded them into its genes—and created the world that created us. It holds the world steady.

—Edward O. Wilson, 1992[1]

THEY SAY nothing in life is certain except death and taxes. I'd add two more to that. First, no matter how you want to define "nature" or "natural," a stark fact is that Earth still has some magnificent ecological regions. These include not only the parks such as those we've looked at in the past few chapters, but also many other lightly populated places that are "holding the world steady," places that are thriving to various degrees as they have for thousands of years, even much longer. Second, those places, and everywhere else on Earth, will change more in the next couple of generations than they have in thousands of years, and in ways that are unprecedented, largely due to global warming and the interactions of warming with other human-imposed pressures.

Warming itself is very likely going to cause some of the most dramatic changes. That's what Jack Williams, Steve Jackson, and John Kutzbach found when they teamed up to forecast what Earth's ecological future might hold over the next century.[2] Williams and Jackson are paleoecologists at the University of Wisconsin-Madison and the University of Wyoming, respectively, in the business of figuring out what past ecological changes mean for the future. Kutzbach, also at Madison, is a climate scientist who has spent a good part of his long career building models to understand the relationships between past, present, and future climates and species. Familiar climates are likely to disappear in many places and novel ones likely to appear, they concluded, causing loss of species and loss of some of the most biodiverse ecosystems on the planet. By "familiar climates," they mean combinations of temperature, rainfall, and other climatic parameters that characterize at least some part of Earth today; by "novel climates," they mean combinations of climatic parameters now experienced nowhere on Earth. Of course, there will also be many places where one so-called familiar climate will be replaced by a different familiar climate, with attendant ecological changes.

Mix that in with other kinds of changes humans continue to cause—cities, dams, agriculture, and so on—and you have the recipe for a very different world indeed. Already, the human footprint, as measured by proximity of roads, towns, and other signs of people, directly influences at least 83 percent of the land surface—and that doesn't include the effects of climate change.[3] The oceans, too, feel a surprisingly heavy direct human impact by such activities as coastal settlements, fishing, pollution, and invasive species. When you add in recent effects of global warming, there is not one square kilometer of ocean that has not been influenced by humans.[4] As climate continues to warm at unprecedented rates, that influence will only increase, both on land and sea.

We can anticipate, then, huge changes in Earth's ecosystems, both locally and globally. Locally, the changes will transform ecological interactions in small ways and large. On the planetary scale, the consequences will be extinctions, loss of biodiversity, invasions of new species, and loss of entire ecosystems. The net effect could be a black-and-white, monophonic version of the living technicolor, surround-sound global ecosystem we now live in.

What that means was driven home to me on a recent trek through one of the world's last remaining tropical rainforests, Tambopata Nature Reserve on the border of Peru and Bolivia. You get to Tambopata by flying into Puerto Maldonado in southeast Peru, not too far from the Bolivian border. As is usual in January, our plane landed in between rainstorms, so as we made our way past the blue-tarp-covered Mercado Central (the central market) toward the Tambopata River, motorized rickshaws and motorcycles—the main means of transport—threw sprays of water off their tires onto our windshield. Down at the river, my wife Liz, our two daughters Emma and Clara, and I pulled on knee-high rubber boots and tightrope walked down a wobbly plank to the oversized canoe that was to take us five hours by river to the nature reserve. As we pushed off, another downpour began, and our boatmen rolled down the clouded visqueen plastic to keep the worst of the rain out. Not that it mattered much—in the tropics you get used to getting wet from the inside out, as humidity near 100 percent keeps all your clothes soaked anyway. First down the Tambopata to its junction with the Rio Madre de Dios, then down the Madre de Dios to the Heath River, and finally up the Heath to *la media de la nada*—the middle of nowhere.

In the morning we woke up under mosquito nets to a strange kind of alarm clock—howler monkeys signaling the dawn with a roar that sounded a lot like jet engines winding up, and a dawn chorus supplied by varying combinations of more than a hundred species of birds—Tambopata is home to one-ninth of all the bird species in the world. That was the beginning of the surround-sound, technicolor world that our guide, Javier, showed us over the next few days. Early one morning out on a lake we were startled by how loud a splash a nine-foot fish makes as it clears the water; another afternoon we heard the crunch of fish bones in giant otter jaws as the otters fed and frolicked off the canoe's prow. Amidst the buzzing of cicadas, the chirping of frogs, and the stacatto drips and plops that each rain flurry orchestrated, we watched hundreds of bright red, blue, and yellow macaws cluster on a red clay cliff, and, as we canoed down the river, came eye-to-eye with pig-sized rodents called capybaras. In the forest were jaguars, and at night, glowing green in the beam of our flashlights, were the pinpoint eyes of spiders, some of them looking all the world like tarantulas, except they were accompanied by a flock of baby spiders the mom takes care of for four years.

By the time we were heading out in the worst of the rainy season, it had been pouring for nearly thirty hours. That last morning as we paddled our canoe across an oxbow lake, it filled from the rain almost as fast as we bailed. At the end of the lake we slogged two kilometers (1.2 miles) down to the Madre de Dios, wading a trail that had turned into a swamp in flat places and a running river on the slopes, with rainwater streaming off our hats and ponchos, in the darkness of twilight even though it was midmorning. Caiman alligators camouflaged themselves as logs—as 15-year-old Emma found out when she stepped on one and it suddenly reared up, a prehistoric-looking reminder of how important the rains were to the native species there. The caimans were using the floodwaters as highways to disperse into new habitats. When we got to the Madre de Dios, the river had risen around three meters (ten feet), carrying in its chocolate waters whole trees that collected and swirled in the back eddys.

All of this, our guide Javier told us, was pretty typical of what he'd seen as a guide in the area over ten years, and over the thirty-three years—his whole life—that he had spent there altogether. So he was surprised when our conversation turned to a couple of studies that dealt specifically with what global warming might do to his home, this UNESCO nature preserve, this place to which people come from all over the world to see species that are already extinct nearly everywhere else—like the jaguars and giant otters mentioned above, and ocelots, giant armadilloes, and harpy eagles. Tambopata, it turns out, is located right at the edge of Amazonia, and that makes it one of the places that may well disappear with global warming, at least the Tambopata we saw and that Javier grew up in. When his kids reach his age, they may be living and guiding not in a rainforest, but in a savannah of grassland punctuated by an occasional stand of trees.

Ultimately, the rainforests in Amazonia are there because the rainy season is so dependable from year to year, and average temperatures, though hot, are not hot enough to evaporate critical amounts of water out of soaked soils. At Tambopata, for example, the wet season starts in November, a month when 200–250 millimeters of rain falls (8–10 inches), and gradually intensifies through February; rain tapers off in March, heralding the dry season of April through October, when only 50–150 millimeters (2–6 inches) of rain falls in any given month. All that adds up to around 2,000–2,500 millimeters

(80–100 inches) of rain per year, which is enough to keep the soil very wet, even with year-round average temperatures close to 25°C (77°F), a little warmer during the rainy season, a little cooler during the dry season.[5]

What's being forecast for the next few decades is a change in that balance between rainfall and evaporation, with global warming adding enough heat to dry out soils in some rainforests even if precipitation does not change. Dry those soils enough, and what used to be rainforest becomes savannah.

Those forecasts come from Brazilian climate and vegetation modelers Luis Salazar, Carlos Nobre, and Marcos Oyama.[6] Like other modelers, their goal is to try to anticipate the magnitude of the changes we might be facing as the globe warms. That's a fundamentally different kind of science than most of what we've seen in earlier chapters, which is based on actual observations of what has been happening over the past few decades and how that differs from what came earlier. Modelers, too, rely on observations of climatic and biological processes we can observe today and what's been recorded for the recent past, but then they convert those observations to equations that describe, for example, the physics of the atmosphere, or the correlation between a certain species' presence and key climatic parameters. Finally, they plug various numbers into those equations to see what would happen given different scenarios.

The various scenarios for the future of global warming are based on different assumptions about what people are going to do in the future. Those scenarios run the gamut from assuming that people will not do anything much different than they always have— business-as-usual scenarios—to assuming worldwide changes that would markedly reduce the amount of greenhouse gases that are pumped into the atmosphere. The IPCC has formalized these scenarios into "storylines" and "scenario families" abbreviated A1, A2, B1, and B2.[7] By and large, B1 is the best we can hope for (think "B" for best). A2 and a variant of A1 called A1F1 are the worst-case scenarios (think "A" for awful—my memory aid, not the IPCC's). The elements that go into each scenario include assumptions about how much the human population will grow, the standards of living worldwide, economic growth, the extent to which countries will either cooperate or operate in isolation, and the extent to which new technologies will be developed to replace reliance on fossil fuels. All of the scenarios are worst-case in the sense that they assume there will be no additional climate initiatives, such as those advocated by hundreds of cities, dozens of states, and thousands of corporations, or by the United Nations Framework Convention on Climate Change or the emissions targets of the Kyoto Protocol.[8]

The B1 world sounds like a happy place: population does not increase very much over what is the case today. Economic development is focused on service and information technology and new technologies that are resource efficient. Global solutions are implemented for such big problems as social and environmental sustainability and equity between nations—yet CO_2 doubles and then it stabilizes by 2100. The B2 world differs in putting less emphasis on global solutions. Population increases a bit more than in the B1 world, with slower and more diverse technological change. Environmental protection and social equity are pursued in this scenario, but more at the local and regional levels than at the global level. CO_2 more than doubles and is still growing at 2100.

Some version of the A storylines seems to be the world we're headed for if business goes on as usual. The world that would result from the A1 storyline is not all bad, by any means. Population peaks in the middle of the twenty-first century, then begins to decline. There is rapid economic growth, and rapid introduction of new, more efficient technologies. Per capita income per nation moves closer to parity, as cultural and social interactions increase. There are three different energy-use scenarios within the A storyline: continued heavy reliance on fossil fuels (the A1F1 scenario), heavier reliance on non-fossil resources to fuel technology (A1T scenario), and a balance between fossil and non-fossil fuels (A1B). A2 is the one I view as the selfish world: where countries continue to work in isolation, where population continues to increase rather than level off, where economic growth continues to be unevenly distributed among countries, and where technological growth is more uneven and slower than in other storylines.

Modelers don't necessarily favor one world over another in interpreting what comes out of their models—they simply plug in the
numbers that each model implies about, for example, each person's
carbon footprint, then they let the equations crank, and see what
comes out the other end. Neither do they try to place too much
reliance on a single model, particularly when it comes to climate
analysis. There are, in fact, many different groups that have developed sophisticated climate models—the IPCC lists 23 of them, based
at research institutions in many different nations around the world.[9]
Depending on how the models are built—that is, what equations are
put into them and how the linkages among the equations are assembled—the forecasts of one model often differ from those of another.

That's why modelers tend to speak in terms of probabilities. Any
single forecast from a model is subject to the assumptions that go into
the model (such as the scenarios about how the world will change)
and to the way the model itself operates. So modelers are not trying
to forecast specific future events, or trying to settle on one answer.
Instead, they try to define a range of probable outcomes by examining many different scenarios with multiple models. When all of the
models began to converge on the same answer—as is the case for a
general trend in warming of the globe, for example—the confidence
that the answer is right becomes higher, though never 100 percent
certain.

In that respect, modeling studies are a lot like life: there are some
things you can predict with reasonable certainty, so you proceed
accordingly, even though you are not 100 percent sure. You are pretty
sure, for example, when you get into your car to drive to the grocery
store or anywhere else, that you will make it there and back without
an accident. But, insurance companies have calculated that you have
a 3 percent chance of being wrong on that score sometime in the
next year (or, to put it another way, three drivers in every hundred
will have a car accident over the course of the year).[10] Statistically
speaking, you are taking a chance, but you drive to the grocery store
anyway, because you trust that you will not be among that unlucky 3
percent.

So too with using modeling studies of climate and ecological change to guide future actions. Modelers and others whose business it is to think about the future think almost exclusively in probabilities, usually with a strictly defined vocabulary to prevent confusion. When you hear words like "very high confidence" from the IPCC, for example, there is a numerical probability associated with it: it means there is a 90 percent chance of whatever condition they are talking actually coming to pass.[11] Whether you believe that a 90 percent chance is enough to prompt action is of course subjective, but here's a question to ask yourself: If there were a 90 percent chance that a plane for which you had a ticket would blow up, would you get on the plane?

How about a 75 percent chance? That is the likelihood that by 2080 not only the Tambopata rainforest but many rainforests throughout tropical South America will be mostly savannah, according to the Salazar team's study. Their approach was to take 15 different climate models chosen to represent the wide variation in answers that can result from using differently constructed models. They also determined the statistical correlation between today's climate and where rainforest and savannah presently grow. Then, they ran the climate models using the IPCC B1 scenario to represent the least-warming scenario for the future (which I'll call the best case), and the A2 scenario to represent the highest warming (one version of the worst case). For each scenario, they looked to see where the predicted climate would allow rainforest to grow, and where effective drying would mean that savannah would replace rainforest in the decades of ahead.

All of the models agreed that temperature would increase in South America—between 1–4°C (1.8–7.2° F) for scenario B1 and between 2–6°C (3.6–10.8°F) for scenario A2. And 75 percent of them agreed that Tambopata Nature Reserve could be dying as early as the 2020s, because even if rainfall stays the same, the warming trend there will increase evaporation enough to dry soils past the point where they can support widespread rainforest.

Using a climate model to interpret what will happen on a particular patch of real estate, like Tambopata, has a high margin of error.[12] As the geographic scale increases, however, the regional picture, like the prognosis for South American rainforests in general, becomes more robust. The consensus of the models that the Salazar team ran was that even under the best-case scenario (B1), tropical forests in South America will decrease 2.6 percent by the 2020s, 5.1 percent by the 2050s, and 8.2 percent by the 2090s. The A2 scenario is of course worse, suggesting tropical forest reductions for the respective decades of 3.1 percent, 9.3 percent, and 18 percent. That means that by 2090, somewhere between one-tenth and one-fifth of all of South America's tropical rainforests could disappear. And remember, that is only as a result of global warming—an even quicker decimator of tropical forests is logging, which is taking them out at the rate of about 325 square kilometers (125 square miles) per day. To put that in perspective, if you started logging at that rate in Tambopata, the whole thing would be clearcut in 31 days.

For the part of Peru and Bolivia where Tambopata is located, the extent of habitat destruction will almost certainly grow: as we motored down the Madre de Dios, we saw where chain saws had already felled the forest and where gold-mining dredges were processing the river mud with mercury, and we were told about the construction underway on the Interoceanic Highway, which will pave the connection between Brazil and the Pacific gateway of Puerto Maldonado.[13] That will open the entire region to even heavier logging and land transformation pressures, virtually ensuring that the nature reserve itself will be a last outpost of native rainforest—except that Tambopata seems to lie right in the path of a global warming–driven encroachment of savannah.

Ironically, the shrinking of rainforests exacerbates global warming itself, the very thing that promises to shrink them in the first place. Rainforests are carbon sinks, which means that as all the plant life within them photosynthesizes, they draw huge amounts of CO_2 out of the atmosphere and keep it locked up in the vegetation. As the rainforests die back, that carbon is released into the atmosphere, thus increasing greenhouse gases even further, and thereby also increasing the warming that is causing the forest dieback to begin with—an example of a positive climatic feedback loop.

If there were no Amazon forest dieback in a warming world (and no more deforestation by logging and the like), those forests would keep 10.3 gigatons of carbon out of the atmosphere. A gigaton of carbon (GtC) is one billion tons of carbon—that is roughly equivalent to the weight of 25,000,000 semi-trucks (those big 18-wheeled tractor-trailer rigs), which, if parked nose to tail, would wrap around Earth's equator about nine and a half times. With the predicted dieback by the year 2090, those Amazonian forests will release 35.6 GtC back into the atmosphere, and that is only the amount from forests lost to global warming (you can mentally add some unknown, large quantity of gigatons from what will also be lost due to logging, which this study did not take into account).[14] That 35.6 GtC is a significant chunk when you realize that at the beginning of 1999, the entire atmosphere contained around 765 GtC.

If that weren't bad enough, there is yet one more feedback loop associated with rainforest dieback. Rainforests make their own moisture, so to speak, as the evapotranspiration that takes place within them keeps recycling the rain over them. As forest disappears, so too does its local contribution to clouds and the rain budget, which means that more local heating and less overall precipitation will occur. Which kills more forest.

It is not only the study by the Salazar team that points to many rainforests disappearing through global warming. That also was one of the key findings of the analysis by Williams, Jackson, and Kutzbach, mentioned earlier, a study that drives home the point that what happens on a local scale is inextricably interwined with what happens globally. The Williams group didn't used climate models to figure out exactly *what* changes were going to occur at each place on Earth. Rather, they wanted to assess *how much* each place was going to differ from its present climate state, which familiar climates were going to disappear from the planet (termed "disappearing climates"), and where novel climates, those that living humans have never seen, were going to arise. Typical of model-based studies these days, they bracketed the range of likely outcomes by examining what might happen under the future scenario afforded by the IPCC's B1 storyline (a semblance of the best-case scenario), and the A2 storyline (on the worst-case end of the spectrum), looking about a century down the road to the year 2100.

They found the places most at risk of changing dramatically were those currently covered by tropical rainforests, including Tambopata and the rest of Amazonia.[15] In the scenario of greatest change (A2), Tambopata and the rest of Amazonia showed up as places that would switch over to novel climates, that is, climates to which none of the world's vegetational communities are currently adapted. The expected ecological changes became even more dramatic when they took into account both the distance that separates where species are today from where they would have to disperse to get to a climate that would suppport them in 2100, and also the barriers that prevent that from happening. With these considerations factored in, even the best-case (B1) scenario indicated that the coming climate patterns will not support current associations of Amazonian rainforest species.

On the global landscape, the Williams team found that rainforests weren't the only places to be affected.[16] In fact, their forecasting maps indicated high liklihood that, besides Amazonian rainforests, late twenty-first-century climates will be unable to support current species associations in northern and southern Patagonia, most of Africa, the Rocky Mountains and Pacific Northwest of North America as well as much of California, the whole southern tier of Eurasia, and the parts of Australia that are not already deserts (especially under the A2 scenario and factoring in the inability of species to move across barriers to dispersal).

Other studies point to similar conclusions. For example, in 1997 a research team led by Pat Bartlein at the University of Oregon used the Canadian Climate Center model and known correlations between various tree species and climate to examine what might happen locally in Yellowstone National Park under the global scenario of doubled CO_2 in the atmosphere, a situation that is even less severe than is projected to occur by 2100 under A2 and most of the A1 scenarios.[17] Their simulations suggested that both winter (January) and summer (July) temperature would rise up to 10°C (18°F) in Yellowstone, January precipitation would increase, and July precipitation would not change much. The net effect would be a warmer, drier park overall, with milder, moister winters, similar to climates now found in the Wasatch Range of Utah. Projected changes in vegetation include marked reduction or loss of whitebark pine (*Pinus albicaulis*), and, assuming they could migrate into the area fast enough, addition of species not presently found in the park: Gambel oak (*Quercus gambelii*), western juniper (*Juniperus occidentalis*), bigtooth maple (*Acer grandidentatum*), Ponderosa pine (*Pinus ponderosa*), western larch (*Larix occidentalis*), western hemlock (*Tsuga heterophylla*), and western red cedar (*Thuja plicata*). The resulting combination of species would be a vegetational community the Yellowstone area has not seen in millions of years, if ever.

The findings of such global and local modeling studies make it clear that global warming is driving us toward huge changes in all of the world's ecosystems, even—maybe especially—those that humanity has been trying to protect as the last vestiges of something wild, of nature more as it was before humans proliferated so widely, of a past that links us with our origins. Losing those vestiges of nature would be bad enough, but there's another big problem hidden in that loss, which the Williams team also uncovered: the places on Earth where global warming will likely wreak the most ecological havoc include most of the world's biodiversity hotspots, which may simply disappear as we know them. As they summed it up:

> . . . [T]he projected development of novel climates and the threat that the climates particular to some biodiversity hotspots may disappear globally, create the strong likelihood that many future species associations and landscapes will lack modern analogs and that many current species and associations will be disrupted or disappear entirely . . . standard conservation solutions (e.g., assisted migration and networked reserves) may be insufficient to preserve biodiversity. . . ."[18]

In order to fully appreciate what losing biodiversity hotspots means, it is helpful to step back and think about what biodiversity actually is, how it arises, and how climate influences it. Biodiversity is, in simple terms, how many different kinds of living things, and which living things, make up a particular ecosystem. There are many different ways that scientists measure biodiversity—the number of species (which is called species richness), the number of populations within a species, and the genetic variation within and among populations, to name just a few. In fact, we still have a lot to learn about all these measures; that's not too surprising when you realize that the word itself—"biodiversity"—was virtually unknown before 1986, even in scientific literature, despite nowadays commonly being used in the media and in many households.[19] What we do know is that climate is one of biodiversity's main determinants, figuring prominently in everything from where an individual species can survive, all the way up to the global distribution of species richness (recall Chapter 2).[20]

We also know that climate is not the whole story for biodiversity: in any given patch of real estate, events that take place over many different time and spatial scales build biodiversity, and climate is only one of the contributors. Other biodiversity builders include factors like how varied the landscape is (this is called habitat diversity)—the more variable, the more species. Also important is how long species have been evolving in a certain place; all else being equal, the longer evolution proceeds, the more branches multiply on the evolutionary tree. There are also factors like how big a continent (or ocean) that contains an ecosystem is, and the degree to which ecosystems have been isolated from exchanging species with other ecosystems: on bigger continents, more species tend to occur than in similar ecological settings on small continents, and in general, the more isolated a place, the fewer species it has.

To create a biodiversity hotspot, then, requires many different dynamics coming together over vast amounts of geological time, measured in millions of years: the building of habitat diversity, the evolution of species, and, depending on the continent (or ocean), either persistent isolation from or connection with other areas. Therein lies one big problem with losing biodiversity hotspots, and losing biodiversity in general, through the abnormally fast ecological disruption of global warming (and the same holds true for other ways humans cull biodiversity): there is simply no way the builders can keep up with such fast-acting destoyers.

There's a second big problem, too: given that each biodiversity hotspot is built by a unique combination of circumstances over millions of years, there is no one-size-fits-all solution to fixing a hotspot once it begins to break down. That was demonstrated, for example, by research that contrasted biodiversity in North America's oldest national park—Yellowstone—with its counterpart in Argentine Patagonia, Parque Nahuel Huapi, one of South America's oldest parks.[21] Both are biodiversity preserves for the ecosystems of which they are part (though not technically biodiversity hotspots in the global sense). As it turns out, Yellowstone's biodiversity was built by millions of years of both evolution and trading species with other continents and surrounding landscapes; Nahual Huapi's was built primarily by local species evolving and multiplying in relative isolation.[22]

Parque Nahuel Huapi has become much less isolated today than it has been for millions of years as the people who settled Patagonia imported (and continue to import) the plants and animals that made them feel at home. For example, in Nahuel Huapi and surrounding areas the backcountry has roses and scotch broom in such profusion that you forget these are Northern Hemisphere plants. The Rio Limay, typical of all of the clear, swift rivers in the region, is filled with trophy trout, also imported from the Northern Hemisphere, but hardly any native fish—in fact, nobody even knows what all the native fish were because the trout quickly ate them.[23] And the mammal fauna includes such North American and Eurasian exotics as axis deer (*Axis axis*), fallow deer (*Dama dama*), wapiti elk (*Cervus elaphus*), wild boar (*Sus scrofa*), European hares (*Lepus capensis*), and European rabbits (*Oryctolagus cuniculus*), all of which started out on game farms and subsequently escaped into the wild.

At the same time that Nahuel Huapi has been importing species, Yellowstone has become more isolated. A sharp, clear boundary now separates logged and agricultural surroundings from the native habitats of the park, turning it into essentially its own island, and in many cases people strictly regulate which species enter and leave. For instance, bison that step too far outside the Yellowstone Park boundary are shot, the goal being to control transmission of disease to domestic livestock. Same thing with wolves, to prevent direct killing of livestock. And woe to the elk that forgets where the park boundary is during hunting season.

Now throw today's global warming on top of that. For the Yellowstone ecosystem, just when species need to be the most fluid across the landscape in order to track their requisite climate, they are instead the most restricted. For the Patagonian ecosystem, native species are now forced, for essentially the first time, to compete with exotic newcomers, just when warming climate is making competition fiercest.

The combination of global warming stripping away the climate in which biodiversity hotspots and biodiversity preserves evolved, while we simultaneously change the rules of the species dispersal game with all of our man-made barriers, makes it a whole new world, and not necessarily a better one. For the first time in at least millions of years, decadal-scale drivers of what determines biodiversity in an ecosystem may be overtaking the more important (until now) million-year drivers, just like a wrecking ball breaking down in hours a building that took years to construct. Under these circumstances, today's rapid global warming is even more of a wild card than we have thought: as it helps accelerate the loss of biodiversity, it brings us, species by species, closer to losing critical ingredients of life's recipe, critical parts of the ecological machine.

Chapter 11 ⟟

Losing the Parts

Imagine trying to understand the ecology of tropical rainforests
by studying environmental changes and interactions among the
surviving plants and animals on a vast cattle ranch in the center
of a deforested Amazon.

—Nancy Knowlton and Jeremy B. C. Jackson, 2008[1]

AS CIRCUMSTANCE would have it, I live in
the heart of California's Silicon Valley, arguably the entrepreneurial
capital of the world. This is the place where two guys started a company in a garage and flipped a coin to see whether it should be named
Packard-Hewlett or Hewlett-Packard. And where later, in another
family garage, two other guys named Jobs and Wozniak started to
build personal computers and named their company after Jobs'
favorite fruit, the apple. It's the home of the start-up company, where
you pitch a wild vision to a venture capitalist, or develop a caffeine-
fueled idea with your friends, and if things work out as planned, you
become a millionaire virtually overnight. When I got there in the
1990s, the dot-com era was gearing up, and the start-ups included
companies with strange names like Yahoo! and Google.

Although Silicon Valley takes its name from the silicon chips of the computer industry, that's not the only kind of entrepreneurism evident there. In 1976, a San Francisco venture capital firm got behind an idea to use the then brand-new dream of genetic engineering to make medicines, pitched by Stanford University biochemist Herbert Boyer and venture capitalist Robert Swanson, an idea that very soon turned into Genentech. Now the region is swarming with biotech firms. And then there's the recent Silicon Valley biotech buzz, a start-up called 23andme,[2] which bills itself as "a web-based service that helps you read and understand your DNA," and has the tagline "genetics just got personal."[3] A swab of saliva, they claim, is all it takes for them to tell you everything your genetic code has to say about your ancestry, what diseases you might be susceptible to, what drugs will be best tailored to help you stay healthy, and so forth.

What most people don't realize is that there's a hidden fact behind virtually every one of these biotechnology breakthroughs. They owe their existence to the preservation of biodiversity, which traces back to the decision of the U.S. Congress more than a century ago to create and protect Yellowstone National Park. In 1872 when the park was established, they didn't call it biodiversity, of course; they called it "a public park or pleasuring-ground for the benefit and enjoyment of the people" and gave the Secretary of the Interior the authority to develop "regulations as he may deem necessary or proper for the care and management of the same. Such regulations shall provide for the preservation, from injury or spoliation, of all timber, mineral deposits, natural curiosities, or wonders within said park, and their retention in their natural condition."[4] In short, preserve the landscape and the species—the biodiversity—within the park boundaries.

Because of that, genetic engineering actually moved from the realm of dream to reality. John Varley, longtime chief of research in Yellowstone whom we met in Chapter 7, chronicled this transformation in a delightful piece in *Yellowstone Science* from which I'll give you the punch lines.[5] Varley pointed out that on December 22, 1989, the journal *Science* featured on its cover what it called "The Molecule of the Year." Inside, it sang the praises of the Taq polymerase molecule. Taq is shorthand for the species *Thermus aquaticus*, a bacterium. A polymerase molecule is the one that *T. aquaticus*, and every other living organism, needs as an enzyme to copy its DNA by a process called polymerase chain reaction, or PCR. In biotech circles PCR is now common vocabulary, because in 1983, Kary Mullis, then a biochemist for Cetus Corporation at the north end of Silicon Valley, figured out how to make PCR happen in the lab.

The basic idea is you take a strand of DNA, which you can imagine as a zipper twisted into a spiral, then you cook it in a stew that has ample amounts of the polymerase enzyme. You spice the stew with certain sugars, phosphates, and nitrogenous bases that make up all DNA. Picture each tooth on the zipper as one of those bases: there are four different kinds. One tooth links to its partner depending on which base it is. Cooking unzips the zipper, so now you have two separate strands, each side of the zipper floating separately in the genetic stew. As the stew cools, each side of the zipper begins attracting those free-floating bases, sugars, and phosphates you stirred in earlier, matching each base zipper-tooth by zipper-tooth, like so many tiny magnets attracting each other, until voilà, you now have two identical complete zippers floating around, one that was built by the original left side of the zipper attracting the mates for each of its teeth, and the other that was built by the right side of the original zipper attracting mates for each of its teeth. Then you reheat the stew, breaking apart both of those zippers, and the process repeats until you have four complete zippers. And so on into the millions. By changing the recipe of the stew, you can target replication of just certain parts of the original long zipper—that is, certain sequences of genes—in which you might be interested.

It is that PCR process that makes possible virtually every breakthrough in applied genetics, from sequencing the human genome, to developing effective pharmaceuticals, to understanding the genetic relationships between species and populations, to understanding whether you are likely to develop breast cancer or why you may like celery and hate asparagus. That's why Kary Mullis's discovery of PCR won him a Nobel Prize. The problem he still had in 1983, when he actually hit on the idea, was that the polymerase molecule, that critical enzyme needed to make the whole replication process happen, is usually destroyed at the high heat needed to separate the two strands of the DNA molecule. The 1983 version of the solution, to keep dumping in more and more polymerase from the bacterium *E. coli* after each cooking cycle, was just not very practical for widespread application.

Cut to Yellowstone Park. There is a hot spring there called Mushroom Pool, and there was a microbial ecologist named Thomas Brock. To make a long story short, in the 1960s Brock was interested in how temperature affected photosynthesis in microorganisms, and he liked the outdoors. So he developed a project to use the streams and hot springs of Yellowstone as natural laboratories in which to conduct his studies.[6] At the time, it was common wisdom that the upper temperature at which life could exist was around 73°C (163°F). Brock found that was indeed the limit he was finding for photosynthetic life, but not for life itself. To get a better handle on the photosynthesizing microbes living right at the limit, he zeroed in on Mushroom Pool in Yellowstone's Lower Geyser Basin, where the lodgepole pine forest is broken up by patches of bare, parched ground, orange and white in color, where dead gray pine trunks point to the sky as steam eerily rises from pools of hot water. This is a place where you walk in the footprints of bison, because you know that if the thin crust of ground covering the near-boiling waters below can support an animal that heavy, it can also support you. In Mushroom Pool the water temperature was right near that limit for photosynthesis, 73°C, so Brock sampled the microbes and cultured them to see what was there. On September 5, 1966, with undergraduate helper Hudson Freeze, he collected a sample that would become known as YT-1, and from which they would culture and name a bacterium new to science: *Thermus aquaticus*.[7] Years later, that culture and that bacterium was specified in a patent for which the pharmaceutical giant Hoffman-LaRoche paid more than $300 million dollars.

Since *T. aquaticus* had evolved in those very hot waters, natural selection had given it a polymerase enzyme that remained very stable even at the high temperatures at which DNA had to be cooked by Mullis's PCR technique. That high-temperature stability was just what was needed to make PCR commercially viable. Mullis hadn't yet made the connection between Brock's work and his own when he first conceived of PCR. But not too long after, the biochemists at Cetus took a great interest in papers published in the late 1970s by other biochemists to whom Brock had begun sending his cultures.[8] Those papers were the ones that demonstrated the stability of *T. aquaticus*' enzyme in the high temperatures PCR required. By that time the name of the enzyme had been shortened to Taq (for *T. aquaticus*) polymerase, or simply Taq.

The rest, as they say, is history. In 1989, the same year *Science* named Taq as its first "Molecule of the Year," David Gelfund of Cetus filed patents on both PCR and Taq. In 1993, Mullis got his Nobel Prize. Ten years later, we had a map of the human genome. By the year 2000 the biotechnology industry had grown to contribute 437,000 jobs, $47 billion in revenues, $11 billion in research and development spending, and $10 billion in tax revenues in the United States alone.[9] The discovery of *Thermus aquaticus* was directly responsible for all that, and for myriad benefits to humanity: diagnoses of diseases like Alzheimer's, atherosclerosis, and cancer; DNA fingerprinting that helps to solve crimes; and the potential to understand who you are and how your life might unfold at the level of your DNA. In short, it was preservation of biodiversity in Yellowstone that brought the miracles of molecular biology right into your living room. As John Varley put it:

> Steven Spielberg aside, it would be hard to concoct a story this unlikely. . . . The fact is that *Thermus aquaticus* was available for discovery there in Mushroom Pool because the feature and its basin were not available for more destructive, short-term uses. Taq would have had a vastly diminished chance of discovery, indeed of survival, in New Zealand, Iceland, Chile, Nevada, California, or almost any of the world's other once-major geothermal areas, because they were not protected, and are now sadly unproductive. Our celebration of Taq is thus tinged with a vague sense of waste: what else, around the world, have we lost already, and how much more can we afford to lose?[10]

Yellowstone, of course, is not the only biodiversity reserve to which we can anchor economic, medical, and technological success stories. Drugs for high blood pressure, ovarian cancer, leukemia, Hodgkins and non-Hodgkins diseases, as well as a host of others come from plants and animals discovered in other nature reserves or similarly intact ecosystems. Approximately 25 percent of all prescription drugs in the United States are derived from plants discovered first in the wild, and the global market value of pharmaceuticals originating from wild genes is in the neighborhood of $75–150 billion per year.[11] In the oceans, the fishing industry is almost entirely dependent on natural biodiversity to generate $67 billion in yearly world exports and $63 billion in imports.[12] And in tropical agricultural systems, there is growing evidence that proximity to areas of natural biodiversity increases crop yields.[13]

In a broader sense, biodiversity hotspots tend to correspond closely with areas that provide the highest-value ecosystem services.[14] "Ecosystem services" is the name ecologists have given to the world's ecological interactions that support and fulfill human life by providing food, clean water, health products, recreational opportunities, decomposition of waste products, and so on.[15] In 1997 it was calculated that the dollar value of natural ecosystem services worldwide was somewhere between $16 and $54 *trillion* per year.[16] Those numbers are not uncontested, but still, $54 trillion is about the same as the 2007 Gross World Product (GWP).[17]

Economic and health reasons are not the only reasons that people value biodiversity, of course.[18] For some, the moral imperative is even stronger: we share the Earth with other species and it is simply unacceptable to destroy them. And for others, it is the pure aesthetics of biodiverse places. While it is possible to put a dollar value on the aesthetics of biodiversity—for example, Jackson Hole, Wyoming, has the highest vertebrate biodiversity in the entire Greater Yellowstone ecosystem, and also the highest prices for its real estate—aesthetic value in the strict sense is priceless. In that sense, biodiversity is not unlike great art. You can put a dollar value on it, but its real value comes in making you feel good. And also like great art, lost biodiversity is irreplaceable, because creating it takes a unique combination of circumstances and a long, long time. Once you destroy it, it's gone forever.

All of that, important as it is, pales by comparison to one other reason to worry about declining biodiversity: the danger of losing keystone species along the way. Loss of a keystone species can cause ecological collapse at local scales; add up enough of those local losses, and you get collapse of the global ecosystem, in a way that can reduce how many people can live on Earth.

As the name implies, keystone species are those that, although represented by relatively small numbers of individuals, have an inordinately important effect on keeping their ecosystems in functioning order. Elephants serve to illustrate how keystone species work. As is typical of very large animals, they are represented by relatively few individuals in the ecosystems of which they are part. But their effects on those ecosystems are tremendous. Their large size means they have a voracious appetite for vegetation, including tree seedlings. That, combined with trampling and knocking over small trees, prevents forests from establishing on landscapes where elephants live; take out the elephants, though, and the whole ecosystem transforms as grassland turns into woodland or forest. In Kruger Park, for example, at densities below about one elephant per 2.5 square kilometers (about a square mile), elephants convert what would otherwise be woodlands into grasslands, an interaction repeated throughout elephant range in general. That, in turn, determines the presence or abundance of a whole host of other species, from other large mammals, to birds, beetles, butterflies, ants, spiders, parasites, and so on. By opening up woodlands, elephants have been documented to increase the presence or abundance of grazing species such as Grevy's zebra and oryx, and where they open up dense thickets, they also increase the abundance of browsers like kudu and eland. It goes the other way too—too many elephants on a patch of land, and those browsing species decline.[19]

Keystones occur in almost every kind of ecosystem on Earth. Documented examples include certain species of starfish, snails, birds, and sea otters in the rocky intertidal marine zone; baleen whales, gray whales, sea otters, rays, and walleye pollack offshore;

various fish, sea urchins, and starfish in coral reef systems; trout, bass, minnows, salamanders, and beavers in freshwater rivers and streams; elephants, rabbits, gophers, prairie dogs, and rinderpest (a disease organism that kills large mammals) in grasslands; seed-dispersing ants, fig trees, flying foxes (also known as fruit bats), and wolves in forests; snails, kangaroo rats, and tuco-tucos in deserts; snow geese in arctic marshes; and rabbits, pikas, and snowshoe hares in tundra, taiga, or alpine environments.[20]

The intricate ways in which global warming may delete keystones, and the potential cascading effects, become clear by looking at scenarios for places where we have lots of information. Consider, for example, one keystone species in Yellowstone National Park, the whitebark pine (*Pinus albicaulis*). Whitebark pine occurs at low abundance compared to other pines, yet its presence supports grizzlies, black bears, red squirrels, and Clark's nutcracker and other granivorous birds directly. The trickle-down effects of removing it would have enormous consequences. In fact, some studies go so far as to say that the survival of grizzly bears in Yellowstone is contingent on the survival of whitebark pine.[21] That is because the grizzlies rely on the whitebark pine seeds to get them through a part of the year when other food resources are scarce, in the late summer and early fall, just as they are building their fat reserves in preparation for hibernation. Indirectly, Yellowstone's whitebark pine anchors the entire subapline forest ecosystem, as it builds habitat for a host of other species through rapidly establishing and promoting tree islands in the harsh conditions near tree line.

As we saw in the last chapter, the prognosis for whitebark pines in Yellowstone is not good given the climate models. At a minimum, the area in which it can live will be much reduced, and it is possible that its preferred climate may be entirely lost within the park. But we may not have to wait until the year 2100 to see how its disappearance cascades through the Yellowstone ecosystem. Some rapid, global warming–induced species interactions seem to be decimating whitebark pines much faster.

Dendroctonus ponderosae, otherwise known as the mountain pine beetle, is a small, nondescript black insect that bores into pine tree trunks. By doing that, it turns whole forests from healthy green to sickly yellowish-orange, then to bare brittle sticks reaching for the sky as the trees die over the course of a year or so. Luckily for white-bark pines, mountain pine beetles have seldom run rampant through them because the life cycle of the beetle requires warmer winter temperatures than typically are found in the subalpine and tree-line zones where the pines grow. Until recently, that is. With the warmer temperatures of the past few years, mountain pine beetles are beginning to rage through the whitebark pine forests of the Greater Yellowstone ecosystem. By the year 2000, mountain pine beetles had arrived in those forests, but only 2,000 acres were infected. As of 2006, a minimum of 171,160 acres (that's 16 percent of the 1,064,600 acres of whitebark-pine-dominated forest stands, or about three quarters of a million trees) had trees dying from mountain pine beetles.[22] That promises to get worse. Climate maps show that in the Greater Yellowstone's whitebark pine areas there was nowhere the beetles could survive under 1951–1980 conditions. Under current climatic conditions (average of 1981–2006), the beetle's survival zone has moved into most of the whitebark pine areas in the northwestern part of the park. Projected warming (average of modeled conditions for 2031–2060) expands the beetle survival zone through most of the western two-thirds of the ecosystem.[23]

Mountain pine beetles aren't the only problem that whitebark pines face. They also have to deal with blister rust, a fungal disease. Blister rust is caused by a pathogen, *Cronartium ribicola*, which has been making its way eastward after being introduced by mistake (like so many exotic species) into British Columbia in 1910. By the year 2000 it was increasing in the southern end of Yellowstone, and may spread even faster under some predicted climate-change scenarios.[24] That alone is of concern; add mountain pine beetles into the picture, and the trees are in real trouble. In Glacier National Park, where the ranges of blister rust and mountain pine beetles already overlap, more than half of the whitebark pines are dead or dying as the trees suffer attacks from both species.[25]

In effect, removing or adding keystone species pushes ecosystems across thresholds into what are known as alternative states. The consequences are obvious in cases like the switch from woodland to grassland in Africa, or from vegetated wetlands to the Sahara Desert mentioned in Chapter 2.[26] Consequences are not so obvious when we are dealing with something that has never happened in human experience, like removing whitebark pines from Yellowstone. That is the situation we will increasingly face as keystone species are disrupted by global warming. In principle, we can be pretty sure that some big effects will percolate through the rest of the ecosystem, but we won't know the details until they happen. What we can be sure of is that when keystones are gone, those ecosystems will look very different from what we have today.

The extent to which ecosystems resist moving into an alternative stable state is called ecosystem resistance. Think of resistance as the ability of an ecosystem to withstand the stresses to which it is subjected, either at the hands of humans or otherwise. A related concept is ecosystem resilience. Resilience is the ability of an ecosystem to return to its normal state after it is perturbed. If you think of an ecosystem as an elastic cord, resistance is how hard you have to pull to get it to break, and resilience is how fast it will snap back into shape before it breaks. As it turns out, ecosystem resistance and resilience are other reasons to worry about global warming's contribution to loss of biodiversity, regardless of loss of keystone species.

More biodiverse ecosystems tend to be more resistant and more resilient. But not in an exactly linear way, which makes the whole relationship a little more frightening when you think about the future. At first you can keep plucking species out of most ecosystems without actually changing the way the ecosystems work, assuming you don't pluck out a keystone species. But, if you take out one too many species, the ecosystem snaps, and there you are, in an alternative ecosystem state, which you may not like. Nancy Knowlton and Jeremy Jackson, for example, point out that this breaking point is exactly where we find ourselves with coral reefs. Already stressed by the rapid depletion or removal of species through fishing and pollution, pulling out just a few more species will push coral reefs over the brink—they simply will cease to exist.[27]

Resistance and resilience mean that ecosystems tend to be pretty stable in the natural course of things. But from a human perspective, ecological resilience and resistance hide what is really going on as we pluck species from ecosystems one by one. Even though every species deletion leads to an overall weakening of both resistance and resilience, nothing observable (from the human perspective) really happens until one too many species is hit, making us think everything is still all right when in fact, just like those coral reefs Knowlton and Jackson talk about, whole ecosystems are about to disappear.

The reason that the reduction in biodiversity takes us by surprise is because nature, like airplanes and spaceships, is built with lots of extra buttressing and backup systems—as engineers like to call it, redundancy. That redundancy comes in two forms. One is simply making the airplane stronger than the minimum needed to fly. It's that concept that is behind what is known as the rivet hypothesis of ecosystem stability, based on an analogy that Paul and Anne Ehrlich came up with about the nonlinear relationship between numbers of species and stability of ecosystems.[28] They likened species to rivets in the wing of an airplane. If you lose a few, no problem. If you lose too many, the wing comes apart and you end up as a ball of fire. The second form of redundancy is having multiple ways of performing the same critical function. If you're flying across the Pacific in a Boeing 747 jumbo jet and one engine goes out, you stay in the air. Drop a second, and you may still hobble along, although the distance you can fly, your altitude, and your maneuverability are severely compromised. Drop a third, and you drop with it.

So it is too with species in ecosystems. If one species becomes extinct (one part fails), another species might be available to take over the function that the extinct species was performing. Most ecosystems have such redundant species—for example, multiple species of ground squirrels in Rocky Mountain ecosystems, or multiple grazing fish in a coral reef ecosystem. Pulling out the last redundant species is like losing that last engine. The redundancy hypothesis recognizes that "species may be segregated into functional groups; those species within the same functional group are predicted to be more expendable in terms of ecosystem function relative to one another than species without functional analogs."[29]

The redundancy hypothesis is borne out by both theoretical and empirical studies.[30] We still don't know, though, just how many and which redundant species are present in each kind of ecosystem. What we do know is that they are there, and if we eliminate too many of them, ecosystems will dramatically change in how they look and how they function, and they will likely deliver less to us in the way of ecosystem services.[31] Over the past couple hundred years, we have been plucking species out one by one, and there is no end in sight.

That's why John Varley titled his article about the Taq discovery "Saving the Parts," to emphasize that, when it comes to preserving ecosystem interactions and services, pioneer conservationist Aldo Leopold hit it right on the money when he said, "The first step in intelligent tinkering is to save all the parts." For building ecosystems, species *are* the parts, and the problem now is that we are losing the parts faster than we are learning what they do, in fact, faster than we can even discover them. Extinction rates today seem to be much more rapid than normal (as we saw in Chapter 4—at best estimate, some 17–377 percent too fast). The looming problem is that global warming seems on track to accelerate even these already high rates of species extinction. For example, as we saw in the last chapter the biomes that will be most changed by global warming are the same biomes that hold most of the world's biodiversity. And we've also seen that for every nature reserve examined in previous chapters, reduction in number of species seems assured by the combination of dramatic climate changes and species' inability to disperse, because human-dominated landscapes usually act as impenetrable barriers between suitable habitats.[32]

Not only do the modeling results and empirical data we've seen in previous chapters point to global warming as speeding up the loss of biodiversity, but so does the relationship between biodiversity, extinction, and global warming through the long course of time— like the last 520 million years. To work out that relationship, evolutionary ecologist Peter Mayhew and his colleagues Gareth Jenkins and Timothy Benton assembled the records of temperature change and global CO_2 concentrations through geological time, ultimately from isotope ratios preserved in ocean cores (as briefly explained in

Chapter 2) and other kinds of atmospheric proxy data.[33] They then compared the temperature, atmospheric CO_2 concentrations, and number of families and genera represented by organisms well known as fossils, using paleontological information compiled in two separate databases of fossil occurrences.[34]

The correlation they found does not bode well for the future of biodiversity. Biodiversity generally went down when CO_2 and temperature went up. And four of the Big Five mass extinctions—the late-Devonian event (367 million years ago), end-Permian (250 million years ago), early Triassic (208 million years ago), and end-Cretaceous (65 million years ago)—corresponded with the highest CO_2 and temperature levels. During those events, most of the species living on Earth at the time went extinct: in the late-Devonian, 80 percent of species; end-Permian, 95 percent; end-Triassic, 80 percent; and end-Cretaceous, 75 percent. Looking at it from the perspective of Linnaean families (which are higher-order groups of related species; for example, dogs, coyotes, wolves, and foxes are all in the same Linnaean family), the extinction percentages also are high—22 percent extinction for the late-Devonian, 51 percent for the end-Permian, 20 percent for the early Triassic, and 16 percent for the end-Cretaceous. These are truly impressive numbers, because extinction of families means that whole branches of the evolutionary tree are pruned, not just the twigs that species oftentimes represent. To get a feeling for the amount of biodiversity lost, and the total restructuring of ecosystems that resulted, consider that the least impressive of all of these mass extinctions was the one that killed the dinosaurs some 65 million years ago. That means that in each of the other mass extinctions, the biodiversity loss and resetting of the global ecosystem was even more severe than crossing the threshold from a world dominated by dinosaurs to a world dominated by mammals, and eventually us.

That's not to say that global warming caused each of the past mass extinctions. Indeed, each appears to have had its own unique trigger—in the case of the dinosaurs, for example, an asteroid impact. Nevertheless, that asteroid hit a world that, according to the Mayhew group's correlations, was expectedly low in biodiversity because

CO_2 levels and temperature were relatively high. Or, in the terminology we were using in the previous paragraphs, a lot of redundant
species, and maybe some of the keystones, were possibly already missing. Most of the other mass extinctions seem to have occurred on the
same kind of globally warmed, biodiversity-depressed world stage.
The vagaries the fossil record make it difficult, if not impossible, to
reconstruct the details of how global warming influenced these past
mass extinctions, but what we do know—that there is a correlation
between globally high CO_2, globally high temperatures, and lowered
biodiversity and mass extinctions—is far from comforting. Now we're
at around 380 ppm (parts per million) of CO_2 in the atmosphere, up
from around 280 ppm 1,000 years ago, and from 315 ppm in 1958.
IPCC projections say that by the year 2100, in the best case, we'll be
at 550 ppm, more likely near 750 ppm, and in the worst case, at about
1,000 ppm. The 1,000 ppm scenario makes the atmosphere look like
it did when the dinosaurs died.[35] If we can project the recognized
relationship between past CO_2 levels, biodiversity, and extinction
into the future, it would seem prudent to stay as far below that 1000
ppm mark as we can.

That brings up the spectre of global warming's role in what many
scientists think we're already in the midst of: the world's next mass-
extinction event. Instead of the Big Five, it's going to be the Big Six,
in this view. Just how bad number six gets depends on just how many
unfortunate events come together at once in the wrong way, as we'll
discuss in Chapter 13. What seems clear already, though, is that
global warming is now adding its own weight to all the other forces
driving us toward dwindling biodiversity. Add that push on the throt-
tle, and the train speeding us toward the sixth mass extinction can do
nothing but accelerate. What rises from the wreck will depend on
what evolution has left to work with.

Chapter 12

Skeleton Crew

We shall best understand the probable course of natural selection by taking the case of a country undergoing some physical change, for instance, of climate.

—Charles Darwin, 1859[1]

It's very iffy. Can't trust it. Dover, PA—they're not sure about evolution. Here in New Jersey, we're countin' on it.

—Bruce Springsteen, 2005[2]

HALLUCIGENIA is just downright weird. It looks like its name—a wormy body with a mushroom-shaped blob on one end that might be the head, might be the tail. Spikes sticking out of the top of the body, like two rows of straight pins with the pointy ends out, give you the sense you wouldn't really want to pick the thing up, though you could—it's only a few centimeters long. Corresponding rows of spiky-looking things project from the bottom of the body, but those are apparently its feet, or what passes for feet on an animal that lives in the sea. That's another odd thing—you'd expect to find *Hallucigenia* walking around in a tropical forest in South America, if you were to judge by where its relatives live. Or at least, what people think its relatives are: velvet worms, or more technically Onycophorans (because they belong to the phylum Onycophora).[3] Yet here we were, at the only place where *Hallucigenia* is known, with neither tropical forest nor sea in sight, and certainly not in South

America. We had been hiking uphill for six hours and 900 meters (3,000 feet) and were finally balanced at what seemed like the top of the world, high in the Canadian Rockies and surrounded by snow-capped mountains that looked like they went on forever. Right above us, mountain goats licked salts out of the gray-brown slabs of shale that coated the steep scree slope and shifted under our feet as we scrambled the final few meters up the mountain.

Those slabs sustaining the goats and crunching underfoot were the Burgess Shale, the modern-day remnant of a 530-million-year-old seafloor. The Burgess Shale is famous for its exquisitely preserved fossils that show us that most of the animal phyla that are common today had evolved by Cambrian time, approximately 543–490 million years ago.[4] It was in that Burgess sea that *Hallucigenia* had lived and died, along with some of the oldest-known species of the phyla Arthropoda (today containing 80 percent of all known animal species, including insects, spiders, crabs, and the like), Cnidarians (jellyfish and corals), Ctenophora (comb jellies), Brachiopoda (clamlike animals but with symmetrical shells), Mollusca (clams and snails), Annelida (various segmented worms), Priapulida, (predatory, unsegmented marine worms), Porifera (sponges), Echinodermata (starfish and sea urchins), Hemichordata (acorn worms), and Chordata (including vertebrate animals, like you and me). All of these animals—representing 119 different genera—were swimming in the ocean or crawling through marine mud near the edge of a huge, steep-edged reef, down which underwater mudslides occasionally cascaded and buried the animals in such a way that even delicate soft parts of their bodies were preserved as fossils. Today, as you pry apart the laminated shale layers at the Walcott Quarry high in these Canadian Rockies, you can look to the northeast and see the remnants of that reef shoved up by tectonic forces to form the Cathedral Escarpment running between Mount Field and Wapta Mountain.

The Walcott Quarry is so named for its discoverer, Charles Walcott. Walcott was a paleontologist at the Smithsonian Institution and liked to spend summers with his family: hiking, camping, mapping the geology, and looking for fossils in the Canadian Rockies. The story goes that while traversing the low part of the same treacherous scree slope where we had watched the mountain goats, one of his family's horses kicked over some slabs of shale. Something caught Walcott's eye. His field notes from that day, August 31, 1909, scrawl what looks like a routine entry: "Out with Helena [his wife] and Stuart [his son] collecting fossils from the Stephens Formation . . . we found a new phyllopod crustacean . . . took a large number of fine specimens to camp." The following day, they continued collecting, and by September 2 Walcott was "working high up on the slope, while Helena collected near the trail." Walcott had apparently located the source of the fossils, the outcrop at which we were standing ninety years later, and which would become known as the Walcott Quarry. The day after Walcott located the quarry, one of Murphy's Paleontological Laws kicked in, which states that you always find the best things too late in the field season to finish up. The weather turned, as it is wont to do in early September in the Canadian Rockies. Thursday, September 3, 1909: "High clouds, cold wind . . . Out in the collecting ground but driven in by the cold."

Such quick weather-changes, the mountains all around the quarry, the glaciers we saw on them, the rugged topography that we traversed, the goats, and we ourselves of course, all are testaments to how much things had changed since *Hallucigenia*'s time. In the 530 million years since *Hallucigenia* had wandered through those tropical seas, the slow but steady forces of plate tectonics had moved the spot where we were standing from a position just south of the equator, and along the way shoved the ancient seafloor upward some 2,300 meters (7,500 feet) above sea level.

Over the aeons through which that slow-motion tectonic sliding inexorably transformed the physical landscape, life too was being transformed, through the process of evolution.[5] Wonderful Life, Stephen Jay Gould called it, in writing about the evolutionary journey that eventually led from those Burgess animals to modern *Homo sapiens*.[6] The animals of the Burgess Shale were themselves the products of a long history of evolutionary change, ultimately tracing their ancestry back to the first single-celled organisms some 3.5 billion years ago. From that beginning, life diversified, one important milestone being the development of the several basic body plans that first become evident in the Burgess fossils (now also known from other fossil deposits of similar Cambrian age).[7] Once those body plans were in place, evolution worked out countless variations on those few basic themes, until today we have somewhere between three million and thirty million species on Earth. (There aren't enough taxonomists to count all the species, so the number of unknown species has to be estimated from the numbers of those we do know.)

Evolving from creatures like those of the Burgess sea to the diversity of life today proceeded in a series of fits and starts, as we now know from observations based on a rich fossil record, experiments in the laboratory and field, and knowledge of the genetic relationships between living (and in some cases fossil) organisms. Those observations verify that the multiplication of life-forms we call evolution results from a tangled web of interactions: between molecules, individual organisms, the environment, and dumb luck. Molecules come into the picture because it is the DNA molecule itself that changes through mutation, with substitutions and changes in the order of the base pairs that build DNA. Individual organisms (all the plants, animals, bacteria, and so forth) are important because it is the individual organism that has to survive in a given environment in order to produce new offspring. And it is at the organismal level that reproduction takes place, typically accomplished by recombination of genes from each parent, which causes new traits that make each new individual unique, and thereby provides abundant variation for natural selection to sort through as various environmental pressures come into play. Those environmental pressures limit the reproductive success of some individuals, the "least fit," more than that of other individuals, the "most fit." And dumb luck—more properly termed gene flow and random drift, in this evolutionary context— changes gene pools not by any selective pressure, but simply through random chance.[8]

It doesn't take much of a leap to realize that if natural selection and random chance are parts of the evolutionary equation, global warming will have evolutionary impacts. With current climatic changes occurring much faster than in the past and making Earth hotter than usual, and global warming driving adjustments in geographic ranges and population sizes, selection pressures for many species have accelerated and are stronger than has been typical. The shifting geographic ranges and population declines we're observing are just the recipe to change gene pools quickly—think, for example, of those pikas and bighorn sheep being isolated on mountaintops with ever-decreasing population sizes that were discussed in Chapter 3. Those, and other examples of new climates and shifts of species around the landscape that we've seen so far, are just the proverbial tip of the iceberg compared to what's on the way in just the next few decades. Global warming thus seems poised to influence the evolutionary trajectory of life dramatically. The question is how.

Answering that depends on which dimension of evolution you are thinking about. I like to think of the critical dimensions as innovation, diversity, and experimentation. These three dimensions of evolution are important to recognize, because global warming promises to affect each differently.

By innovation in evolution I mean the building of whole new designs in nature, like those phyla that had appeared in the Burgess sea by 530 million years ago. Innovations result from mutations at the molecular level coming at the right place and right time. Mutations occur when DNA molecules are changed base by base (that is, zipper-tooth by zipper-tooth, as described in Chapter 11), either by the occasional odd bit of UV light or other environmental contaminant hitting them just the wrong way, or through random mistakes that occur when the DNA molecule replicates itself in the process of cell division.[9] Such mutations sometimes alter the instructions written in the genetic code, often disastrously, but occasionally the end result for the organism can be a new developmental pathway (like the sequence or pattern in which cells split, for example) that may in turn result in a new trait (like a stronger fin on a fish, for example). If that trait allows the organism to occupy a previously unoccupied ecological niche (like the land before amphibians, or the sky before flying insects, reptiles, or birds), an entirely new world opens up for the evolution of life.

The emergence of the whole new designs in nature that characterize innovations are the rarest events in evolution, largely because their underlying driver requires the right mutation hitting the right part of the right genome at the right time in Earth history. The "right genome" is one that has not already developed so much complexity that little tweaks in the genetic program have lethal results. The "right time" is when the world happens to have the right kind of open ecological space. The odds of those random events aligning are infinitesimal, and explain three things we know about the innovations. First, they are exceedingly rare—if we consider animal and bacteria phyla along with plant and fungi divisions (divisions are the botanical equivalent of phyla) as representing those major innovations, about 80 of them have arisen in 3.5 billion years. That's roughly one every 44 million years (although in reality, as the Cambrian Burgess shale shows, the origin of innovations seems clustered at certain times rather than randomly distributed). Second, all of the big innovations (phyla and divisions) arose when genomes and thus developmental pathways were relatively simple—the basic body plans (phyla) of every species on Earth seem to have already appeared by hundreds of millions of years ago. Third, innovations at that grand scale seem largely decoupled from past climate changes—that is, they appear to be purely a toss of the evolutionary dice. This means that any evolutionary effects of global warming will play out in a world that has long settled into interactions between organisms with a limited number of basic designs. Changing those basic designs is simply not within the realm of what global warming, or any other climate change, can do.

The second dimension of evolution is building diversity. Given the fixed amount of basic designs to play with, evolution builds diversity by taking whatever basic plan is available and modifying it in little but important ways as selection and chance dictate—for example, altering the genetic code that makes a clam a clam to produce many different kinds of clams. Those different "kinds" are what we call species, like the million-plus arthropod species that are variations on the theme of an exoskeleton (an outer shell with joints), or the 47,000 (more or less) vertebrate species, all variations on the theme of an internal backbone.

The actual derivation of a new species is called speciation. When speciation happens, a new species splits off from an existing one, somewhat like a new branch budding off an old branch of a tree. Just like innovations, speciation ultimately requires mutations at the level of the genetic code. For most species this is a slow process—by some estimations, about one mutation in five hundred generations, and the vast majority of those are neutral, meaning that they have no detectable effect on the organism. For that reason, even though the appearance of a new species may look fast in geological time, and fast relative to how long the species persists, it still typically takes hundreds of thousands of years in real time.[10] Calculations of how long it would take genetic mutations to accumulate to the extent needed for a new species to arise suggest that unusually fast speciation could take as little as few thousand years (cichlid fishes in lakes), but "fast" in most cases means something less than 300,000 years (other kinds of lake-dwelling fish) or 600,000 to 1 million years (island birds and arthropods). For mammals, reptiles, and amphibians, the speciation process as inferred from molecular evidence typically seems to average 2.2 million years; for birds, 2.0 million years, and the fossil record bears out those molecular-based estimates.[11, 12]

The effect of these slow mutation rates is to limit the speed at which selective forces—like climate change—can stimulate the building of new species. That explains why times of relatively slow climate change—like some of the tectonic-scale climate changes mentioned in Chapter 2, which take place over hundreds of thousands to millions of years—seem to correlate with bursts of speciation. In those cases the rate at which climate changes is well matched to the mutation rate, so as the selection pressure of a changing climate pushes, evolution can keep up and new species evolve. For faster climate changes, like the Milanković oscillations that caused the glacial-interglacial transitions, there is a mismatch in rates—climate simply changes too fast for mutation rates to keep pace.[13] That is the situation that global warming is forcing today, with the rate of climate change outpacing mutation rates of most animal and plant species by a far greater margin than we have ever seen. Under those circumstances, the evolutionary opportunities are reduced to whatever genetic changes are possible by mechanisms other than mutation: which leaves recombination as the main game in town.

Recombination is the reason that, if you look at the students sitting in a classroom, or at your coworkers on the job site, some are tall,
some are short, some have blue eyes, some brown, some have dark
hair, some have light, and so on. Those differences arise from novel
combinations of genes (a set from each parent that together "recom-
bine") expressing themselves differently in each generation (such
that each kid looks at least a little different from Mom and Dad).
Recombination provides the variation upon which natural selection
can act. Natural selection in a sense is the opposite of recombination:
rather than enhancing variation, as recombination does, it acts to
reduce variation, by trimming the least-fit individuals—because they
don't reproduce as frequently—from the whole spectrum of variation
that recombination produces.[14] Recall the classic example used to
illustrate natural selection: what happened to peppered moths in
England as the Industrial Revolution got going full steam and coal-
fired plants spewed out pollution that darkened tree trunks. The
light-colored moths got picked off the tree trunks by birds, since they
were easier to see; the dark-colored ones blended in and were spared.
It did not take too long for that kind of natural selection to reduce
variation such that moth populations contained only dark individuals.

The reason that recombination and selection can drive evolutionary changes even when climate change is outpacing mutation
rates is because species don't represent just one big, well-mixed gene
pool. Instead, they are broken up into many little gene pools (called
populations), and it is in each of those little gene pools that the third
process in evolution—experimentation—dominates. The gene pools
can exist side by side with some rivulets connecting them (the
rivulets being individuals that travel between populations), or at the
other extreme they can be totally isolated (no individuals dispersing
in or out). Each gene pool is constantly brewing its own little evolutionary experiment in balancing the effects of recombination and
selection, producing populations with, on average, a brighter-colored
flower here, a smaller leaf there, and so on. If a new selective force
begins to hit those populations—such as a change in climate that
favors smaller leaves over larger ones—the favored trait can rapidly

spread throughout the population. The smaller the population, the faster the spread can be, because the genes for the new trait get less swamped by genes from the other individuals that don't have the trait. If selection is strong enough, and widespread enough, and isolation is not total, then the new trait can rapidly jump from one gene pool to the next and thereby spread throughout the entire species.

That sort of change is exactly what evolutionary biologists are observing in response to global warming in some species: recombination and selection seem to be working their magic to change genotypes. Interestingly, in almost every well-documented case, the actual selection pressure induced by global warming has to do with phenology[15]—recall from earlier chapters that phenology is the interaction of some biological trait like reproduction with the timing of seasons. In the Yukon, for example, global warming means earlier arrival of spring, and as a result red squirrels (*Tamiasciurus hudsonicus*) have been advancing their breeding season. In 1998 they were breeding 18 days earlier than they had in 1989, which works out to an advance in breeding date of 6 days per generation. Of that, 0.8 day per generation seems to result from evolutionary changes in their genetic hardwiring.[16]

The actual pathway by which global warming stimulates evolution within a species can be circuitous, as another example serves to illustrate. There is a warbler ranging through much of Europe called the European blackcap. As the name implies, males have what looks like a black cap on their head, contrasting with the mostly gray body; females wear a brown cap. As with many insect-eating birds, blackcaps have evolved in concert with climate such that the chicks are born just about the time in the spring when lots of caterpillars hatch. This is a bit tricky, because the genetically hardwired cue for the birds to lay eggs is actually a certain day-length, whereas the cue for the caterpillars to hatch is a certain temperature. It is even trickier because the birds don't spend the whole year in the places where they lay eggs—they migrate, spending the winter in say, Spain, after laying their eggs and rearing their young in southern Germany. There is also a bit of genetic hardwiring that tells the birds to fly back to Spain when it's time to leave for the winter again. The upshot is that there has been a long evolutionary dance between the bird populations and caterpillar populations such that when the days get long enough in Spain, the birds head north to Germany and lay their eggs; by the time the chicks hatch, the temperature is just right for the caterpillars to hatch as well, so there is lots for the chicks to eat (not such a great deal for the caterpillars, though). The problem with global warming, as far as the birds are concerned, is that over the past thirty years it has been getting warm in Germany earlier and earlier in the spring, stimulating caterpillars to hatch before the birds' genetic, day length–controlled trigger tells them to leave Spain. By the time many of the birds get to the nesting ground, the caterpillars have turned into butterflies, and the blackcap chicks starve.

In that German nesting ground there also happen to be a few birds with the genetic hardwiring to send them to England instead of Spain when it comes time to migrate. England, being farther north, experiences an increase in day-length earlier in the spring than does Spain. So those English blackcaps head for Germany a few days earlier, and their chicks hatch before the caterpillars are gone. Not too hard to see why, as the warming trend has progressed over the past thirty years, more and more of those English blackcaps survive. In this case, recombination and selection are causing the English migrants to spread their genes wider and wider through the gene pool of that German breeding ground. Of course, that sort of evolution will come to an end if the English migrant gene is spread through 100 percent of the population, yet warming advances the caterpillar season ahead of the day length–triggered migration cue for even the English blackcaps.

Whether or not those genes actually spread any farther than that German breeding ground depends on whether any individuals from that population interbreed with birds of other populations from other breeding grounds. That jumping of traits from one population to the next as individuals disperse is gene flow. Recently, it's been discovered that global warming affects how much gene flow actually takes place within various species. This finding comes from the unlikely world of fossil DNA.

That world is more like Holocene Park than Jurassic Park. The

Holocene encompasses the last ten thousand years and that geologic age is the origin of the three-millennia-old fossil bones from Lamar Cave in Yellowstone Park (see Chapter 7). The ancient DNA from those bones gives us insights into what happened to gene flow in various Yellowstone species as climate warmed during the Medieval Warm Period, about 1,150 years ago. DNA typically degrades quickly after the death of an organism,[17] but under the right circumstances, as in the sealed dry deposits of caves, it can last several thousands of years. Liz Hadly took some of the fossil pocket-gopher bones (*Thomomys talpoides*) to a molecular biology lab at UCLA where she and ancient-DNA pioneer Bob Wayne, working with others in the lab to replicate results, found that indeed there was DNA preserved in the fossils.[18] With that knowledge, Hadly's Stanford University team started looking for a genetic response to climatic change in other species from the cave, and eventually found it not only in pocket gophers but also in salamanders, grebes, ground squirrels, and three species of voles. They found that what happens to gene flow when climate changes is not always what's expected. It depends a lot on what kind of species you are.[19]

At one end of the scale are montane voles (*Microtus montanus*). These are little brown mice with soft fur, very short tails and chubby tummies. Voles are born to run, so to speak, and thus are natural dispersers. As soon as they grow big enough, they scamper off along their vole runways (you can see these in mountain meadows, little paths where the grass is flattened in long tracks about half a hand-width wide), searching out new territory. That frequently brings them into contact with other populations of voles. So as you might suspect, genetic diversity in vole populations can be quite high. What you wouldn't suspect simply by looking at modern vole populations is that when global warming causes a population to decrease in size, vole genetic diversity actually increases. That was the counterintuitive discovery that the Stanford team found for voles of the Medieval Warm Period in Yellowstone. The explanation is that as local climate change kills off the voles in a population by shrinking their favored habitat, voles from other populations disperse into the area. In the short run, that increases diversity locally; but in the long run, it doesn't do much for the species as whole, for that area becomes a diversity sink—meaning that although new voles frequently come in, they don't survive in high-enough numbers to build up population sizes and send dispersers out.

At the other end of the dispersal scale are pocket gophers, those little guys that cause a lot of trouble in alfalfa fields and maybe in your garden. They are fossorial, meaning they live their life primarily underground in burrows, and they are fiercely territorial. Pocket gophers are the Sylvester Stallones of rodents, all upper body, because they spend their lives moving dirt with their arms. Their big front teeth are framed by whiskers that help them sense the sides of their burrows; their rodenty eyes are even smaller and beadier than usual for rodents, and their ears (at least the outer parts) are tiny so the gophers don't get hung up as they push their way through tight, dark spaces. Born in the burrow, they stick close to home, and seldom make a break across open ground (where hawks, owls, coyotes, and the like are waiting to eat them) where they might disperse into other gophers' territories. That, as you may expect, means that genes don't flow very freely from one gopher population to the next. You might also expect it means that if a population declines in size, genetic diversity in that population also declines. And you would be right—that's exactly what the Stanford team found. With the onset of the Medieval Warm Period, the moist-soil habitats favored by pocket gophers shrank, and so too did the number of pocket gophers around Lamar Cave. And correspondingly, genetic diversity decreased—and it's still at those low levels in today's population there.

Low genetic diversity is a bad thing for evolution, not to mention for actual survival of a species, and even for survival of ecosystems.[20] That global warming can actually decrease genetic diversity in populations and species spells trouble, especially for species in which genetic diversity is already low. These typically are the big, warm, fuzzy ones. At highest risk are those charasmatic species whose specieswide genetic diversity is very low: animals like cheetahs on land and northern elephant seals in the sea. At some point, maybe as far back as the time of those megafaunal extinctions some ten thousand years ago (see Chapter 5), the effective breeding population of cheetahs dropped to just a few animals—maybe as few as seven. From them, all living cheetahs have descended; in the wild, an estimated eight to ten thousand animals.[21] Northern elephant seals almost went extinct in the 1890s when hunting culled their effective breeding population to fewer than thirty animals; from them, population sizes gradually grew back into the thousands.[22] That means that the genotype of one cheetah or one elephant seal is just about identical to the next. In such species, there simply isn't much raw material for recombination to work with. Throw too strong a selection pressure at them, and the outcome of extinction is pretty certain.

Not to say that you might not see some changes even in species with limited genetic diversity before they go extinct, from something that looks like evolution but really isn't. That something is called phenotypic plasticity, which occurs when environmental differences cause a particular genotype to be expressed differently, even though the gene pool of the population is not really changing. As you may recall from Chapter 4, "phenotype" means any observed trait of an organism, like how it looks, how it develops, or even in some cases how it acts. "Plasticity" means that whatever trait is being observed can vary within certain limits for a given genotype. A classic example of phenotypic plasticity is adult body size: malnourished animals (including humans) grow up to be smaller adults than their well-nourished neighbors or siblings. So it goes with certain climatic influences as well—recall, for example, the Irish elk of Chapter 5, and there are many other examples: in Norway, red deer (*Cervus elephus*) born after warm winters are smaller than those born after cold winters;[23] around Yellowstone Park, pocket gophers (*Thomomys talpoides*) living in moister areas are bigger than those living in drier areas;[24] in various birds the egg-laying date varies with temperature (warmer temperature equals earlier egg laying);[25] incubation temperature of reptile eggs affects sex ratios and other traits of hatchlings (for example, in hot nests sea turtle eggs produce 80 percent females, in cool nests 90 percent males);[26] and in North Carolina, the perennial herb *Plantago lanceolata* develops lighter-colored, more-reflective flowers under warmer temperatures.[27] It is, in fact, phenotypic plasticity that actually accounts for most of the advance in the breeding season of the red squirrels in the Yukon that I mentioned earlier (3.7 days earlier per generation). That means that you probably will be seeing some changes in your favorite species as things warm up in your part of the world: for example, you might notice subtle color changes in your flower garden, and maybe the gophers you trap there might start looking a bit smaller (or bigger, depending on where you live), or you might hear baby birds chirping earlier in the spring. Those phenotypically plastic changes will very soon stop, however, even though climate keeps changing. Phenotypic plasticity allows traits to vary only within certain limits (just as there is an upper limit to how tall your child will grow even given the best nutrition). It can give some false hope that things are changing in the right direction, but without recombination to produce some new variation, it very soon reaches its limit.

The problem even with recombination, however, is that without sufficient mutation, it too is just a temporary fix. Recombination can stimulate some evolution within a species, but it generally stops at the species boundary. Furthermore, nothing is ever simple: a given recombination may produce a beneficial trait but at the same time counteract it with a deleterious one.[28] An even bigger problem though, is that without mutation, you eventually run out of raw genetic variation, so evolution grinds to a stop. How long that takes depends to a large extent on how much genetic variation the species started with, the species' generation time, and how many offspring are born at each reproduction. Species like blackcaps, red squirrels, and montane voles are lucky—in today's world they already have lots of genetic variation distributed through many populations, and they reproduce with multiple offspring yearly, so they can probably expect their evolutionary "free ride" (evolution without mutation) to continue for a while at least. Even luckier are the species capable of actually diversifying as global warming pushes them hard; the downside here (for us, anyway) is that these are not species that people typically like. They are the ones that are extremely numerous in terms of individuals, that have extremely fast generation times (days instead of months or years), and that produce hundreds or thousands of offspring with each mating event.

I'm talking about flies, mosquitoes, and other species we tend to regard as vermin. Strong selection pressure like global warming is just what these kinds of species need to kick into high evolutionary gear, because they are not limited by mutation rate, which is directly related to generation time and number of offspring produced in each generation. The importance of generation time and numbers of offspring in influencing evolutionary rates is easy to envision when you think of mutation taking a shot at each new individual that is born. If you have lots and lots of individuals born, mutation gets lots of chances, and even though the proportion of lucky hits stays the same, the actual number of lucky hits increases. It is for that reason that the only species whose evolutionary rates seem to be keeping up quite nicely with global warming, in terms of substantial change at the DNA level, are fruit flies and possibly mosquitoes.[29] You can imagine the other kinds of species that fit the description of lots of individuals and fast, prolific reproduction: many of them have six or eight legs. Of the four-legged variety, a lot of them are small and furry, with beady eyes and long, scaly tails.

The bottom line is that the evolutionary prognoses for global warming are not very encouraging. First, global warming is already introducing climatic selection pressures that outpace mutation rates in many of the species that humans tend to like. This has the net effect of decreasing genetic diversity. And that, in turn, will increase the numbers of species on the road to extinction. In a very real respect, we are creating what paleontologist David Jablonski has called "Dead Clades Walking."[30] Clades are whole branches of the evolutionary tree, and what Jablonski was referring to is what seems to have happened after each of the Big Five mass extinctions. Evolutionary branches that were very bushy got pruned by the extinction events so that only a few twigs survived. But they were "dead clades walking" in the sense that those surviving twigs inevitably withered and died: ultimately, genetic variation and numbers of individuals were simply reduced too much for evolution to generate new sprouts. Second, the only kinds of organisms for which global warming seems capable of actually stimulating significant evolutionary diversification are what we normally call pests. That is another lesson from the last Big Five mass extinctions: the widespread and seemingly insignificant species survive to take over the world.[31]

If you project those trends into the foreseeable future, you get the sense that today biodiversity is actually being hacked down to the bare bones. What will be left for evolution to work with in a world of global warming is a skeleton crew of species, some very biased fraction of the diversity of life that now provides the raw material for generating and maintaining biodiversity. Rebuilding biodiversity fast under those circumstances is not something that evolution is equipped to handle—after each past mass-extinction event, it took some ten million years for biodiversity to build back up to pre-extinction levels.[32] Global warming in that light is not only doing its part to diminish biodiversity substantially within a century or so, it is also limiting the future evolutionary potential of Earth. In that, it finds itself in some very bad company, as we'll see in the next chapter.

Chapter 13

Bad Company

At currently measured rates of human resource consumption, it is virtually assured that eventually the human population will consume so much energy that there will be little or none left for other species.

—Brian Maurer, 1996[1]

PUERTO MONTT is a gateway to Chilean Patagonia, one of the most beautiful places on Earth. High, wild, snow-capped mountains are cut deeply by spectacular gorges through which clean rivers tumble, or which fill with the deep blue sea along the coast. The town is just about as far south as you can go on the Pan American highway, literally near the end of the road. There is an irony there, because Puerto Montt is also near the beginning of the road that led to peopling the Americas.

Today you can get to where it all started by driving west out of the town, first following the shoreline of Reloncaví Sound where brightly colored houses and shops—blue, yellow, pink—cling to a steep hillside on one side of the street and vendors' stalls line the other, then heading through agricultural fields and an occasional tiny remnant of the distinctive type of rainforest (called Valdivian rainforest) that once covered the region. If the clouds and rain break at the right time, you can catch good views of the Osorno Volcano, which two hundred and fifty years ago Charles Darwin watched "spouting out volumes of smoke. This most beautiful mountain, formed like a perfect cone, and white with snow, stands out in front of the Cordillera."[2] The day was startlingly clear when we saw Osorno; the mountain rose with Mount Fuji–like grace above the fringe of *Nothofagus* trees that framed it in the foreground. A few side roads later, we arrived at Chinchihuapi Creek, a small stream carving scarps of dun-colored gravel and dark brown peat out of the otherwise green, rolling hills. Only a few cows and horses mill around today, but archaeological evidence paints a very different picture of what was going on there some 14,600 years ago. This is the site of Monte Verde, the earliest accepted sign of humans in the Americas. Some 1,600 years before Clovis hunters found their way to North America, people at Monte Verde were weaving cord from plants, and building huts by stretching animal skins over wooden frames and staking them into the ground. They ate mastodons and seaweed, and placed plugs of boldo leaves—a medicine said to relieve stomach pains and cold symptoms—in a wishbone-shaped structure that some have interpreted as an altar. Monte Verde also yields pieces of vegetation that show those ancient Americans were importing plants from the high Andes, the Pacific Coast, and other places up to 400 km (250 miles) away.[3]

Jump back in the car and drive south from Monte Verde for about an hour, and you are on Chiloé Island, where the Pan American Highway really ends. Chiloé Island is the big reason that Puerto Montt is southern Chile's fastest growing city. All around the island, sitting in the water like sunken feedlot fences (which in fact they are), are rectangular enclosures, each one packed chock-full of salmon, the mainstay of Chile's multi-billion dollar aquaculture industry. It is the second-biggest salmon-farming enterprise in the world (the first is in Norway), run primarily by the same international aquaculture firms that run salmon farms worldwide, firms like Marine Harvest and Mainstream, with Chilean affiliates such as AquaChile.

That road from Monte Verde fifteen thousand years ago to Chiloé Island today encapsulates, in many respects, how humans have changed the Earth as a whole, and why global warming is in "bad company," which even before global warming entered the scene, already had three bad actors. The first of those is habitat destruction and fragmentation. Around Puerto Montt, and just about anywhere else you care to look on Earth, you see habitat loss in the replacement of the native forest with croplands and logged hillsides, not to mention all the cities, roads, factories, dams, and so on. The second bad actor is our propensity to introduce species into ecosystems where they wouldn't normally end up their own, exemplified here by those salmon around Chiloé Island. And the third is the ever-growing number of people on Earth, each of which needs to consume his or her share of Earth's resources, as exemplified by growth of Puerto Montt itself. The problems with the first bad actor—habitat destruction—have been mentioned frequently in previous chapters; here, it is worth thinking about the effects of the other two in order to fully appreciate the world stage onto which global warming has now entered.

People's habit of moving species they like all around the world—resulting in "introduced species"—goes back a long way, as the plants found at the 14,600-year-old settlement at Monte Verde indicate. People also inadvertently move species they don't like, such as various weeds, parasites, and pathogens. Over and over, introduced species escape and go wild, in the worst cases transforming whole landscapes and seascapes as the invaders get out of control and push out the natives, much to the detriment of ecological function, ecosystem services, biodiversity, economics, and aesthetics.[4, 5]

For example, the salmon in the feedlots off Chiloé are not even from the right ocean—they are Atlantic salmon, transplanted to leaky pens in the Pacific.[6] And, like so may other introduced species, they are the source of major ecological problems, which now are having economic, environmental, and social impacts.[7] In this case the most recent problem is an epidemic of Infectious Salmon Anemia, or ISA.

Salmon infected with ISA exhibit a variety of symptoms: lethargy, hemorrhaging organs, swollen eyes and spleen, pale gills. Then they die. ISA is highly infectious: all parts of a sick fish are contagious, "especially blood and mucus, as well as other body fluids, muscle, viscera, trimming, feces."[8] It is spread by just about any kind of contact with sick fish that you can imagine: fish-to-fish contact; contact with any part of an infected fish, including the waste from processing plants; contact with equipment that processed infected fish; and by contact with people who handled infected fish, parts of fish, equipment those fish came in contact with, or people who have been on ISA-infected sites. If this were a disease that humans could catch—thankfully it's not—it would be one of those where infected people were quarantined in isolation chambers, and where those who tended them wore those CDC hazmat (short for "hazardous material") suits. For the salmon of course, there is no quarantine possible, largely because another non-native species that came along with them, sea lice, carry ISA from one infected salmon enclosure to the next.

The sea lice are natural parasites on salmonid fishes (and one species of louse parasitizes fifty other species of marine fish), but until humans started caging them (the salmon, that is), the sea lice were not much of a problem. Wild salmon in their native habitats are born in freshwater streams, swim out to the ocean to spend most of their lives, then swim back into the freshwater streams where they originally hatched in order to spawn. Sea lice can't stand freshwater; they die on the wild salmon's journey home. Salmon farms circumvent that natural cleansing, and in fact promote epidemic outbreaks of sea lice, because so many fish are crammed into such a tight space. Those sea lice disperse and carry ISA not only to other salmon enclosures but also to the wild fish right outside the cages of the salmon farms. Significantly elevated levels of sea lice swarm onto fish such as wild salmon, trout, and char near fish farms, to the extent that "78–97 percent of all parasitic lice found in coastal waters of Scotland, Ireland, and Norway come from salmon farms (the remainder come mainly from escaped farm salmon)."[9]

ISA was once a disease confined to the Northern Hemisphere and the Atlantic Ocean, primarily around the salmon farms off the coasts of Norway (where it first cropped up in salmon farms in 1984), Scotland, Ireland, and eastern Canada (where the first major outbreak was in New Brunswick in 1996). In 1999 Chilean salmon farms had the dubious honor of hosting the first known occurrences of ISA in the Southern Hemisphere and also the first in the Pacific Ocean.[10] And in late 2007, ISA had finally grown to the epidemic proportions that prompted this newspaper report:

Following the example of industry leader Marine Harvest, a second major salmon company has now broken a virtual vow of
silence that for months shrouded ongoing sanitary problems in
Chile's US$2.4 billion farmed fish sector. . . . [T]he top Chilean
representative of the salmon company Mainstream said Chile's
sanitary problems are "real" but by no means limited to just
Infectious Salmon Anemia (ISA). . . .[11]

The initial solution was to kill and to attempt to dispose of 90
percent of the fish from farms where the ISA outbreak was identified
in summer 2007—millions of fish, tens of millions of dollars. When
that didn't work, the next solution was to move the salmon farms
from the "overcrowded and disease-ridden waters of Chiloé" south to
some of Patagonia's most pristine and "disease-free" marine waters,
near Aysén.[12] The announcement to move operations to Aysén came
on November 22, 2007. Barely one month later, December 21, 2007,
came this headline: "Salmon Disease Detected in Chile's Aysén
Region," and this report: "Mainstream-Cermaq has destroyed 100
percent of its stock on a fish farm near Region XI's Charrecué Island,
the Norwegian-owned farmed fish company revealed this week . . .
after an initial test determined the presence of Infectious Salmon
Anemia (ISA). . . ."[13]

Even without global warming, such introduced species are ecological nightmares; with the addition of global warming, we add a
whole new set of opportunities for introduced species to get out of
control. Basically, new climates mean new opportunities for invaders.
I've mentioned one example already, the mountain pine beetles
interacting with blister rust to decimate whitebark pine and other
trees (Chapter 11). Gypsy moths tell the same kind of story. They
were inadvertently introduced from Asia or Europe to a neighborhood near Boston, Massachusetts, in 1868 or 1869, and quickly
spread throughout the Northeast and into the Midwestern United
States. In one year they can defoliate areas of forest larger than
Rhode Island, Massachusetts, and Connecticut combined, but so far
they have done so no farther west than the Midwest.[14] With global
warming, however, by the year 2085 they may even be defoliating

aspen trees in Utah. Studies show that as of 2006, gypsy moths had not yet established viable populations in Utah, not because they had never been sighted there, but because climate has been unsuitable for them to reproduce (largely because of cold winters). While in 2006 only 10 percent of the aspen stands were at risk in the sense of being in a suitable climate zone, by 2085 that gypsy moth–friendly climate will expand to cover 90 percent of the aspen range.[15]

Hiding underneath such species-by-species examples is a more wide-ranging problem: as we introduce the same species to different places, the world's biota is becoming more and more alike everywhere. What has kept global biodiversity high through the ages is the separation of biotas in different parts of the world; we are now overriding that as we move species around the globe.[16] When we do that, we inevitably decrease world biodiversity—just as we are doing with global warming itself—bringing us ever closer to those dangerous ecological thresholds discussed in earlier chapters.

The reason that introducing species into ecosystems that have never seen them ends up decreasing world biodiversity, rather than increasing it, is that an ecosystem only has so much energy to go around. Think of it as a fixed amount of food that can be divided only among so many bodies. That means, in general, the only way you can add individuals from a new species is to take away individuals belonging to an old species, which has the net effect of limiting populations of natives even in the best cases. In the worst cases, and all too commonly these days, the same weedy species—usually termed "invasives"—tend to grab much of the energy in the suitable ecosystems into which they are introduced, and as a consequence the native species end up disappearing.[17]

That there is only a fixed amount of ecological energy to go around brings us to ecology's third bad actor: the sheer numbers of us. Every day, enough people are added to the world to fill another city with 210,000 people. Think of it as plopping down another city about the size of, say, Rochester, New York, or Akron, Ohio, or San Bernardino, California, every day at about 5:00 p.m. Each new human on Earth adds his or her own contribution of greenhouse gases to the atmosphere (primarily through driving their car, heating their homes, using electricity, and so on), thus increasing the problem of global warming, but besides that, as human populations grow, people inevitably have to co-opt energy from the global ecosystem. That co-opting can be by indirect methods like those salmon farms around Chiloé Island grabbing resources from the native marine fauna, or from direct impacts like the growing numbers of people in Puerto Montt covering soil with pavement, thus taking large areas out of play for primary producers like plants. The bottom line is that each new person that is added to Earth ultimately reduces the energy and resources available for the rest of the planet's ecosystem.

That's what prompted Brian Mauer to make the statement that opens this chapter. Maurer, an ecologist at Michigan State University, writes books with modest titles like *Untangling Ecological Complexity*. He's one of those brilliant yet affable guys who can speak in equations just as fluently as in English, and moreover, who can translate from one to the other so you can actually understand what he's talking about. A boyish grin and a glint in his eye belie the seriousness with which he views the ecological predicaments that inevitably come out of those equations he thinks about. In the 1990s, Maurer and other big-thinking scientists, like Stanford ecologist Peter Vitousek and his colleagues, were pondering deeply the predicament of there being a limited amount of energy to fuel ecosystems: what happens when we begin to use it up?[18] The equations so clearly graphed by Maurer showed a worst-case scenario where we end up reducing biodiversity all the way down to just one species—us. Neither he nor other scientists think we'd ever be able to go that far. There are too many other things likely to limit our population—disease, hunger, war, and, we have to hope, our own intelligence and foresight—before we entirely consume the world's resources. But Maurer's graph does serve to illustrate a very important concept: there is only so much energy to go around on Earth.

For ecosystems, that energy comes from the sun. The way that solar energy is translated into energy for ecosystems is primarily by photosynthesis: plants convert the solar energy into organic matter— that is, plant tissue. Those plants, at the bottom of the food chain, then transfer the energy to other species as herbivores eat the plants, carnivores eat the herbivores, and so on. Ultimately then, the energy that powers ecosystems is the total amount of solar energy that is converted to organic matter, minus the energy it takes for the cells in plants to make the conversion. The resulting number can be expressed as something called Net Primary Productivity, or NPP, typically expressed in weight as petagrams of biomass (biomass typically being the weight of all the organic material produced).[19] One petagram equals 10^{15} grams, equivalent to 1,102,311,310 tons (or some 27.5 million tractor-trailers)—so one petagram is a lot of biomass. Since NPP is governed primarily by the amount of sun striking the Earth and is also somewhat influenced by other climatic parameters, it varies a little on very long-term scales, but modeling studies suggest that global NPP will not change much over the next century, even with global warming. The worst case, though, is that it will decrease drastically.[20]

All that becomes relevant when you realize that the way species slice the energy pie can be figured out by estimating how much NPP they use. A group of scientists led by Vitousek did just that.[21] By reviewing the NPP that was actually measured in a few plots representing the world's major biomes, then multiplying those values by estimates of the surface area of each biome, they came up with as reasonable a set of numbers as it is possible to get: a global NPP of 224.5 petagrams (a mass equivalent to the number of tractor-trailers it would take to wrap around the equator about 2,343 times). That is the NPP that the world's ecosystems have to work with. Of those 224.5 petagrams, Vitousek's group calculated that humans grabbed about 25 percent of global NPP for themselves, and about 40 percent of terrestrial NPP (the terrestrial contribution to NPP is about 132.1 petagrams). They also pointed out that the only way for human populations to increase in number is to take NPP from other species, which, if this proceeded unchecked, would have the inevitable result of causing those others to dwindle in number and eventually to go extinct.

Maurer picked up where Vitousek's group left off and estimated how many humans would have to be on Earth to use all of the NPP: that number is about 20 billion. By Maurer's calculations, we'd reach

20 billion people on Earth by the year 2200 at today's population-growth rates, but he recognized that our growth rates will probably slow. More realistic projections used by the IPCC in their various global-change scenarios (Chapter 10) suggest that our present nearly seven billion people will multiply to almost nine billion by 2050, and then, depending on how demographics play out after that, the population will either drop back down to seven billion, or rise to fifteen billion people by the year 2100.[22] It's a little unnerving to realize that the high end of the IPCC's estimate is only five billion people below what Maurer estimated would wipe out all other species on Earth. Any of those numbers above seven billion are very worrisome, because Maurer's graphs also showed their own version of a threshold event: as humans grabbed more and more of the energy pie by consuming more resources, extinctions of other species would proceed at a more or less constant rate until human populations were big enough to require about 66 percent of global NPP—which would happen when our population reached fifteen billion, the IPCC's high-end estimate for 2100. Then we'd see a truly dramatic and overwhelming rapid crash in biodiversity—perhaps not unlike what happened on a local scale on Easter Island after people settled there a little over a thousand years ago.

Easter Island, the most remote place on Earth in terms of distance from other inhabited places—it is five hours by jet from Santiago, Chile—has long been famous for the enormous stone statues erected by its prehistoric settlers. More recently, with the publication of Jared Diamond's book *Collapse*, the island has also become famous as a classic example of exactly the kind of ecological crash that Maurer's calculations predict.[23] Following the growth of Easter Island's human population to as many as 15,000 people and the intensive agriculture, fishing, hunting, and deforestation that resulted on the relatively small island, not only did the native ecosystem collapse, but also the sophisticated society that built the statues. All the forest that formerly covered much of the island disappeared; native plant diversity fell from around 69 to 48 species; all six of the native land birds went extinct; and the soils were overused to the point they no longer are very productive. Today the island supports only around 4,000 people, and those only because virtually everything they need is imported from the mainland.

The idea of an energy limit causing a crash in biodiversity, pushing the global ecosystem across an ecological threshold, also seems to be upheld by the Pleistocene extinction event discussed in Chapter 5. Recall that between 11,500 and 50,000 years ago, extinction took most of the world's species of the largest mammals. That happened just as human numbers really began to shoot upward; it seems that when the world population of Homo sapiens reached a critical level, other megafauna species crashed hard, falling well below the baseline levels for biodiversity that had characterized the previous hundreds of thousands of years.[24] If you are looking for a global ecological threshold event, there it is.

After the Pleistocene crash, the global ecosystem shifted into a new state: instead of megafauna recovering such that many different species filled megafauna niches, as was the case before, a single megafauna species—us—came to dominate, augmented by the domestic species we use to support ourselves (sheep, goats, cows, pigs, etc.). When numbers of individual animals are converted to biomass (in this case, the estimated total weight of all humans and all other animals that are megafauna), something interesting comes out: it appears to have taken thousands of years for megafauna biomass to build back up to precrash levels. Therein lies another lesson: global ecosystem shifts do not rectify themselves within just a few human generations.

The final part of this story becomes a bit more chilling, because it takes us out of the past and into the future. Beginning with the Industrial Revolution, the biomass of humans and their domestic animals all of a sudden began to skyrocket by orders of magnitude above the natural megafauna biomass baseline that had existed even before the Pleistocene crash. That skyrocketing became possible because we began adding something new to the world's ecological energy budget, something besides the solar radiation that had held the monopoly as ecological fuel throughout the history of life on Earth. The new energy source was what we dug out of the ground: first coal, then eventually oil and natural gas, all of which are ultimately just solar energy that has been in long-term storage. Boosting the globe's total ecological energy by adding that stored fossil-fuel energy to the traditional source (sunshine) is what allowed human populations (and their domesticated species) to so greatly exceed the limits on megafauna biomass that applied before the Industrial Revolution. That fossil-fuel boost to current solar energy is what makes it possible for record numbers of humans to exist on Earth today. The chilling part is that, by using up fossil fuels, we have been (and still are) deficit-spending the global ecological energy account, to the extent we are almost out of the extra energy we have grown to rely on. Projections for how long fossil fuels can keep augmenting the energy available to the global ecosystem at current levels vary, but it looks like we have around 50 more years for oil, 200 years for natural gas, and 2,000 years for coal.[25] If we don't replace them by alternative energy sources, the next biomass crash is imminent.

Since we are the main species being supported by the "extra" energy now provided by fossil fuels, it doesn't take too much thought to realize that such a crash would kill huge numbers of human beings, as it did when the Easter Islanders ran out of their essential resources. Of course, that next biomass crash would likely also include rapid extinction of a wide spectrum of other species, as the root cause would be a net reduction in global ecological energy (current solar energy plus fossil fuels) that ultimately is distributed among all organisms, not just humans. Furthermore, burning up those fossil fuels fast is just about the worst thing we can do if we want to slow global warming, as it is their CO_2 emissions that are warming's primary cause. The moral here is obvious: we don't really have any choice about developing alternative energy sources. We can do it now, and thereby save many species, including perhaps our own, and Earth's ecological health; or we can do it later, after many species, and many people, are dead. But anyway you cut it, we are going to have to do it.

All that puts us squarely at the intersection of a series of unfortunate events, to steal a phrase from children's literature, and more recently, Hollywood. This is our moment in history. Global warming, with its own method of ecosystem demolition, has joined the company of the other three bad actors—habitat loss, introduced species, and population growth—that have long been recognized as the world's big ecological problems. Now we can think in terms of the Gang of Four. Each gang member by itself is a major problem. Put all four together, and the problem becomes much bigger than the sum of its parts. Recognizing this, of course, is the first step in fixing it. It's not like there's no hope. It just takes the right mix of human ingenuity, human determination, and stepping back to take a different, bigger-picture perspective than we're used to.

Chapter 14 ~

Geography of Hope

Never doubt that a small group of thoughtful, committed citizens can change the world.® Indeed it is the only thing that ever has.

—Margaret Mead[1]

What I want to speak for is not so much the wilderness uses, valuable as those are, but the wilderness idea, which is a resource in itself.

—Wallace Stegner, from his "Wilderness Letter," 1960[2]

"HEY MAN, things change." How many times have you heard that, accompanied by a shoulder shrug? It's true, things do change, and that's maybe the one constant in life. Change in itself is not a bad thing—in fact, as we've seen in earlier chapters, some change through time is entirely normal for ecosystems, and even, maybe especially, for our perception of nature. What is not normal, however, is so much change so fast that entire ecosystems and nature as we've known it disappears. With the Gang of Four (global warming, habitat loss, invasive species, and population growth) working together, those are the very real possibilities we now face. How to save the particular ecosystems we value and, in the larger scheme of things, nature itself, is the challenge we now face in the Age of Global Warming.

By "nature," I really mean three different (but related) ways that people perceive Earth's ecological interactions. One perception is nature as ecosystem services, like clean water and productive soils, that people need in order to survive; another is nature as particular constellations of species in particular ecosystems—like Yosemite, Yellowstone, Tambopata, and others, whether or not they are formally recognized as protected reserves. The third perception of nature is as a feeling of wilderness, as Wallace Stegner articulated so eloquently in his "Wilderness Letter," quoted at the head of the chapter.

As we've seen from the examples in earlier chapters, the major threats that global warming poses for all these perceptions of nature are twofold. First, by changing climates faster than species can adapt to them and causing essential climates to disappear in various places, it accelerates extinctions and thereby is a major contributor to one of Earth's biggest problems: loss of biodiversity. Ultimately, loss of biodiversity enormously degrades ecosystem services to humanity. Second, climate change irrevocably changes the places we have marked as special for preserving nature, whether they are formally designated as protected reserves or not. The species we are used to seeing in such places—no matter how remote or protected—will no longer be able to live there, raising tricky questions about how best to save certain species on the one hand, and wilderness itself on the other.

Daunting as the challenge of saving nature is under such circumstances, it is not impossible—if we put our minds to it and make it a priority. Meeting that challenge requires that we do three things: slow global warming as fast and as much as we can; recognize that saving species and saving wilderness is no longer the same thing; and apply new conservation strategies that take into account the new forces of a globally warming world.

Slowing global warming as fast as we can is essential because the train has already left the station: our world has warmed, and it will continue to warm for at least a couple of decades. Even if we quit increasing the amount of greenhouse gases today, Earth would continue to heat up because there is a lag time between putting the greenhouse up and how long it takes for temperature to reach its maximum. The built-in lag time means we would still get 0.2 °C

(0.4°F) hotter by the year 2040 if we could hold greenhouse gas emissions at what they were in the year 2000. But of course we can't, because we're already past that. It looks most likely that by 2040 we'll be around 0.4°C (0.7°F) hotter than today, when you factor in the lag time from greenhouse warming already in the works with the amount of greenhouse gases we're likely to continue to emit. Interestingly, it doesn't really matter which of the IPCC scenarios you use, they all come up with about that answer for 20 years down the road.[3] What happens after that, though, is highly dependent on which scenario plays out. In the best case (the B1 scenario), we'll likely be 0.8°C (1.4°F) hotter in the year 2100 than we were in 2000. Even that seemingly inevitable 0.8°C makes the world hotter than it's been since humans evolved. In the worst case (A1F1 or A2), we'll be approaching 4°C (7°F) hotter—and recall that that's hotter than it's been since just about any species you can name has been on Earth. Recall also that the faster the rate and higher the magnitude of warming, the more detrimental are the effects on ecosystems. Even in the best-case scenario, ecosystems are going to have a tough enough time keeping up with heating the globe to 0.8°C hotter in 90 years, already a much faster rate of change than they normally experience. Heating things up five times faster, as in the worst-case scenario, is a really bad idea.

There are many simple actions that each of us can take that, when multiplied by billions of people, will have a huge impact in helping to slow the pace of global warming: things like changing incandescent lightbulbs to CFLs, turning the thermostat down a degree or so in winter and up a degree or so in summer; and many more that have been detailed in numerous recent articles, books, and Web sites (summarized in the Appendix). Besides individual actions, as many writers have pointed out, it will take serious corporate initiatives, governmental policies, the cooperation of nations, and the development of alternative energy sources to mitigate the problem of global warming. But the bottom line is this: slowing global warming is eminently achievable if we have the will, while delaying action not only postpones dealing with an inevitable problem, it makes that problem worse day by day. Either we slow global warming now, or we will see the window of opportunity slam shut on saving not only particular ecosystems that the world has long sought to protect (like those in national parks throughout the world), but nature in all the primary ways we now perceive it.

Just as critical, of course, is that we need to attack the synergy of the Gang of Four. Slowing down any one of them—global warming, habitat fragmentation, invasive species, or human population growth—will help in minimizing the ecological impacts of global warming. In some instances, because of feedback effects, slowing one will slow others—for example, slowing population growth slows all the other three. Of course, this works the other way around too: exacerbating global warming also exacerbates habitat fragmentation, for instance, and speeding up population growth makes all the other three worse.

Simply slowing down the train, however, does not change the reality that major ecological changes have already been set in motion, which, like it or not, will continue to gather momentum at least for several decades as the Age of Global Warming unfolds. And as those changes proceed, we inevitably face the prospect of transforming nature itself into something we hardly recognize—not only by degrading ecosystem services globally and losing certain species in particular ecological preserves, but also by losing wilderness, either by neglect or design. If that happens, we lose connection with the wilderness world in which we became human.

Our connection with wilderness runs surprisingly deep, as I found when asking a wide variety of people, of different walks of life and a broad range of ages, to tell me what "nature" means to them. Of course it means different things to different people, and has dictionary definitions that are commonly some variant of "the material world that surrounds man and is independent of his activities," or "primitive wild conditions," or "a simple life without the conveniences or distractions of civilization."[4] But the theme that emerged when people told me about the kind of nature they thought really needed to be saved was this: nature has leaves instead of concrete; round edges instead of square corners; freedom instead of fences; chance instead of plans; risk instead of security; tranquility instead of stress; species that, for the most part, were there before people, instead of species that were put there by people; and freedom from heavy guidance by *Homo sapiens*. With such views, most people (at least the many I've talked to) seem to define nature pretty much as Stegner's "wilderness idea": that is, as ecosystems that haven't been mainly overrun by humans and that give us the feeling of being in a wild place. And people seem to value nature in this sense because it gives them a feeling of peace and of being connected to the nonhuman part of the world in a way they find nowhere else.

Examples of ecosystems that preserve that sort of wilderness are still to be found in many places, and not all are bureaucratically protected parcels, by any means.[5] Some are truly remote—like Antarctica, Siberia, and the Gobi Desert, which are vast, lightly populated, and, to most humans, inhospitable tracts of land. Others are well known for their special beauty and are visited annually by millions—many national parks fall into that category. And still others are somewhere in between, not physically remote or climatically extreme, not legislatively protected with a mandate of strict preservation, but nevertheless not used so heavily by people that they have lost their natural character, places like national forests, state lands, or in some cases, even private holdings. Unarguably, not all such places, if any of them, are free of the human hand. But, that's okay, as far as the idea of wilderness goes. As Stegner put it:

> I am not moved by the argument that those wilderness areas which have already been exposed to grazing or mining are already deflowered, and so might as well be "harvested." . . . [T]hey are only wounds; they aren't absolutely mortal. Better a wounded wilderness than none at all.[6]

Stegner was making the point that despite some human disturbance to landscapes, that feeling of wilderness, of nature, can remain as long as what is wild outweighs what has been disturbed. I would extend that point to the changes we've already made to Earth's atmosphere, and to those that are still building. What does move me are some other words of Stegner's, because they capture for me, more than any other reasoning, why it is so critical to save the wilderness aspect of nature:

> Something will have gone out of us as a people if we ever let the remaining wilderness be destroyed; if we permit the last virgin forests to be turned into comic books and plastic cigarette cases; if we drive the few remaining members of the wild species into zoos or to extinction; if we pollute the last clear air and dirty the last clean streams and push our paved roads through the last of the silence. . . . We simply need that wild country available to us, even if we never do more than drive to its edge and look in. For it can be a means of reassuring ourselves of our sanity as creatures, a part of the geography of hope.[7]

More pragmatically, those remaining wild areas are also critical ecological pulse points. They are the only places we have left where we can watch and learn how sustainable ecosystems are supposed to operate, where we can pick up the early warning signs that something is going wrong in the global ecological picture—not unlike watching canaries in a coal mine, whose death would tell miners that poisonous gas levels were getting dangerously high. In that respect, we need wilderness not only to keep us sane, but to keep track of Earth's ecological health and thereby keep us alive. How, then, do we actually go about saving the wild in this Age of Global Warming, and how does saving wilderness fit in with saving particular ecosystems and the global ecosystem in general?

This is where it becomes important to recognize the three faces of nature I've distinguished above. In reality, we are talking about saving three different kinds things, however much they overlap: ecological function that provides the services humanity needs for survival (the global ecosystem); certain species and assemblages of species (particular ecosystems); and wilderness. Sure, we could get by, at some basic level, by settling for the first without the other two; or by concentrating on the first two without the third; but the geography of hope lies in keeping as much as we can of all three. To do that, we need a fundamental shift in how we think about protecting our environment, to an explicit recognition that saving nature as humans fully value it will require something different from saving individual species, saving particular ecosystems, or maintaining a basic level of ecosystem services.

As we've seen in earlier chapters, it is inevitable that global warming will, in just a few decades, significantly alter climates that support assemblages of species we love in many of our favorite nature reserves, and that because of the other three in the Gang of Four, there will be no place for many of those species to run to as that happens.[8] That reality means that what used to be a one-stop-shopping conservation solution—preserve a parcel of land and the species in it, and you also preserve a particular ecosystem and, by extension, nature itself—no longer will work, because a parcel of geography won't preserve a particular assemblage of species if their needed climate at that locus disappears. At least not without some heavy management by people, which, of course, by definition undermines nature as "wilderness." All of a sudden we are faced with two different questions. How do we actually preserve species whose last stronghold is in protected areas and other natural areas under siege by climate change? And what exactly are we trying to keep whole in those ecologically important areas?

It is primarily the first question—how do we preserve species, and assemblages of species that we think ought to live together—that is causing ecologists and reserve managers to think outside the box and discuss some bold new ideas, and that could help in dealing with the detrimental effects of global warming. One of those is called assisted migration.[9]

Here's a typical story. One of the most famous insects in conservation biology is the Bay checkerspot butterfly (*Euphydryas editha bayensis*), because its long history of study in the San Francisco Bay region showed it was being decimated by a succession of human actions. Formerly widespread through California, the butterfly's range was dramatically reduced when invasive plant species, introduced in hay for domestic stock, outcompeted plants on which the butterfly depended. Then housing developments destroyed butterfly habitats that had been distributed through the hills up and down the San Francisco peninsula. On top of that, by 1998 global warming led

to the demise of one of the few remaining (and one of the most studied) populations, at Stanford University's Jasper Ridge Biological
Preserve, by upsetting a delicate phenological balance. Now continued warming in California threatens to do the same to the last populations of the checkerspots. There are, however, climatically suitable
places where the butterflies could thrive, the only problem being that
there is no way for them to get there on their own. In former times,
the butterflies probably could have leapfrogged along from one suitable habitat patch to the next and kept pace with the climate
changes underway. Now they can't, because humans have destroyed
suitable habitats between where they are and where they need to be.
The proposal on the table is help them along, by putting them in a
car and driving them to a new home.

That, in a nutshell, is assisted migration, and you can imagine it
being done for just about any species. Assisted migration provides a
way to guard against individual species losses due to global warming,
but it is not as clean a solution as you might hope. We know that
species do not exist in a vacuum—how many species must we move
from one ecosystem to the next in order to ensure survival of the target species? And what about the effects on other species that already
are present in the ecosystem to which the assisted migrant is moved?
In Chapter 13, we saw some of the problems that inevitably occur
whenever humans take nature into their own hands by moving a
species from a place where it lives naturally to a place where it's never
been; indeed, introduced species are a key member of the Gang of
Four.

An even bolder proposal, so far argued primarily for the U.S. but
in concept applicable anywhere, goes by the name of Pleistocene
rewilding.[10] This is not to be confused with simply "rewilding" or
"ecosystem restoration," which reintroduces species into ecosystems
where we know they were historically, such as putting wolves back in
Yellowstone. Instead, Pleistocene rewilding aims at "the resurrection
of the foraging behavior of animals now buried in the graveyards of
near time," as paleoecologist Paul Martin put it.[11] The proposal for
Pleistocene rewilding starts by recognizing that we live in ecologically abnormal times—abnormal in the sense of lacking, in most

places, all those big-bodied animals, which growing human populations and climate change drove to extinction at the end of the Pleistocene (see Chapters 5 and 13). We've spent most of our time as a species in the company of those big animals. Moreover, the logic goes, megafauna everywhere were integral in structuring ecosystems for tens of millions of years before we were on the scene, just as, for example, elephants presently act as a keystone species in Africa. Now megafauna are missing from nearly every ecosystem except some African ones (and in small pockets in India and Asia). The idea is that resurrecting Earth's ecosystems as they "should be" will require refilling those megaherbivore and megacarnivore niches. That refilling would take the form of replacing lost species with their nearest-living ecological analogs. For example, in the American West, we might see wild horses and burros taking the place of the many species of extinct Pleistocene horses that once roamed there, camels that today live in the Middle East shipped in to replace the extinct camels that were native to North America, herds of elephants as analogs for the mammoths and mastodons that the first North Americans hunted to extinction, and African cheetahs and lions to keep all of those megaherbivores in check. Pleistocene rewilding would transform vegetation as well, just as the large herbivores in Africa keep woodlands in check and promote the growth of some shrub and grass species over others.

Pleistocene rewilding is not without its ecological downsides, to put it mildly.[12] Among the risks are importing parasites along with exotic megafauna. Also, the introduction of exotic megafauna could, through competitive and other species interactions, actually decrease local diversity in ecosystems that have been maintained megafauna-free for thousands of generations—which would have the effect of decreasing global diversity, not increasing it. Critics also question whether intermingling species that have never lived together really would reproduce the ecological interactions that disappeared thousands of years ago. Trying to engineer those interactions with exotic species may well be like trying to piece together an egg that fell out of the nest: with enough work and some putty and paint, we might be able to get the shell to look right, but ultimately it is not possible to put the chick back inside so that it will hatch. And of course, there are numerous social and political issues to address—for example, issues about costs, land acquisition, transforming familiar landscapes, public acceptance of living next to large predators, and so on.

All that notwithstanding, proponents argue that Pleistocene rewilding has the direct conservation benefit of increasing the geographic range of many presently endangered species, thereby increasing their chances for survival and minimizing the overall loss of global biodiversity, especially of remaining megafauna. In a globally warming world, those increases in geographic range are doubly important if we are to maximize the overlap of endangered species with climatically suitable places.

Neither Pleistocene rewilding nor assisted migration actually has left the drawing board yet, but they could be important new tools in the fight to save species—if they are applied in the right way. That "if" is a big one, because it is here that we run smack-dab into a conundrum we are faced with in the Age of Global Warming: that what we need to do to save species and what we need to do to save the wilderness aspect of nature are diverging. Pleistocene rewilding and assisted migration could help in saving species, but, if improperly applied, could destroy the wilderness, because they potentially lay a heavy management hand on previously little-managed landscapes. Saving wilderness requires preserving ecological processes that operate in the absence of significant human interference.

In fact, we view the Pleistocene ecosystem we lost as special precisely because humans hadn't yet acted as the architects and construction crew to engineer it. Likewise what makes the ecosystems where we can still experience wilderness at its best so special— including the Krugers, the Kalaharis, the Yellowstones, the Yosemites, the Patagonias, the Tambopatas, and many others that are still out there—is the relatively light touch of people, the sense that the ecological interactions that evolved before people dominated are still playing out. By planting species in such places through assisted migration or Pleistocene rewilding, we begin to wipe out the very wildness—a critical aspect of nature—that those places were set aside to preserve. At the most basic level, what difference is there between a landscape in which the major ecological interactions have been arranged by the hands of humans, and a very elaborate zoo?

Recognizing that tension between the actions that will save species (moving them artificially) and the actions that will save wilderness (a hands-off philosophy of let-come-what-may) adds a new twist to conservation biology in the Age of Global Warming. The idea that has implicitly guided conservation biology—that it is possible and desirable to maintain or recreate conditions that prevailed when parks and other reserves were first set aside, or at any other arbitrary point in time—just no longer applies.[13] And a new twist is that saving species and saving wilderness can no longer be viewed as always overlapping. Instead, as climate changes faster than our fragmented landscapes will allow species to track it, the preservation of species and the preservation of natural ecological processes will become mutually exclusive in more and more cases. How, for example, do we maintain a diverse large herbivore community in Kruger when the dry season becomes too dry to support the large herbivores? Do we provide water tanks? Truck species to wetter habitats in other parks seasonally? Or truck in from other places species that can withstand the dry times? Or do we just let Kruger alone, and see what happens under the new climatic regime? Those kinds of thorny questions mean that we have to recognize that saving species and saving wilderness become two different goals, towards which we will have to work in parallel, rather than regarding them as a single goal that a single kind of action—like fencing off a nature preserve—will accomplish.

Likewise, saving particular species and saving wilderness are goals that in concept are different from the goal of sustaining ecosystem services (the global ecosystem) at the minimum level needed to support humans. Sustaining ecosystem services does have maintaining biodiversity as a major goal, but preserving nature is not a necessary prerequisite for that. For example, one forward-looking notion about how to sustain ecosystem services recognizes the economic value of ecological necessities we take for granted and so puts a price on them.

As reported by Stanford ecologist Gretchen Daily and writer Katherine Ellison, people are already trading in carbon offsets, basically buying and selling credits for keeping CO_2 out of the atmosphere, as well as restoring natural river courses to add value to neighborhoods and cities, and protecting watersheds from being covered by housing developments for economic gain.[14] The latter is what New York City does because, amazingly, keeping watersheds unpaved is more cost-effective than building water treatment plants that would be needed if rain and melting snow were not filtered through the soil before eventually coming out of Manhattan's faucets.[15]

Another example of keeping global biodiversity healthy while not necessarily preserving wilderness is an approach championed by University of Arizona ecologist Michael Rosenzweig, one which he dubbed "win-win ecology" or "reconciliation ecology."[16] In this approach, human-dominated places would be designed to incorporate and conserve species that would otherwise be imperiled.[17] For instance, Rosenzweig explains how planting native vegetation in yards and city parks increases habitat for native species, and how ecologists are working with the military to promote native landscapes on Eglin Air Force base in Florida. The Eglin reconciliation-ecology effort includes replacing exotic sand pines and slash pines with newly planted native longleaf pines, the tree on which endangered red-cockaded woodpeckers depend. The woodpeckers need mature longleaf pines, with wood that has been softened by a fungus, in order to excavate their nests. While waiting for the trees to get old enough such that this occurs naturally, the "eco-military" alliance has been drilling holes in the hard young longleaf pine trunks, a simple action that has resulted in a 6 percent increase in woodpeckers in just two years.

Both the ecosystem-services approach and win-win ecology will be critical in maintaining a globally viable ecosystem, but each, by itself, could easily let the third face of nature, wilderness, slip through the cracks. Indeed, reconciliation ecology actually argues there's no getting around that eventuality: "We must give up romantic notions about reserves as wilderness. . . . It will be almost like admitting that wilderness itself is no more. Yet we must grit our teeth and do it."[18] I disagree wholeheartedly with that (and so would Stegner, I suspect). The key to developing a comprehensive strategy toward saving nature—having it all—is first to recognize that there are in fact three different conservation priorities: sustaining the global ecosystem, saving particular species, and saving wilderness, and that different, but not mutually exclusive, actions are required to accomplish each.

Shifting our perspective to emphasize the tripartite aspect (global, species, wilderness) of the ecological problems we face in this Age of Global Warming, combined with conscious redoubling of some conservation strategies already underway, provides a tractable approach to saving nature as humanity knows it. At the global level, reconciliation ecology and trading in ecosystem services hold good promise; building the infrastructure and opportunities to enhance such efforts will be essential. But it will take more to save many species and wilderness; the action plan for that has to be on the ground where the wild things still are, and boils down to three words: keep, connect, and create.

"Keep" is already encompassed by existing conservation plans. We need to make sure not to lose any more of the 12 percent of Earth's surface that now is protected, in some form or fashion, to preserve nature. That means ensuring that places like national parks, wilderness areas, and the like remain off-limits to destructive uses (logging, mining, oil exploration, and damming, to name a few). Every one of those destructive uses provides just a short-term gain (usually to a vocal and self-selected few) that quickly evaporates, at the expense of forever losing an irreplaceable piece of the world. Under the heading of "keep" also falls actions like keeping ecosystems intact by restoring to them species that we know without a doubt are missing (that is, ecosystem restoration, not Pleistocene rewilding). At one end of the ecosystem restoration spectrum are simple fixes like reintroduction of wolves to Yellowstone; at the other end are efforts to restore massively degraded landscapes, such as restoring West African forests.[19] Those ecosystem restoration efforts, of course, now have to be planned with shifting climate zones in mind. "Keep" also means keeping as many species alive as we can, by whatever means we can—those species are the biodiversity we are banking on for the future, as well as to keep ecosystems running today.

"Connect" is becoming increasingly important in existing conservation strategies, and takes on an even greater urgency in the Age of Global Warming. The only way that endangered species can have a chance of tracking their changing climate from where they are now to where they will need to be is if habitat corridors exist. The idea of habitat corridors has long been a staple of conservation biology. It is simply the notion of finding ways to connect existing ecological preserves with tracts of land in which at least minimal amounts of natural habitat is maintained, such that plants and animals can disperse back and forth between protected areas. That effectively increases the geographic range of the dispersing species and ultimately their chances for survival. Now, in addition, an urgent need in every preserve on Earth is for their respective land managers to evaluate the possibilities for "climate-connection corridors" through which species can move to stay alive. This will require cooperation between climate modelers, ecologists, land managers, and stake-holders, and also the political will to get the job of establishing climate corridors done, something that starts with each one of us. For some reserves, there will be few connection possibilities. For others, like the string of protected areas up and down the Rocky Mountain chain, various parks in Africa, and South American parks in and near the Andes and in the Amazon, potentials for connections are good.

"Create" refers to the new initiatives that will be needed to make saving the global ecosystem, species, and wilderness possible. One category of what we need to create is physical: the more surface of the Earth that is devoted to minimizing human impacts, the better our chances of success. Thus efforts of individuals and of organizations to convert lands from high-impact to low-impact uses are critically important. Recent trends in this direction, represented, for example, by the work done by groups like the Nature Conservancy and Wildlife Conservation Society as well as individual efforts, are encouraging.[20] Particularly necessary is the creation of marine-based nature reserves before it is too late, because the oceans' ecosystems are right now witnessing the same kind megafaunal extinctions that took place on land during the Pleistocene.

The other part of "create" is conceptual: recognition that with global warming shifting climate zones such that species can't follow, preserving wilderness is no longer an automatic outcome of preserving species (or ecosystem services). To preserve all the parts of nature will require nothing less than separating what is now the unitary objective of a "nature reserve" (i.e., preserve the species and you preserve nature) into two distinct objectives, necessitating two kinds of reserves, each equally important. One kind, which would explicitly be thought of as species reserves, would be devoted to the preservation of individual species and certain assemblages of species. The other, explicitly designated as wildland reserves, would be devoted to the preservation of wilderness. The goal of the two would be related, but different: the primary goal of species reserves would be to keep certain species and certain assemblages of species from disappearing; the goal of the wildland reserves would be to preserve ecological interactions that have not been heavily influenced or managed by people, that is, a fundamental wildness.

The reason the distinction between the two is important is because species reserves would require heavy management to maximize survival of species. Programs like assisted migration and Pleistocene rewilding would be important—perhaps critical—elements in their overall conservation strategy. Species reserves would be the places to which species from a climatically unsuitable area might be transplanted. But, given what we know already about the collateral effects of transplanting species, those kinds of reserves would be most viable in areas where human impact on the landscape already has been heavy. For example, a climatically challenged butterfly might be moved to a climatically suitable state park surrounded by housing developments (assuming it was designated as a species preserve), but not to a pristine mountain meadow in Yosemite (assuming it was designated a wildland preserve). In species reserves, our children will have the satisfaction of seeing that species which otherwise would have gone extinct are thriving, albeit sometimes in places where they would never have dispersed without our help. And species reserves will be essential in helping to maintain global biodiversity.

Wildland reserves, on the other hand, would take on the function of keeping existing wild places as free from human manipulation as possible, and stand as the last places where we can monitor Earth's health by watching what happens to ecosystems that aren't under active human control. Importantly, inevitably, and contrary to current conservation strategies in many places, this means that the species in them will change as global warming progresses—some will become more abundant, some will become less abundant, some will drop out altogether, and in lucky cases where enough connections exist, new immigrants will find their way in. In wildland reserves so defined, our children will not see the same species that we see in them today—but they will continue to experience the wilderness aspect of nature as we now value it, a feeling of wildness that grows out of an ecosystem where interactions between species have not been placed there by people. In the best cases, of course, networks of connected wildland reserves on each continent would also do their part to keep endangered species alive in the ecological settings in which they evolved.

The devil is always in the details, of course, and those details will take lots of hashing out by scientists, politicians, and the rest of us. But, the reality is that unless we put this broad-brush plan of keep, connect, and create in place now, it will be too late: what we want to save will be gone. We will have crossed an ecological threshold that, again in Stegner's words, will take us into a world where

> never again can we have the chance to see ourselves single, separate, vertical, and individual in the world, part of the environment of trees and rocks and soil, brother to the other animals, part of the natural world and competent to belong in it. . . . [We will be] committed wholly, without chance for even momentary reflection and rest, to a headlong drive into our technological termite-life, the Brave New World of a completely man-controlled environment.[21]

We have moved even closer to that "termite-life" threshold than when Stegner wrote those words; in fact, we are poised to step across it, with our uniquely human qualities—technology, intelligence, and foresight. Those qualities got us to this dangerous place; but their real power is that they have also made us realize how we've changed Earth's very climate, and how, because of that, we could see many, many species and Earth's ecological health irrevocably slip away. Whether or not we take that final step into a termite-life of ecological loss depends entirely on what actions we pursue—or elect not to pursue—in just the next few years.

Slowing Down Global Warming

Individual Actions

Global warming sounds so big that it's hard to imagine that you as an individual can anything about it ("what I do is such a tiny drop in the bucket it doesn't matter anyway"). But that's where you're wrong: the reason Earth is in peril is because of individual actions—by me, by you, by the person sitting next to you, by the person you bump into on the street. The bad news is that when we put all those individual actions together, it becomes one huge number—big enough to change climate, big enough to change how Earth supports life. The good news—the very good news—is that, just as the problem is the sum of what each one of us is doing, so is fixing the problem. A little action by each of seven billion people makes a huge difference. That means we each hold a little part of the future of the world in our hands, and there are an awful lot of us. In that respect, it's never been easier for you to help change the course of the planet.

Among the easy things you personally can do to slow global warming are:

- changing your incandescent lightbulbs to Compact Flourescent Lightbulbs (CFLs)
- adjusting your thermostat down in winter and up in summer
- washing your clothes in warm water instead of hot, or cold instead of warm

- making sure you turn off the lights and other appliances when you're not in the room
- setting the sleep function on your computer to kick in sooner
- walking or biking instead of driving when you're only going a couple of blocks
- recycling when you have the option
- rather than tossing those pieces of paper that come pouring off your printer, flip them over and use the other side first
- reuse your grocery bags, or better yet, bag your groceries in your own cloth bags
- if you live in a place where clean water comes out of the tap, don't buy bottled water, or if you do, reuse the plastic bottles
- buy locally produced products when possible
- when you replace your car or major appliances, buy energy-efficient models.

I've listed several Web sites and other resources in the endnotes for this appendix if you're interested in the details on why such actions will help so much,[1] but you've probably already noticed that the common theme is reducing the energy that you personally draw from power plants, which in fact can be done without cutting your conveniences much, if any. If you want to go a step further, you can take a half hour to estimate how much you personally contribute to the Earth's carbon budget by logging onto a Web site, and then seeing if you can come up with ways to cut that down by a few percent.[2] Lest you doubt that these individual actions make any difference, consider what happens when you actually multiply out the oft-cited example of simply changing lightbulbs: if each household in just the U.S. replaced thirty incandescent lightbulbs (an average-to-low number for a typical household) with a CFL, we could take 60 coal-fired power plants off-line, and over the course of ten years keep about 2.4 GtC out of the atmosphere—which turns out to be just about the increase that IPCC models suggest that CO_2 emissions would add to the atmosphere over the next decade under business-as-usual models.[3]

Governmental and Industry Actions

Global warming is a world problem, and you can't solve a world problem without world cooperation by national leaders, and also by industries and corporations, especially those that are major contributors to greenhouse gas emmissions. Some first efforts have been tremendously successful—the IPCC, for example, which recently shared a Nobel Prize for their role in bringing the problem of global warming and potential solutions to the public. Others, like the United Nations Framework Convention on Climate Change (of which the Kyoto Protocol is part),[4] still have not gotten the traction they need to impel action on a world scale—but could, if the people of the member nations (especially powerful nations like the U.S.) speak loudly enough to their leaders.

Which brings us back once again to individual actions, things you and I can do. We wield an enormous influence over the world through how we choose to vote and what we choose to buy. Again, it's the power of numbers. If voters hold their leaders responsible for doing something about global warming, it will get done. If most people refuse to buy products from companies that, for example, wrap products in more plastic than necessary, pretty soon the plastic wrapping will stop.

Clean Energy

It will take new technologies to help us shift from fossil fuels to cleaner energy—solar, wind, possibly nuclear, and probably some yet to be invented. Luckily, human ingenuity—especially when coupled with the fact that there are billions of dollars to be made as the clean-energy industry swings into high gear—seems up to the task. Already, venture capitalists have poured vast amounts of money into clean-energy start-ups;[5] if that bellwether leads in the same direction it did for the emerging biotechnology industry in the 1970s and dot-com industries in the 1990s, stablizing greenhouse emissions by reducing the use of fossil fuels is on its way. But it's not here yet, and won't be for at least a few decades. That's why it is so critical to buy some time with the solutions to global warming laid out so far—individual action, national governmental and industry action, and cooperative international action.

Minimizing the Human Footprint

All other things being equal, the emission of greenhouse gases grows as the number of people on Earth grows, because we each contribute our share as we cook, heat our homes, drive, fly in airplanes, and so on—more per person in industrialized countries like the U.S., less per person in third-world countries, but everybody has a carbon footprint. The IPCC estimates that today's human population of around seven billion people will grow to somewhere around nine billion by 2050, and could reach fifteen billion by the year 2100—or it could fall back to our present seven billion, depending on various demographic scenarios. Leveling off at the lower population estimate or even below, rather than at the upper estimate, is clearly necessary if we hope to rein in global warming. But even if we do drop back down to seven billion by 2100, barring global catastrophe it seems unavoidable that Earth will see a period of a few decades around 2050 when two billion more people live on it than is the case now, adding to greenhouse gas emissions. That, and the emergence of presently third-world countries as industrialized nations (where greenhouse gas emissions per person tend to be higher), make it all the more important that actions such as those outlined above be implemented quickly to reduce the carbon footprints of each one us, our children, and our children's children.

Notes

Chapter 1. The Heat Is On

1. Bill McKibben, *The End of Nature* (New York: Random House, 1989). The quote is from the introduction of the 2006 Random House Trade Paperback Edition, p. xiv.

2. The "ice ages" comprise the Pleistocene Epoch, which lasted from about 10,000 to 1.8 million years ago. Glaciers expanded and retreated across the northern half of North America some 39 times during that period. The expansions signal cold times called "glacials" and the retractions signal warm times called "interglacials." The fossil marmots in the Colorado cave occur in different layers of sediments that document both glacial and interglacial times near 900,000 years ago.

3. See the article by David W. Inouye, Billy Barr, Kenneth B. Armitage, and Brian D. Inouye, "Climate change is affecting altitudinal migrants and hibernating species," *Proceedings of the U. S. National Academy of Sciences* 97 (2000): 1630–33.

4. Hansen, now director of the NASA Goddard Institute for Space Studies, made this comment after he finished testifying about the dangers of global climate change to the Senate Committee on Energy and Natural Resources, as related by Bill McKibben in "The Coming Meltdown," *New York Review of Books* (January 12, 2006).

5. Stephen H. Schneider, *Global Warming: Are We Entering the Greenhouse Century?* (San Francisco: Sierra Club Books, 1989). Schneider was a climatologist at the National Center for Atmospheric Research when he wrote the book and now is a professor at Stanford University.

6. Several recent books offer excellent readable treatments of the science behind global warming, and the history of the idea, and how we know that global warming is real. I recommend the following for readers who want more details: *The Weather Makers* by Tim Flannery (New York: Atlantic Monthly Press, 2005); *An Inconvenient Truth* by Al Gore (Emmaus, PA: Rodale Publishers, 2006); *Field Notes from a Catastrophe* by Elizabeth Kolbert (New York: Bloomsbury Publishing, 2006); *Global Warming, A Very Short Introduction* by Mark Maslin (Oxford University Press, 2004); and *Global Warming: The Complete Briefing*, 3rd ed., by John Houghton (Cambridge University Press, 2004). The authoritative Web site for information about global warming is that of the Intergovernmental Panel on Climate Change, http://www.ipcc.ch/.

7. This is a still-to-be-tested idea that has recently been proposed by W. F. Ruddiman, a leading climatologist at the University of Virginia. In 2003 he published "The Anthropocene greenhouse era began thousands of years ago" in the scientific journal *Climatic Change* 61:261–93. A more comprehensive treatment can be found in his book *Plows, Plagues, and Petroleum: How Humans Took Control of Climate* (Princeton: Princeton University Press, 2005).

8. Andrew E. Derocher, Nicholas J. Lunn, and Ian Stirling, "Polar bears in a warming climate," *Integrative and Comparative Biology* 44 (2004):163–76.

9. Robert Roy Britt, "Grizzlies Invade Polar Bear Territory, Outcome Uncertain," *LiveScience.com* (2005) http://www.livescience.com/environment/050309_grizly_north.html, accessed September 25, 2006.

10. D. B. Wolkow, "Climate change the culprit behind grizzly bears in Arctic," *ExpressNews* (April 1, 2005), University of Alberta. http://www.expressnews.ualberta.ca/article.cfm?id=6500, accessed Sept. 27, 2006.

11. Li Yu, Qing-wei Li, O.A. Ryder, and Ya-ping Zhang, "Phylogeny of the bears (Ursidae) based on nuclear and mitochondrial genes," *Molecular Phylogenetics and Evolution* 32 (2004):480–94. Calculating how many years ago the two species diverged depends on what assumptions one makes about the molecular clock and which genes are used in estimating the divergence. However, even 1.5 million years is a recent split in terms of mammalian history.

12. Ibid., endnote 8.

13. See R. L. Peters and T. E. Lovejoy, p. xviii, and also M. E. Soulé, pp. xiii–xvi, in Peters and Lovejoy, eds., *Global Warming and Biological Diversity* (New Haven, CT: Yale University Press, 1992).

Chapter 2. Behind Nature's Heartbeat

1. A. G. Tansley, "The use and abuse of vegetational concepts and terms," *Ecology* 16 (1935):284–307, p. 299. In full the quote reads: "It is the systems so formed which, from the point of view of the ecologist, are the basic units of nature on the face of the earth." By "systems so formed" Tansley was referring to "not only the organism-complex, but also the whole complex of physical factors," which further down the page he makes clear he is calling the "ecosystem."

2. Bill McKibben, *The End of Nature* (Random House, 1989).

3. Ibid., endnote 1.

4. This particular variant is from the Canadian Forest Service, http://ecosys.cfl.scf.rncan.gc.ca/definition-eng.asp, accessed April 1, 2008.

5. The relationship between basal metabolic rate and January temperature was first pointed out by Terry Root in "Environmental factors associated with avian distributional boundaries," *Journal of Biogeography* 15 (1988):489–505 and "Energy constraints on avian distributions and abundances," *Ecology* 69 (1988): 330–339.

6. The life span of mammal species has been calculated from the fossil record, and represents the range given by the following studies. J. Alroy, "Constant extinction, constrained diversification, and uncoordinated stasis in North American mammals," *Palaeogeography, Palaeoclimatology, Palaeoecology* 127 (1996):

285–311; J. Alroy, "New methods for quantifying macroevolutionary patterns and processes," *Paleobiology* 26 (2000):707–33; M. Foote and D. M. Raup, "Fossil preservation and the stratigraphic ranges of taxa," *Paleobiology* 22 (1996): 121–40; E. S. Vrba and D. DeGusta, "Do species populations really start small? New perspectives from the Late Neogene fossil record of African mammals," *Philosophical Transactions of the Royal Society of London* B 359 (2004):285–93. Similar studies based on the fossil record have not been done for other kinds of animals or plants.

7. This particular tectonic-scale event was called Miocene Climatic Optimum. From 18.5 million to 17 million years ago, the mean global temperature rose 3–4°C (5.4–7.2°F), and those warm conditions persisted until 14 million years ago, when tectonic-scale global cooling began.

8. The Intergovernmental Panel on Climate Change estimates that warming between 1990 and 2100 will be somewhere between 1.1°C (2°F) and 6.4°C (10.5°F), most likely between 1.8°C (3.2°F) and 4.0°C (7.2°F). The lower estimates are based on optimistic scenarios that include more reliance on energy sources other than fossil fuels, lower population growth, and common global goals; the upper estimates reflect scenarios where we carry on pretty much as we are now. See IPCC, 2007: "Summary for Policymakers," in *Climate Change 2007: The Physical Science Basis. Contribution of Working Group I to the Fourth Assessment Report of the Intergovernmental Panel on Climate Change*, ed. S. Solomon, D. Qin, M. Manning, Z. Chen, M. Marquis, K. B. Averyt, M. Tignor, and H. L. Miller (Cambridge University Press, 2007). Available at http://www.ipcc.ch/, accessed April 1, 2008.

9. A key paper describing the transfer function technique for extracting sea surface temperature from foram assemblages is: J. Imbrie and N. G. Kipp, "A new micropaleontological method for quantitative paleoclimatology: Application to a late Pleistocene Caribbean core," in K. K. Turekian, ed., *Late Cenozoic Glacial Ages* (New Haven, CT: Yale University Press, 1971), pp. 71–182. See also David B. Ericson and Goesta Wollin, "Pleistocene Climates and Chronology in Deep-Sea Sediments," *Science* 162 (1968):1227–34; and Harvey Maurice Sachs et al., "Paleoecological transfer functions," *Annual Review of Earth and Planetary Sciences* 5 (1977):159–78. An important early application of transfer functions was the CLIMAP project, which provided some of the first global reconstructions of ice age climates; see CLIMAP Project Members, "The Surface of Ice Age Earth," *Science* 191 (1976):1131–37.

10. http://nobelprize.org/nobel_prizes/chemistry/laureates/1934/urey-bio.html, accessed April 1, 2008.

11. S. Epstein, "The Role of Stable Isotopes in Geochemistries of All Kinds," *Annual Review of Earth and Planetary Sciences* 25 (1997):1–21, p. 8. See also J. R. Arnold, J. Bigeleisen, and C. A. Hutchison Jr., "Harold Clayton Urey, April 29, 1893–January 5, 1981," *Biographical Memoirs* 68:363–411 (Washington, DC: National Academy of Science Press, 1996), pp. 375–76, http://books.nap.edu/openbook.php?record_id=4990&page=375 [accessed April 1, 2008]; and also K. P. Cohen, S. K. Runcorn, H. E. Suess, H. G. Thode, "Harold Clayton

Urey, 29 April 1893–5 January 1981," *Biographical Memoirs of Fellows of the Royal Society* 29 (1983):622–59 and 643–45.

12. S. Epstein (1997); K. P. Cohen et al. (1983), as cited in endnote 11.

13. At Columbia Urey had published seminal papers on cosmology, and he later went on to make major contributions in planetary science and the origin of life—he is the Urey of the famous Miller-Urey experiment that demonstrated how organic compounds could form from an inorganic primordial soup. Zachary D. Sharp, in *Principles of Stable Isotope Geochemistry* (Englewood Cliffs, NJ: Prentice-Hall, 2005), chap. 6, http://epswww.unm.edu/facstaff/zsharp/505/carbonates%201.pdf, p. 1. [accessed April 1, 2008], relates the following anecdote about a possible stimulus for Urey to use isotopes as a paleothermometer. In 1947, catching up after the Manhattan Project and the move to Chicago, Urey was finally getting around to fulfilling a lecturing commitment he had made to the Royal Society of London. "He was speaking about the physical fractionation of stable isotopes between ideal gases and simple aqueous solutions. He finished his lecture at ETH Zürich and accepted a question from Paul Niggli, the renowned Alpine geologist. Niggli asked if the fractionation between carbonates and water might be large enough and sensitive enough to temperature variations so that they could be used for reconstructing ancient marine temperatures. The story goes that Urey thought a second, said that he didn't know, but it seemed reasonable."

14. As related in: Spencer R. Weart, *The Discovery of Global Warming* (Cambridge, MA: Harvard University Press, 2003), http://www.aip.org/history/climate/forams.htm, accessed April 1, 2008.

15. The cores that Emiliani analyzed at the University of Chicago labs were recovered by expeditions from Columbia University, the Oceanographic Institute at Göteborg, Sweden, and the Scripps Institution of Oceanography in California.

16. After Emiliani's seminal work, Willi Daansgaard, Nick Shackleton, and others showed that the amount of water held in glacial ice also influences the oxygen isotope ratios in foram shells. Basically, the light isotope oxygen-16 is depleted during glacial times because it more easily evaporates from the oceans. It is caught in snow that falls at the poles and ends up turning into glacial ice; thus, during glacial times, instead of oxygen-16 being recycled back into the ocean as rain or snowmelt, a substantial portion of it is locked up in glacial ice. Subsequent research refined paleotemperature curves by comparing the oxygen isotope ratios to transfer functions and later on magnesium/calcium ratios of forams in the same cores, and by adjusting equations to estimate the amount of oxygen-16 locked up in ice sheets. If you are interested in the details of how isotopes are used as paleothermometers, the following sources will lead you deeper. Spencer R. Weart, *The Discovery of Global Warming* (Cambridge, MA: Harvard University Press, 2003), available online at http://www.aip.org/history/climate/forams.htm; Dirk Nürnberg, "Taking the Temperature of Past Ocean Surfaces," *Science* 289 (2000):1698–99; James Zachos et al., "Trends, Rhythms, and Aberrations in Global Climate 65 Ma to Present," *Science* 292 (2001):686–93 (see especially Web Supplement Note 2 in this article); William F. Ruddiman, *Earth's Climate: Past and Future* (New York: W.H. Freeman. 2001); R. S. Bradley, *Paleo-*

climatology: Reconstructing Climates of the Quaternary (San Diego and London: Academic Press, 1999).

17. Milanković was building on earlier work by James Croll, a Scottish scientist who supported himself as an insurance agent and a janitor before he was appointed keeper of maps at the Geological Survey of Scotland in the mid 1860s.

18. Eccentricity refers to variation from a perfectly circular orbit. The shape of Earth's orbital path around the sun in fact is not a perfect circle but more of an oval (actually, an ellipse), which you can envision as pulsating very slowly, such that sometimes the oval is compressed (becoming least like a perfect circle), and sometimes it is expanded (becoming most like a perfect circle). In addition, the sun is closer to one end of the oval than to the other. The shape of the oval changes on a regular basis in a couple of different ways over time periods of about 100,000 and 413,000 years.

Axial tilt (also called obliquity) is how much the Earth is tilted in relation to the plane of its orbit around the sun. Picture a spinning top, slightly tilted—the tilt is what we are talking about. Each single spin of the top around its axis would be analogous to the Earth rotating one complete 24-hour day. As Earth makes its daily rotations, it is presently tilted at an angle of about 23.44°; however, through time, that tilt accentuates to as much as 24.5°, and then straightens up to as little as 21.5°. The swing from minimum to maximum tilt and back takes about 41,000 years.

Now keep picturing the spinning top, but picture it slowing down until it starts to wobble. As it turns out, Earth is constantly wobbling like that—but very slowly, with each wobble taking about 26,000 years. That wobble is called precession.

What Milanković (and Croll before him) realized is that these orbital irregularities meant that different amounts of solar insolation were striking Earth, depending on what phase each of the three cycles was in. And they realized that there were complex interplays between the cycles: superimposed on the slow eccentricity cycle was the faster tilt cycle, and superimposed on that was the even faster wobble cycle. Those complex interplays produce dramatic, and calculable, climatic effects. For example, when eccentricity is at its maximum (the orbital path least like a circle), there is maximum difference in how much sunlight hits the Earth in summer versus winter, meaning more dramatic differences in seasonality, that is, between summer and winter temperatures. Combine that with the wobble factor, and you get even more effects on seasonality. When the eccentricity and wobble cycles line up such that the wobble points the northern hemisphere right at the sun just as Earth is closest to the sun in its eccentric orbit, northern summers are really, really hot and northern winters are really, really cold—that is, the difference between summer and winter in the northern hemisphere is enhanced. At the same time in the southern hemisphere, the difference between summer and winter decreases.

19. J. D. Hays, J. Imbrie, and N. J. Shackleton, "Variations in Earth's Orbit: Pacemaker of the Ice Ages," *Science* 194 (1976):1121–32.

20. The standardization of rates involves plotting the log of the per-hundred-year temperature change against the log of the number of years over which the

temperature change was measured. This produces a line on a graph that starts high on the left (measurements over short time intervals) and drops as you move to right (measurements over long time intervals). The line defines the average rate of warming over a given measurement interval. Rates of climate change such as the fast tectonic rates (e.g., the Mid Miocene Climatic Optimum mentioned in endnote 7), glacial-interglacial transitions, and the Medieval Warm Period represent the fastest natural rates and plot as outliers from the main cluster of points that define the line. The projected rates for global warming over the next century plot even farther above the line, i.e., they are outliers even compared to the fastest past rates, which indicates that they are abnormally fast even when adjusted for measurement interval. See A. D. Barnosky, E. A. Hadly, and C. J. Bell, "Mammalian response to global warming on varied temporal scales," *Journal of Mammalogy* 84 (2003):354–68.

21. See M. S. Scheffer and S. R. Carpenter, "Catastrophic regime shifts in ecosystems: linking theory to observation," *Trends in Ecology and Evolution* 18 (2003):648–56; and M. S. Scheffer, J. A. Carpenter, C. Folkes, J. A. Foley, and B. Walker, "Catastrophic regime shifts in ecosystems" *Nature* 413 (2001):591–96.

22. The vegetation-climate positive feedback has to do with the albedo (that is, heat reflectivity) of different land surfaces. Vegetation reflects less. Thus as less and less of the Sahara was covered by vegetation, more heat was reflected away from the Earth's surface, which enhanced the summer cooling effect that was already underway by the Milanković-driven gradual decrease in insolation. For details see Peter deMenocal, Joseph Ortiz, Tom Guilderson, Jess Adkins, Michael Sarnthein, Linda Baker, and Martha Yarusinsky, "Abrupt onset and termination of the African Humid Period: rapid climate responses to gradual insolation forcing," *Quaternary Science Reviews* 19 (2000):347–61.

Chapter 3. On Our Watch

1. Joel M. Lerner, "Climate change warms up the plant hardiness map," *Chicago Tribune* Web Edition (August 5, 2007), http://www.chicagotribune.com/news/weather/chi-climateaug05,0,6803183.story, accessed August 24, 2007.

2. See for example the Central England Temperature Record, which shows a notable warming trend over the past couple of decades and the hottest year on record in 2006, followed closely by 1999 and 1990. http://en.wikipedia.org/wiki/Image:CET_Full_Temperature_Yearly.PNG, accessed April 1, 2008.

3. See Richard Bisgrove and Paul Hadley, "Gardening in the Global Greenhouse: The Impacts of Climate Change on Gardens in the UK, Technical Report" (Centre for Horticulture and Landscape, School of Plant Sciences, The University of Reading, November 2002), p. 23.

4. BGCI Plants for the Planet, "Climate Change Observations in Botanic Gardens Around the Globe" (March 2, 2007), http://www.bgci.org/resources/news/0323/, accessed August 29, 2007.

5. See for example the following study: COHMAP Members, "Climatic changes of the last 18,000 years: observations and model simulations," *Science* 241(1988):1043–52.

6. Such logic had already been presented in 1960 by Claude Hibbard, a commonsense Kansan who became one of the greats in paleontological circles. Among other things, Hibbard basically discovered that fossil bones of rats and mice could be recovered in great abundance and had a lot to tell us about past climates. The story that has percolated down through the years is that one time, as a young student on a fossil-collecting expedition, Hibbard had to take his turn to stay back in camp and cook. When boredom overtook him, he poked around in some nearby Pleistocene sediments that were near camp and noticed tiny bones eroding out. When he shook some of the dirt through a screen, there on the screen lay more fossils—many more—than the rest of the expedition had collected all day. From then on, Hibbard concentrated his efforts on interpreting the small-mammal remains, which led him to notice the no-analog pairs of species that indicated to him that summers must have been cooler and winters warmer in Pleistocene Kansas. Paleontologists following in his footsteps—Ernie Lundelius at the University of Texas, John Guilday at the Carnegie Museum in Pittsburgh, and Russ Graham, then at Illinois State Museum, now at Penn State—reached similar conclusions by studying fossil mammals from the Llano Estacado, the Appalachians, and the northern Great Plains, respectively.

7. The Web of Science "indexes over 8,000 of the leading journals in the arts, humanities, sciences, and social sciences, providing searching of footnoted citations. Includes the Arts & Humanities Citation Index, Science Citation Index, and Social Sciences Citation Index" (http://sunsite2.berkeley.edu:8088/ERF/servlet/ERFmain). You can access the Web of Science at http://portal.isi-knowledge.com/. The numbers given in these paragraphs are from database searches conducted on July 9, 2008.

8. Certainly there were people publishing their ideas about how climate change might affect species ranges and populations before these global warming papers began to appear in the early 1990s. Some of the publications go back to 1917 and earlier, as reviewed by C. Parmesan, "Ecological and Evolutionary Responses to Recent Climate Change," *Annual Reviews of Ecology, Evolution, and Systematics* 37 (2006):637–69. Those publications fall into two classes: (a) those of biologists observing changes in the presence, absence, or phenology of species that seemed to correlate with year-to-year weather observations, and (b) those of paleontologists suggesting that past climate changes in large part explained past changes in terrestrial plants and animals, invertebrate marine animals (clams, snails, and the like) and protists (like the foraminifera discussed in Chapter 2.). It was in the late 1980s and 1990s that these two classes of information were integrated, to the extent that ecologists started looking at the effects that changing climate could have on individual species and ecosystems.

9. Up to the end of 2007, searched on July 9, 2008.

10. These statistics come from a search of the Web of Science on July 9, 2008, using the key words "global warming" and iteratively each one of the following: "plants," "mammals," "birds," "reptiles," "amphibians," "fish," "insects," "marine."

11. The actual number of species that are documented to be affected is far

greater than the number of published studies, because many of those publications report on more than one species.

12. Meta-analyses critically review all the information published on a given topic (in this case, correlations between weather records and such ecological characters as phenology and distribution of flora and fauna), extract relevant data, and then treat that data either quantitatively or qualitatively to identify any informative patterns.

13. C. Parmesan and G. Yohe, "A globally coherent fingerprint of climate change impacts across natural systems," *Nature* 421 (2003):37–42. Terry L. Root, Jeff T. Price, Kimberly R. Hall, Cynthia Rosenzweig, and J. Alan Pounds, "Fingerprints of global wild animals and plants," *Nature* 421 (2003):57–60. Besides meta-analyses in the strict sense, since the year 2000 there have also been several informative summaries of the diverse literature on the effects of global warming on biota, among them: L. Hughes, "Biological consequences of global warming: Is the signal already apparent?" *Trends In Ecology & Evolution* 15 (2000):56–61; John P. McCarty, "Review: Ecological Consequences of Recent Climate Change," *Conservation Biology* 15 (2001):320–31; Josep Peñuelas and Iolanda Filella, "Responses to a Warming World," *Science* 294 (2001):793–95; G. R. Walther, E. Post, P. Convey, A. Menzel, C. Parmesan, T. J. C. Beebee, J. M. Fromentin, O. Hoegh-Guldberg, and F. Bairlein, "Ecological responses to recent climate change," *Nature* 416 (2002):389–95; C. Parmesan, "Ecological and Evolutionary Responses to Recent Climate Change," *Annual Reviews of Ecology, Evolution, and Systematics* 37 (2006):637–69.

14. See also a brand-new study that further confirms these meta-analyses: Cynthia Rosenzweig, David Karoly, Marta Vicarelli, Peter Neofotis, Qigang Wu, Gino Casassa, Annette Menzel, Terry L. Root, Nicole Estrella, Bernard Seguin, Piotr Tryjanowski, Chunzhen Liu, Samuel Rawlins, and Anton Imeson, "Attributing physical and biological impacts to anthropogenic climate change," *Nature* 453 (2008):353–58.

15. In the Root collaborative study, out of 1,468 species only about 4 percent (about 62 species) were not birds, insects or other terrestrial invertebrates, or plants. Mammals (12 species), amphibians (10 species), and fish (3 species) each comprised less than 1 percent of the total species analyzed. Marine invertebrates, including plankton species, comprised 4–5 percent of the sample (upward of 37 species). In the Parmesan and Yohe phenology analysis, which looked at more than 1700 species, no mammals, reptiles, or marine invertebrates were included; there were 12 amphibian species and two fish species (0.7 percent and 0.1 percent of the total species, respectively). For the distribution and abundance analysis, there were 70 marine invertebrate species, 60 marine zooplankton, two mammals, seven reptiles and amphibians combined, and 85 fish, which respectively account for around 4 percent, 3.5 percent, 0.1 percent, 0.4 percent, and 5 percent of the total of more than 1700 species that were examined.

16. See R. B. Weladi and Ø. Holand, "Influences of large-scale climatic variability on reindeer population dynamics: implications for reindeer husbandry in

Norway," *Climate Research* 32 (2006):119–27; Anders Mårell, Annika Hofgaard, and Kjell Danell, "Nutrient dynamics of reindeer forage species along snowmelt gradients at different ecological scales," *Basic and Applied Ecology* 7 (2006): 13–30; Nathalie Pettorelli, Robert B. Weladji, Øystein Holand, Atle Mysterud, Halgrim Breie, and Nils Christian Stenseth, "The relative role of winter and spring conditions: linking climate and landscape-scale plant phenology to alpine reindeer body mass," *Biology Letters* 1 (2005):24–26; D. K. Grayson and F. Delpech, "Pleistocene reindeer and global warming," *Conservation Biology* 19 (2005):557–62.

17. D. K. Grayson and F. Delpech (2005) as cited in endnote 16.

18. D. K. Grayson and F. Delpech (2005) as cited in endnote 16.

19. Andrew T. Smith and Marla L. Weston, *Mammalian Species* 352 (1990): 1–8.

20. Prior to the 1990s, the surveys which placed pikas on the Great Basin mountaintops from which they are now absent took place in 1913, 1925, 1934, 1935, 1936, and 1941. Compounding the climatic impacts on pikas may be other human impacts, such as grazing cattle nearby. For details see: E. A. Beever, P. E. Brussard, and J. Berger, "Patterns of apparent extirpation among isolated populations of pikas (*Ochotona princeps*) in the Great Basin," *Journal of Mammalogy* 84 (2003):37–54; and D. K. Grayson, "A brief history of Great Basin pikas," *Journal of Biogeography* 32 (2005):2103–11.

21. Li Wei-Dong and Andrew T. Smith, "Dramatic decline of the threatened Ili pika *Ochotona iliensis* (Lagomorpha: Ochotonidae) in Xinjiang, China," *Oryx* 39 (2005):30–34.

22. Robert Guralnick, "Differential effects of past climate warming on mountain and flatland species distributions: a multispecies North American mammal assessment," *Global Ecology and Biogeography* 16 (2007):14–23.

23. The University of California Museum of Paleontology Web site http://www.ucmp.berkeley.edu/ was brought online in 1993, culminating efforts by Guralnick and his contemporary graduate students and UCMP staff and faculty.

24. In the past, the mountaintop species, unlike their flatland counterparts, did not balance their overall range size by simply populating suitable habitat to the north as it got too hot in the south. Even at the northern edge of their ranges, they couldn't disperse across the intervening hot lowland valleys. With northern populations unable to jump to mountaintops still farther north, southern populations vanishing into thin air as their mountaintops got too hot, and survivors forced into higher elevations for a given latitude, the overall geographic range of many mountain species ended up shrinking dramatically, even if their latitudinal extent increased.

25. Clinton W. Epps, Per J. Palsbøll, John D. Wehausen, George K. Roderick, and Dale R. McCullough, "Elevation and connectivity define genetic refugia for mountain sheep as climate warms," *Molecular Ecology* 15 (2006):4295–302; C. W. Epps, D. R. McCullough, J. D. Wehausen, V. C. Bleich, and J. L. Rechel, "Effects of climate change on population persistence of desert-dwelling mountain sheep

in California," *Conservation Biology* 18 (2004), 102–13; C. W. Epps, P. J. Palsbøll, J. D. Wehausen et al., "Highways block gene flow and cause a rapid decline in genetic diversity of desert bighorn sheep," *Ecology Letters* 8 (2005):1029–38.

26. C. Parmesan (2006) as cited in endnote 13.

27. See the compelling summary of the golden toad's short known history on Earth and the role of global warming in contributing to its demise in *The Weather Makers* by Tim Flannery (New York: Atlantic Monthly Press, 2005).

28. J. Alan Pounds, Martín R. Bustamante, Luis A. Coloma, Jamie A. Consuegra, Michael P. L. Fogden, Pru N. Foster, Enrique La Marca, Karen L. Masters, Andrés Merino-Viteri, Robert Puschendorf, Santiago R. Ron, G. Arturo Sánchez-Azofeifa, Christopher J. Still, and Bruce E. Young, "Widespread amphibian extinctions from epidemic disease driven by global warming," *Nature* 439 (2006):161–67.

29. As quoted by Juliet Eilperin in "Warming Tied to Extinction of Frog Species" (*Washington Post*, January 12, 2006), http://www.washingtonpost.com/wp-dyn/content/article/2006/01/11/AR2006011102121.html, accessed September 13, 2007.

30. The chikungunya outbreak in Italy was reported by *BBC News*, September 6, 2007, http://news.bbc.co.uk/2/hi/health/6981476.stm, accessed September 13, 2007. Another example of a climate-caused pathogen expansion may be the mosquito-borne West Nile virus, which was unknown in the United States before 1999, when people in New York were first infected. In most people, the disease is asymptomatic or like a mild flu, but approximately one out of 150 get really sick—symptoms like high fever, neck stiffness, coma, convulsions, and paralysis. The virus lives in the blood of birds—whose flyways are affected by climate—and in mosquitoes, which bite the birds, and then bite humans. The particular brand of mosquito that is involved, *Culex pipiens*, thrives in the stagnant pools that form as water sources dry up during hot, dry spells, and thirsty birds concentrate to wet their whistle at the same ever-dwindling water sources. Higher percentages of birds thus get infected in such years, which starts the vicious circle of more mosquitos carrying the virus, which means that eventually the odds get high enough that a mosquito who has sucked a bird's blood sucks a person's too. The 1999 outbreak restricted to New York followed just such an abnormally hot, dry spell. Within four years people were being infected all across the United States, and as climate is warming, more are being infected in wide swaths of Canada.

31. Regarding squid, see David W. Sims, Martin J. Genner, Alan J. Southward, and Stephen J. Hawkins, "Timing of squid migration reflects North Atlantic climate variability," *Proceedings: Biological Sciences* 268 (Dec. 22, 2001):2607–11. Regarding mussels and barnacles, see John A. Barth, Bruce A. Menge, Jane Lubchenco, Francis Chan, John M. Bane, Anthony R. Kirincich, Margaret A. McManus, Karina J. Nielsen, Stephen D. Pierce, and Libe Washburn, "Delayed upwelling alters nearshore coastal ocean ecosystems in the northern California current," *Proceedings of the U. S. National Academy of Sciences* 104 (2007):3719–24. Regarding plankton, see Terry L. Root et al. as cited in endnote

13. Regarding coral reefs, see Richard Black, "Gorillas head race to extinction" (*BBC NEWS*, September 12, 2007), http://news.bbc.co.uk/2/hi/science/nature/6990095.stm, accessed September 23, 2008.

Chapter 4. Witnessing Extinction

1. From the article by Hal Bernton, "Up-close View of Dead Zone Shows 'It's Just a Wasteland'" (*Seattle Times*, August 14, 2006), http://seattletimes.nwsource.com/html/localnews/2003185060_deadzone09m.html, accessed September 12, 2007.

2. You can download movies that show you the before-and-after videos of the Cape Perpetua deadzone from: http://oregonstate.edu/media/archives/.

3. See the following for more information: F. Chan, J. A. Barth, J. Lubchenco, A. Kirincich, H. Weeks, W. T. Peterson, and B. A. Menge, "Emergence of Anoxia in the California Current Large Marine Ecosystem," *Science* 319 (2008):920; John A. Barth, Bruce A. Menge, Jane Lubchenco, Francis Chan, John M. Bane, Anthony R. Kirincich, Margaret A. McManus, Karina J. Nielsen, Stephen D. Pierce, and Libe Washburn, "Delayed upwelling alters nearshore coastal ocean ecosystems in the northern California current," *Proceedings of the U.S. National Academy of Sciences* 104 (2007):3719–24.

4. Upwelling along the Oregon coast is driven by a combination of ocean and atmospheric processes, both ultimately controlled by global climate patterns. The ocean-based processes in part depend upon how much nutrient-rich subarctic water enters the California Current (a major southward-flowing ocean current along the west coast of the U.S.), and whether other waters that feed the current are high or low in oxygen. That oxygen content, in turn, is related to how much the surface water has mixed with water at depth, controlled largely by water temperature. Since 2002, there have been more years when the waters feeding the coast are comparatively low in oxygen. The atmospheric processes involve the coast-paralleling winds that normally blow in the spring and summer to drive the upwelling season. In recent years the winds have been abnormal with regard to when they've come in the spring, how long they continue, and how strong they are. The unusual winds, in turn, come from unusual climatic conditions: atypical southward shifts of the jet stream (controlled largely by the difference in temperature between polar air masses and more equatorward air masses), which delay the upwelling winds in the the spring and intensify them in the summer, and also differential heating of the continental land relative to the ocean water, which can make the winds blow harder when they kick in.

5. Recent studies are beginning to document that global warming will cause increased upwelling in other places in the world as well: among them the northwest African coast, the Arabian Sea, the Iberian margin, and the coastal waters along Peru and Chile. See H. V. McGregor, M. Dima, H. W. Fischer, and S. Mulitza, "Rapid 20th-Century Increase in Coastal Upwelling off Northwest Africa," *Science* 315 (2007):637–39. Other studies suggest that hypoxia triggered by a combination of global warming, pollution, and other causes will increase in the future, and that the detrimental effects on marine life have been, if anything, underestimated. See Raquel Vaquer-Sunyer and Carlos M. Duarte, "Thresholds

of hypoxia for marine biodiversity," *Proceedings of the U. S. National Academy of Sciences* 105 (2008):15452–57.

6. These numbers were compiled from searching the IUCN Red List for "marine species" on September 26, 2007.

7. World Wildlife Fund, "Are We Putting Our Fish in Hot Water?" published online at http://assets.panda.org/downloads/fisherie_web_final.pdf, accessed October 4, 2007.

8. S. Elizabeth Alter, Eric Ryne, and Stephen R. Palumbi. "DNA evidence for historic population size and past ecosystem impacts of gray whales," *Proceedings of the U. S. National Academy of Sciences* 104 (2007):15162–67.

9. Global warming is expected to affect marine mammals in a variety of ways. See Mark P. Simmonds and Stephen J. Isaac, "The impacts of climate change on marine mammals: early signs of significant problems," *Oryx* 41 (2007):19–26.

10. Jeremy B. C. Jackson, Michael X. Kirby, Wolfgang H. Berger, Karen A. Bjorndal, Louis W. Botsford, Bruce J. Bourque, Roger H. Bradbury, Richard Cooke, Jon Erlandson, James A. Estes, Terence P. Hughes, Susan Kidwell, Carina B. Lange, Hunter S. Lenihan, John M. Pandolfi, Charles H. Peterson, Robert S. Steneck, Mia J. Tegner, and Robert R. Warner, "Historical Overfishing and the Recent Collapse of Coastal Ecosystems," *Science* 293 (2001):629–38.

11. Jeremy B. C. Jackson, "Habitat destruction and ecological extinction of marine Invertebrates," published online at http://cbc.amnh.org/symposia/archives/expandingthearc/speakers/transcripts/jackson-text.html, accessed October 4, 2007.

12. Jeremy B. C. Jackson et al. (2001) as cited in endnote 10.

13. Kenneth R. Weiss, "A Primeval Tide of Toxins, Part One, Altered Oceans," *Los Angeles Times* (July 30, 2006), http://www.latimes.com/news/local/oceans/la-me-ocean30jul30,0,6670018,full.story, accessed September 23, 2008.

14. Jeremy B. C. Jackson et al. (2001) as cited in endnote 10.

15. J. M. Pandolfi, J. B. C. Jackson, N. Baron, R. H. Bradbury, H. M. Guzman, T. P. Hughes, C. V. Kappel, F. Micheli, J. C. Ogden, H. P. Possingham, and E. Sala, "Are U.S. Coral Reefs on the Slippery Slope to Slime?" *Science* 307 (2005): 1725–26. See also Jeremy B. C. Jackson et al. (2001) as cited in endnote 10.

16. Nancy Knowlton, "The future of coral reefs," *Proceedings of the U.S. National Academy of Sciences* 98 (2001):5419–25.

17. Nicholas A. J. Graham, Shaun K. Wilson, Simon Jennings, Nicholas V. C. Polunin, Jude P. Bijoux, and Jan Robinson, "Dynamic fragility of oceanic coral reef ecosystems," *Proceedings of the U. S. National Academy of Sciences* 103 (2007):8425–29.

18. Jeremy B. C. Jackson as cited in endnote 11.

19. O. Hoegh-Guldberg, "Climate Change, Coral Bleaching, and the Future of the World's Coral Reefs," *Marine and Freshwater Research* 50 (1999):839–66.

20. John M. Pandolfi and Jeremy B. C. Jackson, "Ecological persistence interrupted in Caribbean coral reefs," *Ecology Letters* 9 (2006):818–26.

21. Chris D. Thomas, Alison Cameron, Rhys E. Green, Michel Bakkenes, Linda J. Beaumont, Yvonne C. Collingham, Barend F. N. Erasmus, Marinez Fer-

reira de Siqueira, Alan Grainger, Lee Hannah, Lesley Hughes, Brian Huntley, Albert S. van Jaarsveld, Guy F. Midgley, Lera Miles, Miguel A. Ortega-Huerta, A. Townsend Peterson, Oliver L. Phillips, and Stephen E. Williams, "Extinction risk from climate change," *Nature* 427 (2004):145–48.

22. Thomas et al. (2004), p. 145; see endnote 21 for full citation.

23. Helen M. Regan, Richard Lupia, Andrew N. Drinnan, and Mark A. Burgman, in "The Currency and Tempo of Extinction," *The American Naturalist* 157 (2001):1–10.

Chapter 5. No Place to Run To

1. Stephen Jay Gould, 1974, "The Origin and Function of 'Bizarre' Structures: Antler Size and Skull Size in the 'Irish Elk,' *Megaloceros giganteus*," *Evolution* 28 (1974):191–220.

2. Purportedly the Elk Tombstone was carved by Danish paleoecologist Knud Jessen and Irish geologist Anthony Farrington when they were at Ballybetagh in 1934 to study the paleoenvironmental history of the bog by looking at the fossil pollen, plants, and bones embedded in the sediments. Preceding their studies in the bog were other excavations for Irish elk after the original discovery of elk fossils in 1846 or 1847 as a canal was being dug. Excavations targeted at discovering more Irish elk took place in 1876 (by R. J. Moss of the Royal Dublin Society), 1881 (by W. Williams to find skeletons for sale), and 1914 (by H. Stokes, also to find skeletons for sale).

3. Technically Irish elk are not elk at all, but instead giant deer. Their closest living cousins are the fallow deer, *Dama dama*, which are small in comparison. Of all living deer, fallow deer most resemble Irish elk in various details of their morphology, such as having antlers that are flattened (or palmate, as scientists call them) like those of a moose. That such morphological similarities are more than coincidence has been confirmed by recent studies that compared the fossilized DNA extracted from Irish elk bones to the DNA sequences of living deer—and found that Irish elk sequences most resemble those of *Dama dama*. See the following articles for more detail: A. M. Lister, C. J. Edwards, D. A. W. Nock, M. Bunce, I. A. van Pijlen, D. G. Bradley, M. G. Thomas, and I. Barnes, "The phylogenetic position of the 'giant deer' *Megaloceros giganteus*," *Nature* 438 (2005), 850–53; and Sandrine Hughes, Thomas J. Hayden, Christophe J. Douady, Christelle Tougard, Mietje Germonpré, Anthony Stuart, Lyudmila Lbova, Ruth F. Carden, Catherine Hänni, and Ludovic Say, "Molecular phylogeny of the extinct giant deer, *Megaloceros giganteus*," *Molecular Phylogenetics and Evolution* 40 (2006):285–91.

4. Unlike controlled experiments, which manipulate variables one by one (apply "treatments") to assess what data (results) are produced, natural experiments start with the data that nature has already produced, and work backwards to try to figure out what those data mean. Despite the limitation that we can't systematically control the "treatments," they are the only kinds of experiments that conclusively show us how things play out over time spans longer than human lifetimes and at continental or global spatial scales. Controlled

experiments start with details, and work forward to see what data (results) are produced. They show exactly how specific changes affect systems at a given spatial and temporal scale, but generalizing to effects at larger scales becomes tricky because as scales increase, effects change nonlinearly.

5. See the following articles for a detailed discussion and a long list of literature about the evidence that bears on Pleistocene extinctions: P. L. Koch and A. D. Barnosky, "Late Quaternary extinctions: state of the debate," *Annual Review of Ecology, Evolution, and Systematics* 37 (2006):215–50; A. D. Barnosky, P. L. Koch, R. S. Feranec, S. L. Wing, and A. B. Shabel, "Assessing the Causes of Late Pleistocene Extinctions on the Continents," *Science* 306 (2004):70–75.

6. P. S. Martin, "Pleistocene overkill," *Natural History* 76 (1967):32–38.

7. The quote is from page 585, in Donald K. Grayson and David J. Meltzer, "A requiem for North American overkill," *Journal of Archaeological Science* 30 (2003):585–93.

8. The quote is from page 122, in Stuart Fiedel and Gary Haynes, "A premature burial: comments on Grayson and Meltzer's 'Requiem for overkill,'" *Journal of Archaeological Science* 31 (2004):121–31.

9. In this book I am reporting ages in calendar years, not as radiocarbon ages per se. Radiocarbon ages assume the ratio of C^{14} to C^{12} and C^{13} has remained constant through time. Nowadays, we know that the $C^{14}/C^{12} + C^{13}$ ratio has varied slightly through time, so radiocarbon ages are routinely converted to calendar years by adjusting for that known variation. This adjustment generally pushes the radiocarbon ages back by a few hundred to a few thousand years in the conversion to calendar years, depending on how far back in time the specimens come from. I have converted radiocarbon ages that were reported in primary scientific publications to calendar years using the program OxCal (http://c14.arch. ox.ac.uk/ embed.php?File=oxcal.html, accessed May 12, 2008). It is important to note that what is reported here is only the median of the calibrated age, for the sake of convenience and simplicity—but in actuality, radiocarbon ages are not exact numbers. They always have a margin of error, or "error bar," of plus or minus so many years, which reflects analytical errors and other uncertainties. For example, the error bars on the date I give for the last Irish elk and the beginning of the Younger Dryas in Ireland (the Younger Dryas is the sudden cold snap that occurred just before climate started to warm in earnest at the end of the last glacial time) in the strict sense indicate that, although the median is near 12,500 years, technically speaking we can be 95 percent confident that the actual date falls between somewhere a little older than 13,000 years and somewhere a little younger than 12,000 years.

10. The switch from Alleröd to the colder Younger Dryas was one of those millennial-scale climate wiggles explained in Chapter 2. This particular wiggle was embedded within a part of the Milanković cycles that was just starting to move the world from a glacial into an interglacial time. By the end of the Younger Dryas, the Milanković cycles moved full-on into the interglacial phase, so things warmed and stayed warm—we are still in the same interglacial. It was during our present interglacial, beginning around 11,900 years ago, that the peat

formed on top of the glacial-age sediments that entomb the Irish elk bones.

11. The ~9,000 radiocarbon-year date (closer to 10,100 in calendar years) for human arrival in Ireland is based on work by P. C. Woodman, G. F. Mitchell, and M. Ryan, as cited in A. D. Barnosky, "Big game extinction caused by late Pleistocene climatic change: Irish elk (*Megaloceras giganteus*) in Ireland," *Quaternary Research* 25 (1986):128–35; and in A. J. Stuart, P. A. Kosintsev, T. F. G. Higham, and A. M. Lister, "Pleistocene to Holocene extinction dynamics in giant deer and woolly mammoth," *Nature* 431 (2004):684–90.

12. E. Jansen, J. Overpeck, K. R. Briffa, J. C. Duplessy, F. Joos, V. Masson-Delmotte, D. Olago, B. Otto Bliesner, W. R. Peltier, S. Rahmstorf, R. Ramesh, D. Raynaud, D. Rind, O. Solomina, R. Villalba, and D. Zhang, "Palaeoclimate. In: Climate Change 2007: The Physical Science Basis," *Contribution of Working Group I to the Fourth Assessment Report of the Intergovernmental Panel on Climate Change*, ed. S. Solomon, D. Qin, M. Manning, Z. Chen, M. Marquis, K. B. Averyt, M. Tignor, and H. L. Miller (Cambridge University Press, 2007), p. 456.

13. Some scientists thought that a comet might have exploded over the Great Lakes of North America and contributed to or even initiated the Younger Dryas by accelerating the influx of fresh water into the North Atlantic. Their idea is that the purported comet either actually exploded a huge part of the North American ice sheet, causing fresh water to flood into the North Atlantic, or caused a mantle of dark soot to coat vast areas of ice. The darkening of the ice would cause it to absorb more heat from the sun and thus melt faster than unblemished ice. This idea was published in: R. B. Firestone, A. West, J. P. Kennett, L. Becker, T. E. Bunch, Z. S. Revay, P. H. Schultz, T. Belgya, D. J. Kennett, J. M. Erlandson, O. J. Dickenson, A. C. Goodyear, R. S. Harris, G. A. Howard, J. B. Kloosterman, P. Lechler, P. A. Mayewski, J. Montgomery, R. Poreda, T. Darrah, S. S. Que Hee, A. R. Smith, A. Stich, W. Topping, J. H. Wittke, and W. S. Wolbach, "Evidence for an extraterrestrial impact 12,900 years ago that contributed to the megafaunal extinctions and the Younger Dryas cooling," *Proceedings of the U. S. National Academy of Sciences* 104 (2007):16016–21. So far this idea is not receiving much support: see R. Kerr, "Experts find no evidence for a mammoth-killer impact," *Science* 319 (2008):1331–32.

14. All dated Irish elk fossils from Ireland are from Alleröd time, except for specimens from Castlepook Cave, County Cork, which records the earliest entry of Irish elk into Ireland at between 32,000 and 37,200 radiocarbon years ago. For a listing of dated specimens, see the supplementary material from A. J. Stuart, P. A. Kosintsev, T. F. G. Higham, and A. M. Lister, "Pleistocene to Holocene extinction dynamics in giant deer and woolly mammoth," *Nature* 431(2004): 684–90.

15. A radiocarbon date on one of the bones said that particular animal died about 12,500 years ago, right at the climatic transition. Given the clustering of the Ballybetagh bones near the top of the Alleröd layer, it seems likely that most of the animals died within a century or so (possibly within a few decades) of that dated animal.

16. Antler size is allometrically related to body size in deer, which means the

bigger the body, the bigger the antlers. It turns out that in comparison to other deer, most Irish elk antlers are the size you'd expect given their large body size. However, the Ballybetagh antlers were smaller than the allometric equations predicted.

17. Besides nutritional state, antler size also varies from year to year based on age. Very young and very old animals have proportionately smaller antlers than animals in their reproductive prime. For the comparison of Ballybetagh versus all Irish animals, the average age of the animals in the two samples was the same (see the Barnosky references in endnotes 11 and 22 for this chapter). The age of the fossil animals was assessed by measuring how much their teeth were worn and by measuring the height of the antler pedicle. (The pedicle is the projection on the skull to which the antler is attached—the older the animal, the shorter the pedicle.)

18. That antler growth is triggered by day-length has been established in many living deer and elk species in which the females lack antlers and the males have large ones, for example, red deer *Cervus elaphus* (or as they are called in North America, wapiti or elk), fallow deer (*Dama dama*, the closest living relative of Irish elk), sika deer (*Cervus nippon*), and white-tailed deer (*Odocoileus virginianus*). Likewise, the yearly life cycle of storing fat reserves during the time of spring-summer antler growth, and running a caloric deficit during the rut and ensuing winter, characterizes such living species. The evolutionary relationships between the extinct Irish elk and these living species implies the same sort of genetic controls on antler growth and yearly life cycle in them.

19. R. A. Moen, J. Pastor, and Y. Cohen, in "Antler growth and extinction of Irish elk," *Evolutionary Ecology Research* 1 (1999):235–49, modeled the growth of Irish elk antlers and concluded (p. 235) that "About 6 percent of the calcium and 10 percent of the phosphorus in the antler were resorbed from the skeleton because dietary intake of minerals was insufficient to meet requirements for antler mineralization. The minerals resorbed from the skeleton in summer would have to be replenished by dietary intake over the following winter."

20. See Cedric O'Driscoll Worman and Tristen Kimbrell, "Getting to the hart of the matter: did antlers truly cause the extinction of Irish elk?," *Oikos* 117 (2008):1397–1405.

21. This was supported by the plant and pollen fossils, which showed that the kinds of vegetation needed to sustain healthy Irish elk were decreasing in abundance due to the climate change through which the Ballybetagh elk were living.

22. For more details, see A. D. Barnosky, "Taphonomy and herd structure of the extinct Irish elk, *Megaloceros giganteus*," *Science* 228 (1985):340–44; and A. D. Barnosky (1986) as cited in endnote 11.

23. A. J. Stuart et al. (2004) as cited in endnote 14.

24. Ibid.

25. Richard G. Roberts, Timothy F. Flannery, Linda K. Ayliffe, Hiroyuki Yoshida, Jon M. Olley, Gavin J. Prideaux, Geoff M. Laslett, Alexander Baynes, M. A. Smith, Rhys Jones, and Barton L. Smith, "New Ages for the Last Aus-

tralian Megafauna: Continent-Wide Extinction About 46,000 Years Ago," *Science* 292 (2001):1888–92.

26. Clive N. G. Trueman, Judith H. Field, Joe Dortch, Bethan Charles, and Stephen Wroe, "Prolonged coexistence of humans and megafauna in Pleistocene Australia," *Proceedings of the U. S. National Academy of Sciences* 102 (2005):8381–85.

27. Depending on the geographic region, the last pulse of extinctions in Eurasia started as early as 14,000 years ago. The last survivors of Irish elk hung on until about 7,650 years ago (in Siberia) and mammoths until 4,000 years ago (only on some northern islands). However, most populations of even these late–hangers on disappeared between 11,500 and 13,000 years ago. See discussions in Koch and Barnosky (2006), Barnosky et al. (2004) [citations in endnote 5], and A. J. Stuart, P. A. Kosintsev, T. F. G. Higham, and A. M. Lister, "Pleistocene to Holocene extinction dynamics in giant deer and woolly mammoth," *Nature* 431 (2004):684–90.

28. If the controversial comet explosion mentioned in endnote 13 actually occurred, the end-Pleistocene catastrophe in North America would have been exacerbated, with wildfires possibly further disrupting habitats for a variety of species, over and above the disruptions caused by humans and climate change. However, evidence for the comet explosion is not strong.

29. See M. R. Waters and T. W. Stafford Jr., "Redefining the Age of Clovis: Implications for the Peopling of the Americas," *Science* 315 (2007):1122–26.

30. The end-Pleistocene climate change in North America, as in northern Europe, was characterized initially by the sudden, geologically short Younger Dryas cold snap, when melting glaciers poured fresh water into the North Atlantic and disrupted the flow of currents that keep northern latitudes warm. Then, after a few hundred years, warming ensued in earnest. The Younger Dryas hit North America about 12,900 years ago, a date that is within the 95 percent error bars of the Younger Dryas dates mentioned earlier for Ireland.

31. Extinctions were also severe at the end of the Pleistocene in South America. Details of the chronology there are not yet reliably resolved, but the range of published dates indicates that megafauna populated the continent when humans first arrived as early as 14,600 years ago, and suggest that the last extinctions did not take place until a few thousand years later. Thus some correlation between the time of extinction, first human presence, and global warming seems likely.

Chapter 6. California Dreaming

1. From the writings of Joseph Grinnell, as quoted at http://www.mip.berkeley.edu/mvz/Grinnell/, accessed October 19, 2007.

2. Annie Alexander quoted from http://mvz.berkeley.edu/History.html, accessed October 19, 2007.

3. Annie Alexander was an avid naturalist who used her resources to support programs in paleontology, zoology, and botany. Her life and contributions to science have been chronicled in: *On Her Own Terms: Annie Montague Alexander and the Rise of Science in the American West*, by Barbara Stein (Berkeley: University of California Press, 2001).

4. Joseph Grinnell's description of himself when he was just starting his zoology career. Page 276, in Jean M. Linsdale, "In Memorium: Joseph Grinnell," *The Auk* 59 (1942):269–85.

5. Joseph Grinnell, "Field tests of theories concerning distributional control," *American Naturalist* 51 (1917):115–28.

6. Joseph Grinnell, "The Niche-relationships of the California Thrasher," *The Auk* 34 (1917):427–33.

7. I do not know whether Annie Alexander ever met John Muir. Her social circle certainly included at least one family who also played host to Muir, Judge Theodor Hittel's family in San Francisco, according to Barbara Stein (2001), as cited in endnote 3. Grinnell had met Muir on his 1896 Alaska trip—Muir had been one of the "tourists . . . who had learned of the boy's interest in birds" and had visited to "view the bird skins" of Grinnell's growing Alaska collection, as related by Hilda Wood Grinnell on page 5 of "Joseph Grinnell: 1877–1939," *The Condor* XLII (1940):3–34.

8. Although Yosemite and Sequoia were the second and third national parks, they were actually the country's first protected wilderness reserves: on June 30, 1864, Abraham Lincoln approved "granting Yosemite Valley and the Mariposa Grove of Giant Sequoias to the State of California as an inalienable public trust." Technically, the second national park was Mackinac National Park in Michigan, established in 1875; however, it was decommissioned in 1895. Therefore in 1900, ten years after Yosemite was declared a national park, it was still one of only four in the U.S.: Yellowstone, established in 1872; Yosemite and Sequoia in 1890; and Mount Rainier in 1899. Outside of the U.S. there were two more: Royal National Park had been established in Australia in 1879, and Banff in Canada in 1885. By 1910, the U.S. had added Crater Lake (1902), Wind Cave (1903), Mesa Verde (1906), and Glacier (1910).

9. John Muir, *Our National Parks* (1901), online version published at http://www.sierraclub.org/john_muir_exhibit/frameindex.html?http://www.sierraclub.org/john_muir_exhibit/writings/our_national_parks/, accessed October 27, 2007, quote from fifth paragraph of Chapter 1.

10. Barbara Stein (2001), as cited in endnote 3, pp. 43 and 45.

11. Ibid, p. 47.

12. Jean M. Linsdale (1942) as cited in endnote 4, pp. 270 and 276. The "personal handicaps" Grinnell referred to were being "cocksure," "fresh," and "inclined to be slap-dash."

13. Barbara Stein (2001), as cited in endnote 3, p. 82.

14. Clearly Yosemite and other national parks are not completely untouched by humans—even before Europeans were there, Native Americans used them to some extent, and now there are impacts from roads, visitation, non-native species, and so on. But the fact remains that national parks give a much closer approximation of how ecosystems operate without human alteration than do the human-dominated landscapes surrounding them.

15. "Man-day" is an accurate description. Paradoxically, despite his respect for Annie Alexander's field abilities, Grinnell did not allow women on his crews.

16. Joseph Grinnell and Tracy Irwin Storer, *Animal Life in the Yosemite, an Account of Mammals, Birds, Reptiles, and Amphibians in a Cross-Section of the Sierra Nevada, Contribution of the Museum of Vertebrate Zoology, University of California* (Berkeley: University of California Press, 1924).

17. By the time Grinnell worked in the park in 1914 two mammal species had gone extinct: grizzly bears and mountain sheep. The former had already been hunted out by the time Yosemite was declared a national park in 1890. William D. Newmark, in "Extinction of Mammal Populations in Western North American National Parks," *Conservation Biology* 9 (1995):512–26, notes recolonization by mountain sheep in 1986 and local extinction of mink and black-tailed jackrabbit in 1972 and 1977, respectively. However, both of those purported disappearances are in question. Grinnell and Storer's (1924) record [as cited in endnote 16] of the black-tailed jackrabbit (*Lepus californicus*) was from the Yosemite region, but not from the park itself. Jim Patton informs me (e-mail January 7, 2008) that the black-tailed jackrabbit was never part of the historic record of Yosemite Park, and Craig Moritz noted (e-mail March 29, 2008) that porcupines are now probably missing from the park, but mink have been sighted. Therefore today the park at most lacks porcupines and minks in respect to what was there in Muir's and Grinnell's time, though even those absences are uncertain.

18. As quoted from: Michelle Nijhuis, "The Ghosts of Yosemite," *High Country News* (October 17, 2005), http://www.hcn.org/servlets/hcn.Article?article_id=15837, accessed October 29, 2007.

19. Chris J. Conroy, James L. Patton, Craig Moritz, et al. "A return to Joseph Grinnell's Yosemite transect: mammal community change after 90 years," published online (2006) at http://www.climatechange.ca.gov/events/2006_conference/presentations/2006-09-15/2006-09-15_CONROY.PDF, accessed October 30, 2007.

20. Craig Moritz, James L. Patton, Chris J. Conroy, Juan L. Parra, Gary C. White, and Steven R. Beissinger, "Impact of a Century of Climate Change on Small Mammal Communities in Yosemite National Park," *Science* 322 (2008):261–4.

21. The list is that of Grinnell and Storer (1924) [as cited in endnote 16], updated to current taxonomy: a mole (*Scapanus latimanus*), six species of shrews (*Sorex monticolis, S. ornatus, S. trowbridgii, S. vagrans, S. lyelli, S. palustris*), six species of mice (*Peromyscus maniculatus, P. boylii, P. truei, P. californicus, Onychomys leucogaster, Reithrodontomys megalotis*), two species of wood rats (*Neotoma cinerea, N. macrotis*), five species of voles (*Microtus montanus, M. californicus, M. longicaudus, Lemmiscus curtatus, Phenacomys intermedius*), three species of pocket gophers (*Thomomys bottae, T. monticola, T. talpoides*), three species of pocket mice (*Perognathus parvus, P. inornatus, Chaetodipus californicus*), two species of kangaroo rats (*Dipodomys heermanni, D. panamintinus*), a kangaroo mouse (*Microdipodops megacephalus*), a jumping mouse (*Zapus princeps*), a porcupine (*Erethizon dorsatum*), a mountain beaver (*Aplodontia rufa*), a marmot (*Marmota flaviventris*), four ground squirrels (*Spermophilus townsendii, S. lateralis, S. beldingi, S. beecheyi*), five species of chipmunk (*Tamias alpinus, T. senex, T. townsendi, T. quadrimaculatus, T. merriami, T. speciosus, T. amoenus*),

a flying squirrel (*Glaucomys sabrinus*), a gray squirrel (*Sciurus griseus*), a chickaree (*Tamiasciurus douglassi*), a beaver (*Castor canadensis*), a pika (*Ochotona princeps*), two species of jackrabbits (*Lepus californicus, L. townsendii*), and three cottontail rabbits (*Sylvilagus audobonni, S. bachmani, S. nuttallii*). Note that not all of these species are from Yosemite National Park in the strict sense—the list is for the entire Yosemite transect, some of which fell in the Yosemite region but outside the park itself.

22. I thank Craig Moritz, Jim Patton, and Chris Conroy for providing the information I report here, and thank them and their colleagues for early access to information recently published in their *Science* paper, full citation in endnote 20.

23. At the Yosemite Valley climate station as reported by Conroy et al. (2006) as cited in endnote 19, and Moritz et al. (2008) as cited in endnote 20. Ideally it would be nice to have the same kind of climate data from the exact elevations at which the animals were changing their ranges, but such data do not exist.

24. Also in this "northern species" category are white-tailed jack rabbits (*Lepus townsendii*) and porcupines (*Erithezon dorsatum*), but the data are too sparse for these two to say much about how they have changed since Grinnell's time.

25. See endnote 23.

26. Kim Bonniwell O'Keefe, *A Multiscale Study of the Ecological and Evolutionary Response of* Spermophilus armatus *to Climate Change* (Stanford, CA: Doctoral Dissertation, Stanford University Department of Biological Sciences, March 2007).

27. Ermines (*Mustela erminea*) may provide yet another example of change that is hard to explain by climate: at face value they appear to have shifted their lower and upper elevational boundaries downward 1,200 meters (4,000 feet) and 600 meters (2,000 feet), respectively. However, it is so difficult to sample them that the meaning of that apparent range shift is hard to interpret—it may simply be a sampling artifact. Interestingly, the ermine range expansion correlates in time with the purported disappearance of mink in the park.

28. The northern species are Trowbridge's shrew (*Sorex trowbridgii*), Douglas's squirrel (*Tamiasciurus douglassi*), and the montane vole (*Microtus montanus*). The species restricted to a narrow elevational band in the California Sierra is the lodgepole chipmunk (*Tamias speciosus*).

29. See endnote 17.

Chapter 7. Disturbance in Yellowstone

1. Crawford S. Holling, "Resilience and stability of ecological systems," *Annual Review of Ecology and Systematics* 4 (1973):1–23.

2. R. Reese, "Greater Yellowstone, the national park and adjacent wildlands," *Montana Geographic Series no. 6, Montana Magazine* (Helena, Montana, 1984).

3. Committee on Ungulate Management in Yellowstone National Park, *Ecological Dynamics on Yellowstone's Northern Range* (Washington, DC: National Research Council, The National Academies Press, 2002), http://www.nap.edu/catalog.php?record_id=10328, accessed November 27, 2007.

4. "Yellowstone Fires," *Morning Edition*, National Public Radio Transcript,

available online at http://www.nationalgeographic.com/radiox/yellowstone/yellow_post_transcript_1.html, accessed November 27, 2007.

5. Studies of the foraging range of raptors and mammalian carnivores, censuses of the modern fauna based on trapping, observations, and historical literature, and isotopic studies on the teeth of small mammals in the fossil deposits that show approximately how far away from the fossil deposit they actually lived all serve to document the fidelity of the fossil deposits in recording the composition of the living community. See: E. A. Hadly, "Influence of late-Holocene climate on northern Rocky Mountain mammals," *Quaternary Research* 46 (1996):298–310; E. A. Hadly, "Fidelity of terrestrial vertebrate fossils to a modern ecosystem," *Palaeogeography, Palaeoclimatology, Palaeoecology* 149 (1999): 389–409; Stephen Porder, Adina Paytan, and Elizabeth A. Hadly, "Mapping the origin of faunal assemblages using strontium isotopes," *Paleobiology* 29 (2003): 197–204.

6. Wood rat middens more than 40,000 years old have been found in the southwestern United States. See J. L. Betancourt, T. R. Van Devender, and P. S. Martin, eds., *Packrat Middens: The Last 40,000 Years of Biotic Change* (Tucson: University of Arizona Press, 1990). Fossil wood rat middens in Porcupine Cave, Colorado, described in Chapter 8, are in excess of 800,000 years old.

7. See endnote 9 in Chapter 5. For the way the Lamar Cave radiocarbon dates were converted to calendar years, see E. A. Hadly (1996) and (1999) as cited in endnote 5 in this chapter.

8. See E. A. Hadly (1996) and (1999) and Porder et al. (2003) as cited in endnote 5 in this chapter.

9. Bruce Barcott, "The Rancher and the Grizzly: A Love Story," *OnEarth Magazine*, National Resource Defense Council (Winter 2007), available online at http://www.nrdc.org/onearth/07win/grizzly1.asp, accessed November 27, 2007.

10. Charissa Ried, Tom Oliff, Paul Schullery, and Roger Anderson (interviewers), "The Rewards of Adventurism: The YS Interview with John Varley," *Yellowstone Science* 14, no. 3 (2006):5–18.

11. Kim Murray Berger and Eric M. Gese, "Does interference competition with wolves limit the distribution and abundance of coyotes?" *Journal of Animal Ecology* 76 (2007):1075–85.

12. Christopher C. Wilmer and Wayne M. Getz, "Gray Wolves as Climate Change Buffers in Yellowstone," *PLoS Biology* 3, no. 4 (2005):e92, 571–76.

13. Hawthorne L. Beyer, Evelyn H. Merrill, Nathan Varley, and Mark S. Boyce, "Willow on Yellowstone's Northern Range: Evidence for a trophic cascade?" *Ecological Applications* 17, no. 6 (2007):1563–71; William J. Ripple and Robert L. Beschta, "Restoring Yellowstone's aspen with wolves," *Biological Conservation* 138 (2007):514–19.

14. A. D. Barnosky, E. A. Hadly, and C. J. Bell, "Mammalian response to global warming on varied temporal scales," *Journal of Mammalogy* 84 (2003): 354–68.

15. Generally, medieval times were characterized by temperatures warmer than those of the few hundred years either before or afterward. The exact beginning

and end of what has become known in scientific literature as the Medieval Warm Period seems to have varied by a few tens of years or more depending on where on Earth a particular climate record comes from, and the climatic conditions that prevailed varied from place to place of course, as climate does today. For a thorough discussion of the Medieval Warm Period and its definition and recognition see E. Jansen, J. Overpeck, K. R. Briffa, J. C. Duplessy, F. Joos, V. Masson-Delmotte, D. Olago, B. Otto-Bliesner, W. R. Peltier, S. Rahmstorf, R. Ramesh, D. Raynaud, D. Rind, O. Solomina, R. Villalba, and D. Zhang, "Palaeoclimate," in *Climate Change 2007: The Physical Science Basis. Contribution of Working Group I to the Fourth Assessment Report of the Intergovernmental Panel on Climate Change*, ed. S. Solomon, D. Qin, M. Manning, Z. Chen, M. Marquis, K. B. Averyt, M. Tignor, and H. L. Miller (Cambridge University Press, 2007).

16. G. A. Meyer, S. G. Wells, R. C. Balling, A. J. Timothy Lull, "Response of alluvial systems to fire and climate change in Yellowstone National Park," *Nature* 357 (1992):147–50; G. A. Meyer and J. L. Pierce, "Climatic controls on fire-induced sediment pulses in Yellowstone National Park and central Idaho: a long-term perspective," *Forest Ecology and Management* 178 (2003):89–104.

17. E. A. Hadly (1996) as cited in endnote 5.

18. Brian J. McGill, Elizabeth A. Hadly, and Brian A. Maurer, "Community inertia of Quaternary small mammal assemblages in North America," *Proceedings of the U.S. National Academy of Sciences* 102 (2005):16701–706.

19. Miranda M. Lim, Zuoxin Wang, Daniel E. Olazábal, Xianghui Ren, Ernest F. Terwilliger, and Larry J. Young, "Enhanced partner preference in a promiscuous species by manipulating the expression of a single gene," *Nature* 429 (2004):754–57.

20. W. E. Grant, N. R. French, and D. M. Swift, "Response of a small mammal community to water and nitrogen treatments in a shortgrass prairie ecosystem," *Journal of Mammalogy* 58 (1977):637–52; D. T. Stalling, "*Microtus ochrogaster*," *Mammalian Species* 355 (1990):1–9.

21. J. A. Gennett, "A late Quaternary pollen sequence from Blacktail Pond, northern Yellowstone Park, U.S.A.," *Palynology* 10 (1986):61–71; C. Whitlock and P. J. Bartlein, "Spatial variations of Holocene climatic change in the Yellowstone region," *Quaternary Research* 39 (1993):231–38.

22. These most-recent prairie vole teeth were not dated directly. Other organic materials in the layer from which they came yielded radiocarbon dates that, when converted to calendar years and interpreted in light of error bars, indicated the layer likely contained materials that could be as old as 300 years or as recent as 80 years.

23. As interpreted from data summarized by IPCC Working Group I, Chapter 6, Figs. 6–10; see endnote 15 in this chapter. A useful summary of temperature change since the Medieval Warm Period is also given at: http://www.globalwarmingart.com/wiki/Image:1000_Year_Temperature_Comparison_png, accessed November 27, 2007. The figure at that Web site was compiled from original data from peer-reviewed publications listed on the site.

24. Judsen E. Bruzgul, Webb Long, and Elizabeth A. Hadly, "Temporal

response of the tiger salamander (*Ambystoma tigrinum*) to 3,000 years of climatic variation," *BMC Ecology* 5 (2005):1–7 doi:10.1186/1472-6785-5-7.

25. The vertebral arch in the paedomorphic individuals is less complete than in the metamorphosed ones, and it is vertebrae with fully fused arches that make up the bulk of the salamander sample in the layers from the Medieval Warm Period in Lamar Cave.

26. Sarah K. McMenamin, Elizabeth A. Hadly, and Christopher K. Wright, "Climatic Change and Wetland Dessication Cause Amphibian Decline in Yellowstone National Park," *Proceedings of the U.S. National Academy of Sciences* 105 (2008): 16988–93.

27. The researchers were not allowed to visit seven of the original 46 ponds because the areas were closed to visitation. Even assuming that amphibians might have been found in all seven of those, there was still at least a 35 percent decrease in the number of ponds that supported amphibians. If none of those unsurveyed ponds held amphibians in 2006–2008, the decrease would be 52 percent.

Chapter 8. Mountain Time in Colorado

1. Terry L. Root and Stephen H. Schneider, "Climate Change: Overview and Implications for Wildlife," pp. 1–56 (quote from p. 2), in Stephen H. Schneider and Terry L. Root, eds., *Wildlife Responses to Climate Change: North American Case Studies* (Washington, DC: Island Press, 2002).

2. On August 3, 1986, Don Rasmussen, his wife Jerry, Kirk Branson, and Zach McGuire broke into a room in Porcupine Cave that had never been seen by humans. From the top of a wood rat midden they picked up a rusty tobacco can, the brand being Velvet Tobacco. Inside the can was a note dated June 14, 1939, signed by Lloyd Marshall and Elvis Conner. Branson later located the retired Marshall, who told of sitting outside the cave, writing the note, stuffing it into the can, and leaving it near the cave entrance. The wood rats apparently had dragged it some 45 meters (150 feet) back into the cave, through cracks and crevices too small for humans, into a room that remained sealed even after the miners discovered the main portion of the cave. See the following for a detailed account of this and other discoveries relating to the history of Porcupine Cave: Geraldine J. Rasmussen, Kirk Branson, and John O. McKelvy, "The Historical Context of Porcupine Cave, American Indians, Spaniards, Government Surveyors, Prospectors, Ranchers, Cavers, and Paleontologists in South Park, Colorado," pp. 39–50 (Chapter 4), in A. D. Barnosky, ed., *Biodiversity Response to Climatic Change in the Middle Pleistocene: The Porcupine Cave Fauna from Colorado* (Berkeley: University of California Press, 2004).

3. The Porcupine Cave excavations were conducted initially by crews from the Carnegie Museum of Natural History, then later by the Denver Museum of Natural History and the University of California Museum of Paleontology. The full history of work at Porcupine Cave, and contributions by most of the scientists involved, can be found in: A. D. Barnosky, ed., *Biodiversity Response to Climatic Change in the Middle Pleistocene: The Porcupine Cave Fauna from Colorado* (Berkeley: University of California Press, 2004).

4. Bell is now an associate professor of geosciences at the University of Texas, Austin. His work on the biochronology of the Porcupine Cave voles was reported in his doctoral dissertation for the University of California-Berkeley Department of Integrative Biology, as well as in several papers in the Porcupine Cave book cited in endnote 3 and in numerous other papers cited therein.

5. In actual practice, local magnetostratigraphies are developed by heating or otherwise demagnetizing rock samples from throughout a thick geologic section (say, a hundred-foot high cliff) in equipment that allows the orientation of the magnetic grains in the rock to be identified, and a plot is made of the pattern of magnetically normal and reversed intervals. If this pattern is distinctive enough, it can be matched to the same pattern of reversed and normal intervals in Global Magnetic Polarity Timescale, which has been calibrated with radioisotopic dates, such as Ar-Ar dates. For more information see *Paleomagnetism: Magnetic Domains to Geologic Terranes* by Robert F. Butler, originally published by Blackwell Scientific Publications in 1992, published online in 1998 at http://www.geo.arizona.edu/Paleomag/book/, accessed December 14, 2007.

6. Victor A. Schmidt, Julio Friedmann, Robert Raynolds, and Fred Luiszer conducted the paleomagnetic analyses on Porcupine Cave specimens. See the following for details: S. Julio Friedmann and Robert G. Raynolds, "Magnetostratigraphic Constraints on the Age of Pleistocene Fossiliferous Strata in Porcupine Cave's DMNH Velvet Room Excavation," pp. 57–63 in Barnosky, ed. (2004) as cited in endnote 3; A. D. Barnosky and Christopher J. Bell, "Age and Correlation of Key Fossil Sites in Porcupine Cave," pp. 64–74 in Barnosky, ed. (2004) as cited in endnote 3.

7. The paleomagicians had collected and analyzed the samples from bottom to top of the Pit sequence and had found that the ones from halfway down all the way to the bottom were magnetically reversed—that is, what is north today was south then. They had also found similarly reversed samples from an excavation in another room of the cave—the Velvet Room, where magnetically normal sediments lay on top of the reversed ones. All the paleomagnetic data taken together indicated that the sediments in the Pit and in the Velvet Room recorded the last time the Earth's magnetic field flipped, about 780,000 years ago—a flip the paleomagicians call the Brunhes-Matuyama boundary.

8. For the first million years of the Pleistocene, glacials cycled into interglacials and back about every 41,000 years. Beginning around one million years ago, the cycles began to lengthen, and by 800,000 years ago, a 100,000-year cycle began to dominate, and the differences between glacials and interglacials became much more dramatic. In that topmost transition in the Pit we seemed to have captured one of the most pronounced global warming events that had taken place since the glacial-interglacial metronome first began its rhythm.

9. With "person-year" defined as one person working 40 hours per week 52 weeks per year.

10. Anthony D. Barnosky, Christopher J. Bell, Steven D. Emslie, H. Thomas Goodwin, Jim I. Mead, Charles A. Repenning, Eric Scott, and Alan B. Shabel, "Exceptional record of mid-Pleistocene vertebrates helps differentiate climatic

from anthropogenic ecosystem perturbations," *Proceedings of the U.S. National Academy of Science* 101 (2004):9297–302.

11. Frederic E. Clements, "Nature and structure of the climax," *The Journal of Ecology* 24 (1936):252–84.

12. Henry A. Gleason, "The individualistic concept of the plant association," *Bulletin of the Torrey Botanical Club* 53 (1926):98–117, p. 117.

13. Brian J. McGill, Elizabeth A. Hadly, and Brian A. Maurer, "Community inertia of Quaternary small mammal assemblages in North America," *Proceedings of the U. S. National Academy of Sciences* 102 (2005):16701–706; John M. Pandolfi and Jeremy B. C. Jackson, "Ecological persistence interrupted in Caribbean coral reefs," *Ecology Letters* 9 (2006):818–26.

14. A. D. Barnosky et al. (2004) as cited in endnote 10. Anthony D. Barnosky and Alan B. Shabel, "Comparison of Mammalian Species Richness and Community Structure in Historic and Mid-Pleistocene Times in the Colorado Rocky Mountains," *Proceedings of the California Academy of Sciences*, ser. 4, 56 (Suppl. I) (2005):50–61.

15. To sort species into size and trophic categories, you simply tally how many species there were of small, medium, and large herbivores, how many small, medium, and large omnivores, and how many small, medium, and large carnivores. In the case of Porcupine Cave, this was done for different time slices: the old interglacial (the brown clay that was under the dust that capped the Pit), the old glacial (as represented by the dry dust cap), the historic part of our present interglacial (before Europeans impacted the landscape), and the present. The historic and present conditions were ascertained from written records.

Chapter 9. Africa on the Edge

1. Paul S. Martin, *Twilight of the Mammoths* (Berkeley: University of California Press, 2005), pp. 11 and 118.

2. Kruger National Park in eastern South Africa is now part of the Great Limpopo Transfrontier Park, which unites Kruger, the Gonarezhou National Park in Zimbabwe, and the Limpopo National Park in Mozambique.

3. Recall that those extinctions, the subject of Chapter 5, killed 88 percent of the megafauna in Australia, 83 percent in South America, 72 percent in North America, and 36 percent in Eurasia, whereas even the most extreme estimate would place the African loss at 18 percent.

4. Alfred L. Roca, Nicholas Georgiadis, Jill Pecon-Slattery, Stephen J. O'Brien, "Genetic Evidence for Two Species of Elephant in Africa," *Science* 293 (2001):1473–77.

5. Charles Siebert, "An Elephant Crackup?" *New York Times* (October 8, 2006), http://www.nytimes.com/2006/10/08/magazine/08elephant.html?%20% 255BAU, accessed February 2, 2007. The information about elephants in this chapter was largely drawn from Siebert's article, which reports on the primary research of psychologist and ecologist Gay Bradshaw.

6. Ibid. Interestingly, putting misbehaving male elephants with mature males that have grown up under more normal elephant circumstances almost immedi-

ately causes the errant younger males to behave, as shown by relocating mature males into Pilanesburg National Park in South Africa. See Rob Slotow, Gus van Dyk, Joyce Poole, and Andre Klocke, "Older bull elephants control young males," *Nature* 408 (2000):425–26.

7. Joseph O. Ogutu and Norman Owen-Smith, "ENSO, rainfall, and temperature influences on extreme population declines among African savanna ungulates," *Ecology Letters* 6 (2003):412–19.

8. The dramatic reduction of roan antelope was probably exacerbated by increased predation by lions, which in turn seems to have been triggered by more lions following zebras into the roan antelope range as the zebras moved in response to drought. See endnote 7.

9. The relevant data for post-2002 have not been published.

10. See the 2007 IPCC report "Summary for Policymakers," in *Climate Change 2007: The Physical Science Basis. Contribution of Working Group I to the Fourth Assessment Report of the Intergovernmental Panel on Climate Change,* ed. S. Solomon, D. Qin, M. Manning, Z. Chen, M. Marquis, K. B. Averyt, M. Tignor, and H. L. Miller (Cambridge University Press, 2007). Available at http://www.ipcc.ch/, accessed April 1, 2008.

11. M. Hulme, R. Doherty, T. Ngara et al., "African climate change: 1900–2100," *Climate Research* 17 (2001):145–68.

12. Barend F. N. Erasmus, Albert S. Van Jaarsveld, Steven L. Chown, Mrigesh Kshyatriya, and Konrad J. Wessels, "Vulnerability of South African animal taxa to climate change," *Global Change Biology* 8 (2002):679–93.

13. Barend F. N. Erasmus et al. (2006) as cited in endnote 12. See pp. 679 (for the quote) and 688 (for the population-growth information).

14. The study included species of primates, carnivores, perissodactyls, artiodactyls, hyracoids, tubulidentates (aardvarks), pholidotes (pangolins or scaly anteaters), lagomorphs (rabbits), macroscelideans (elephant shrews), and rodents. See W. Thuiller, O. Broennimann, G. Hughes, J. R. M. Alkemade, G. F. Midgley, and F. Corsi, "Vulnerability of African Mammals to Anthropogenic Climate Change Under Conservative Land Transformation Assumptions," *Global Change Biology* 12 (2006): 424–40.

Chapter 10. Disappearing Act

1. Edward O. Wilson, *The Diversity of Life* (New York: W. W. Norton and Co., 1992), p. 15.

2. John W. Williams, Stephen T. Jackson, and John E. Kutzbach, "Projected distributions of novel and disappearing climates by 2100 AD," *Proceedings of the U. S. National Academy of Sciences* 104 (2007):5738–42.

3. Eric W. Sanderson, Malanding Jaiteh, Marc A. Levy, Kent H. Redford, Antoinette V. Wannebo, and Gillian Woolmer, "The Human Footprint and the Last of the Wild," *Bioscience* 52 (2002):891–904.

4. Benjamin S. Halpern, Shaun Walbridge, Kimberly A. Selkoe, Carrie V. Kappel, Fiorenza Micheli, Caterina D'Agrosa, John F. Bruno, Kenneth S. Casey, Colin Ebert, Helen E. Fox, Rod Fujita, Dennis Heinemann, Hunter S. Lenihan, Elizabeth M. P. Madin, Matthew T. Perry, Elizabeth R. Selig, Mark Spalding,

Robert Steneck, Reg Watson, "A Global Map of Human Impact on Marine Ecosystems," *Science* 319 (2008):948–52.

5. Rainfall and precipitation from the Puerto Maldonado airport, the nearest climate station to Tambopata, as reported at http://en.allmetsat.com/climate/peru.php?code=84658, accessed February 19, 2008.

6. Luis F. Salazar, Carlos A. Nobre, and Marcos D.Oyama, "Climate change consequences on the biome distribution in tropical South America," *Geophysical Research Letters* 34 (2007):L09708, 6 pp.

7. Neil Adger, Pramod Aggarwal, Shardul Agrawala, Joseph Alcamo, Abdelkader Allali, Oleg Anisimov, Nigel Arnell, Michel Boko, Osvaldo Canziani, Timothy Carter, Gino Casassa, Ulisses Confalonieri, Rex Victor Cruz, Edmundo de Alba Alcaraz, William Easterling, Christopher Field, Andreas Fischlin, B. Blair Fitzharris, Carlos Gay García, Clair Hanson, Hideo Harasawa, Kevin Hennessy, Saleemul Huq, Roger Jones, Lucka Kajfez Bogataj, David Karoly, Richard Klein, Zbigniew Kundzewicz, Murari Lal, Rodel Lasco, Geoff Love, Xianfu Lu, Graciela Magrín, Luis José Mata, Roger McLean, Bettina Menne, Guy Midgley, Nobuo Mimura, Monirul Qader Mirza, José Moreno, Linda Mortsch, Isabelle Niang-Diop, Robert Nicholls, Béla Nováky, Leonard Nurse, Anthony Nyong, Michael Oppenheimer, Jean Palutikof, Martin Parry, Anand Patwardhan, Patricia Romero Lankao, Cynthia Rosenzweig, Stephen Schneider, Serguei Semenov, Joel Smith, John Stone, Jean-Pascal van Ypersele, David Vaughan, Coleen Vogel, Thomas Wilbanks, Poh Poh Wong, Shaohong Wu, and Gary Yohe, "Climate Change 2007: Impacts, Adaptation and Vulnerability," *Working Group II Contribution to the Intergovernmental Panel on Climate Change Fourth Assessment Report: Summary for Policymakers, formally approved at the 8th Session of Working Group II of the IPCC* (Brussels: IPCC Secretariat, April 2007), p. 22. The document can be obtained from: IPCC Secretariat, c/o WMO, 7bis, Avenue de la Paix, C.P. No. 2300, 1211 Geneva 2, Switzerland, or is available online at http://www.ipcc-wg2.org/.

8. The United Nations Framework Convention on Climate Change is an international effort to address the problem of global warming. The Kyoto Protocol is a commitment made by some nations to reduce the output of greenhouse gases following a prescribed series of steps and targets. See http://unfccc.int/essential_background/items/2877.php for details; accessed February 19, 2008.

9. D. A. Randall, R. A. Wood, S. Bony, R. Colman, T. Fichefet, J. Fyfe, V. Kattsov, A. Pitman, J. Shukla, J. Srinivasan, R. J. Stouffer, A. Sumi, and K.E. Taylor, "Climate Models and Their Evaluation," in *Climate Change 2007: The Physical Science Basis. Contribution of Working Group I to the Fourth Assessment Report of the Intergovernmental Panel on Climate Change*, ed. S. Solomon, D. Qin, M. Manning, Z. Chen, M. Marquis, K. B. Averyt, M. Tignor, and H. L. Miller (Cambridge University Press, 2007).

10. According to insurance statistics from http://www.floodsafety.com/national/property/risk/index.htm, accessed February 19, 2008.

11. The IPCC has developed the following conventions to describe probabilities associated with forecasting future events and the outcome of modeling studies. For description of confidence in the major statements in their technical

summaries: Very high confidence—at least a 9 out of 10 chance of being correct. High confidence—about an 8 out of 10 chance. Medium confidence—about a 5 out of 10 chance. Low confidence—about a 2 out of 10 chance. Very low confidence—less than a 1 out of 10 chance. For description of likelihood, which is a probabilistic assessment of some well-defined outcome having occurred or occurring in the future: Virtually certain means >99 percent probability of occurrence. Very likely = 90–99 percent probability. Likely = 66–90 percent probability. About as likely as not = 33–66 percent probability. Unlikely = 10–33 percent probability. Very unlikely = 1–10 percent probability. Exceptionally unlikely means <1 percent probability. From *Working Group II Contribution to the Intergovernmental Panel on Climate Change Fourth Assessment Report: Summary for Policymakers*, p. 21; see full citation in endnote 7.

12. The higher margin of error at smaller spatial scales occurs because climate models average conditions for fairly big areas, like patches of the Earth's surface ranging from one to five degrees of latitude and longitude on a side. The maps produced by the Salazar team had a resolution of two degrees of latitude and longitude—each square on their maps encompasses some 49,000 square kilometers (or 19,000 square miles, an area just a little smaller than the U.S. state of West Virginia). Just because Tambopata falls in a certain square doesn't necessarily mean that it and everything else in that square will change in the same way; it simply means that the overall trend for that patch of real estate will be for savannah to replace rainforest as soils dry out.

13. Dominic Hamilton, "The road to riches, the road to ruin," *www.geographical.co.uk* (September 2006) http://www.nomadom.net/words/pages/interoceanica_peru.pdf, accessed February 19, 2006.

14. P. M. Cox, R. A. Betts, M. Collins, P. P. Harris, C. Huntingford, and C. D. Jones, "Amazonian forest dieback under climate–carbon cycle projections for the 21st century," *Theoretical and Applied Climatology* 78 (2004):137–56.

15. As Williams et al. pointed out, the pattern of highest change in the tropics is different from what commonly is expressed by other studies, which show most temperature change taking place in higher-temperate latitudes. That is because the Williams et al. paper defines change in a way more meaningful to characterizing ecological differences: to assess how much each place would change, they standardized the amount of change predicted by the climate models against the amount of interannual variability that is currently characteristic of each place. There is little interannual variability in the tropics today, so even a small temperature increase makes a huge difference to ecosystems that have evolved within that little-varying climate. The converse is true for high-latitude ecosystems, whose organisms have evolved to withstand high interannual variation, i.e., very cold winters and very hot summers.

16. The Williams team came up with the following projections: by the year 2100, under the B1 scenario, 4–20 percent of the Earth's surface will likely experience disappearing climates, and a largely different 4–20 percent will attain novel climates. Under the A2 scenario, the numbers are worse: 12–39 percent and 10–48 percent, respectively. The range in these numbers comes from differences among the models analyzed—all the models agree that the world will get

warmer in the future, but they differ over the amount of warming. Even in areas where there are no disappearing or novel climates, future climates will still be different from those in the area today.

17. Patrick J. Bartlein, Cathy Whitlock, and Sarah L. Shafer, "Future climate in the Yellowstone National Park Region and its potential impact on vegetation," *Conservation Biology* 11 (1997):782–92.

18. Quotes from pp. 5741 and 5738 in Williams et al. (2007) as cited in endnote 2. See Chapter 14 for discussion of networked reserves and assisted migration.

19. In 1987, the word "biodiversity" cropped up in only two scientific articles. But by 2007, biodiversity was mentioned in more than 21,000 scientific articles and has become common vocabulary in the popular media and in a wide sector of the general public (as counted on the Web of Science database, http://apps.newisiknowledge.com/, accessed January 14, 2008). Interestingly, that's pretty much the same trajectory that the awareness of global warming has followed, first reaching the scientific and policy mainstream in the late 1980s, and now becoming household words. That little fact is probably more than coincidence: both global warming and decline of biodiversity are strongly correlated with growing numbers of people on Earth.

20. Climate influences biodiversity not only through its control of average temperature and precipitation in a given place, but also through its role in causing ecological disturbances, i.e., hitting ecosystems with unusual events. On the short timescale, these are things like big storms; on the long scale, things like the relatively sudden shifts from glacial to interglacial cycles. Disturbance is not necessarily a bad thing, because ecosystems seem to need a certain amount of disturbance to reach maximal biodiversity. But too little disturbance, or too much, and biodiversity falls—it seems that intermediate levels of disturbance promote the most biodiversity.

21. Nahuel Huapi was established in 1903 with a land donation to the Argentine government by Perito Moreno and formed the nucleus for a protected natural area. In 1934, a new law created the Argentine National Park System, and with it the formal designation of Nahuel Huapi as Argentina's first national park.

22. For a complete discussion of all the methods, results, and theory behind this study, see: A. D. Barnosky, E. A. Hadly, B. A. Maurer, and M. I. Christie, "Temperate Terrestrial Vertebrate Faunas in North and South America: Interplay of Ecology, Evolution, and Geography with Biodiversity," *Conservation Biology* 15 (2001):658–74.

23. Doris Soto, Iván Arismendi, Jorge González, José Sanzana, Fernando Jara, Carlos Jara, Erwin Guzman, and Antonio Lara, "Southern Chile, trout and salmon country: invasion patterns and threats for native species," *Revista Chilena de Historia Natural* 79 (2006):97–117.

Chapter 11. Losing the Parts

1. Nancy Knowlton and Jeremy B. C. Jackson, "Shifting baselines, local impacts, and global change on coral reefs," *PLoS Biology* 6, issue 2 (2008): 215–20, e54. doi:10.1371/journal. pbio.0060054.

2. See for example: Martin Bashir, "Individual Genetic Risk Factors

Delivered Via Internet," *ABC News* (February 13, 2008), http://abcnews.go. com/ Health/story?id=4284602&page=1, accessed February 24, 2008.

3. Quote from 23andme website, https://www.23andme.com/, accessed February 24, 2008.

4. Quote from the verbatim transcript of the law that enacted establishment of Yellowstone, see: http://www.usnews.com/usnews/documents/docpages/document_page45.htm, accessed February 24, 2008.

5. John Varley, "Saving the parts," *Yellowstone Science* 1, no. 4 (1993):13–16.

6. Thomas D. Brock, "The Value of Basic Research: Discovery of *Thermus aquaticus* and Other Extreme Thermophiles," *Genetics* 146 (1997):1207–10.

7. Thomas D. Brock and Hudson Freeze, "*Thermus aquaticus* gen. n. and sp. n., a Nonsporulating Extreme Thermophile," *Journal of Bacteriology* 98 (1969): 289–97.

8. D. Edgar, A. Chien, and J. Trela, "Purification and characterization of a DNA polymerase from an extreme thermophile, *Thermus aquaticus*," Abstracts, *Annual Meeting, American Society Microbiologists* 75 (1975):151; S. Sata, C. A. Hutchison, and J. I. Harris, "A thermostable sequence-specific end nuclease from *Thermus aquaticus*," *Proceedings of the U. S. National Academy of Sciences* 74 (1977):542–46; J. G. Zeikus and T. D. Brock, "Protein synthesis at high temperatures: aminoacylation of tRNA," *Biochimica Biophysica Acta* 228 (1971):736–45; J. G. Zeikus, M. M. Taylor, and T. D. Brock, "Thermal stability of ribosomes and RNA from *Thermus aquaticus*," *Biochimica Biophysica Acta* 204 (1970):512–20.

9. Ernst and Young Economics Consulting and Quantitative Analysis, "The Economic Contributions of the Biotechnology Industry to the U. S. Economy," *Prepared for the Biotechnology Industry Organization* (May 2000), http://www. bio.org/speeches/pubs/ernstyoung.pdf, accessed February 24, 2008.

10. Page 15 in John Varley (1993) as cited in endnote 5.

11. Science and Development Network, "The Value of Biodiversity," published online at http://www.scidev.net/ms/biofacts/index.cfm?pageid=423, accessed February 25, 2008.

12. World fisheries statistics from the National Oceanic and Atmospheric Administration published online at http://www.st.nmfs.noaa.gov/st1/fus/fus04/ 04_world2004.pdf, accessed February 25, 2008.

13. Taylor H. Ricketts, Gretchen C. Daily, Paul R. Ehrlich, and Charles D. Michener, "Economic value of tropical forest to coffee production," *Proceedings of the U. S. National Academy of Sciences* 101 (2004):12579–82.

14. Will R. Turner, Katrina Brandon, Thomas M. Brooks, Robert Costanza, Gustavo A. B. da Fonsea, and Rosimeiry Portela, "Global Conservation of Biodiversity and Ecosystem Services," *Bioscience* 57 (2007):868–73.

15. For innovative ways people are profiting from ecosystem services, see a book by Gretchen C. Daily and Katherine Ellison, *The New Economy of Nature: The Quest to Make Conservation Profitable* (Washington, DC: Island Press, 2002).

16. R. Costanza, R. d'Arge, R. de Groot, S. Farber, M. Grasso, B. Hannon, K. Limburg, S. Naeem, R. V. O'Neill, J. Paruelo, R. G. Raskin, P. Sutton, and M.

van den Belt, "The values of the world's ecosystem services and natural capital," *Nature* 387 (1997):253–60.

17. The World Fact Book, published online at https://www.cia.gov/library/publications/the-world-factbook/print/xx.html, accessed March 31, 2008.

18. For a good discussion of the many reasons biodiversity is important, see Yvonne Baskin, *The Work of Nature: How the Diversity of Life Sustains Us* (Washington, DC: Island Press, 1997).

19. Norman Owen-Smith, "Pleistocene Extinctions: The Pivotal Role of Megaherbivores," *Paleobiology* 13 (1987):351–62.

20. Mary E. Power, David Tilman, James A. Estes, Bruce A. Menge, William J. Bond, L. Scott Mills, Gretchen Daily, Juan Carlos Castilla, Jane Lubchenco, and Robert T. Paine, "Challenges in the Quest for Keystones," *BioScience* 46 (1996):609–20; Ana D. Davidson and David C. Lightfoot, "Keystone rodent interactions: prairie dogs and kangaroo rats structure the biotic composition of a desertified grassland," *Ecography* 29 (2006):755–65.

21. David J. Mattson and Troy Merrill, "Extirpations of grizzly bears in the contiguous United States, 1850–2000," *Conservation Biology* 16 (2002):1123–36.

22. Ken Gibson, "Mountain Pine Beetle Conditions in Whitebark Pine Stands in the Greater Yellowstone Ecosystem, 2006," *USDA Forest Health Protection Numbered Report* 06-03 (February 2006), http://www.fs.fed.us/r1-r4/spf/fhp/publications/bystate/R1Pub06-03_MPB_Yellowstone_gibson.pdf, accessed February 26, 2008.

23. Jesse A. Logan, "Climate Change Induced Invasions by Native and Exotic Pests," USDA Forest Service, published online at http://www.usu.edu/beetle/documents/Logan06_Abstract.pdf, accessed February 26, 2008. Document available from USDA Forest Service, Rocky Mountain Research Station, 860 N 1200 E, Logan, UT 84321.

24. Laura Koteen, "Climate Change, Whitebark Pine, and Grizzly Bears in the Greater Yellowstone Ecosystem," in *Wildlife Responses to Climate Change: North American Case Studies*, ed. Stephen H. Schneider and Terry L. Root (Washington, DC: Island Press, 2002), pp. 343–411.

25. "Threats," *Whitebark Pine Ecosystem Foundation*, published online at http://www.whitebarkfound.org/threats.html, accessed February 25, 2008; Michelle Nijhuis, "Global Warming's Unlikely Harbingers," *High Country News* (July 19, 2004), http://www.hcn.org/servlets/hcn.PrintableArticle?article_id=14853, accessed February 25, 2006; Jim Robbins, "At Yellowstone, an Ecosystem Teetering on a Tree," *New York Times* (February 8, 2000), http://query.nytimes.com/gst/fullpage.html?res=9A03E7DC173EF93BA35751C0A9669C8B63, accessed February 25, 2008.

26. For more explanation of these and other examples, see Chapter 2; for details see M. S. Scheffer and S. R. Carpenter, "Catastrophic regime shifts in ecosystems: linking theory to observation," *Trends in Ecology and Evolution* 18 (2003):648–56; and M. S. Scheffer, M. S. Carpenter, J. A. Foley, C. Folkes, and B. Walker, "Catastrophic regime shifts in ecosystems," *Nature* 413 (2001):591–96.

27. N. Knowlton and J. B. C. Jackson, as cited in endnote 1.

28. P. R. Ehrlich and A. H. Ehrlich, *Extinction: The Causes and Consequences of the Disappearance of Species* (New York: Random House, 1981).

29. Kris H. Johnson, Kristiina A. Vogt, Heidi Clark, Oswald Schmitz, and Daniel Vogt, "Biodiversity and the productivity and stability of ecosystems," *Trends in Ecology and Evolution* 11 (1996):372–76, p. 373.

30. M. W. Schwartz, C. A. Brigham, J. D. Hoeksema, K. G. Lyons, M. H. Mills, P. J. van Mantgem, "Linking biodiversity to ecosystem function: implications for conservation ecology," *Oecologia* 122 (2000):297–305; Ricard V. Sole and José M. Montoya, "Complexity and fragility in ecological networks," *Proceedings of the Royal Society of London* B 268 (2001):2039–45.

31. Andrew Dobson, David Lodge, Jackie Alder, Graeme S. Cumming, Juan Keymer, Jacquie McGlade, Hal Mooney, James A. Rusak, Osvaldo Sala, Volkmar Wolters, Diana Wall, Rachel Winfree, and Marguerite A. Xenopoulos, "Habitat loss, trophic collapse, and the decline of ecosystem services," *Ecology* 8 (2006): 1915–24.

32. Magnifying the problem is that no species exists in a vacuum—every species that goes extinct will also take with it the species that depend on it. That point was made cogently by a study that estimated the number of "affiliate species" that were projected to go extinct if their host species did. The affiliate species studied were those that have a clear dependence on their hosts: species like butterflies and beetles that depend on certain plants, plants that depend on certain pollinators, parasites that depend on certain birds or mammals, and so on. If all of the 9,600 endangered species that were mentioned in that study were to go extinct, the researchers estimated the collateral damage in the form of extinct affiliates would be an additional 6,300 species. See Lian Pin Koh, Robert R. Dunn, Navjot S. Sodhi, Robert K. Colwell, Heather C. Proctor, and Vincent S. Smith, "Species Coextinctions and the Biodiversity Crisis," *Science* 305 (2004):1632–34.

33. Peter J. Mayhew, Gareth B. Jenkins, and Timothy G. Benton, "A long-term association between global temperature and biodiversity, origination, and extinction in the fossil record," *Proceedings of the Royal Society* B 275 (2008): 47–53. doi:10.1098/rspb.2007.1302.

34. Families are a rank in the Linnaean taxonomic hierarchy, which includes Phylum, Class, Order, Family, Genus, Species. You belong to the genus *Homo*, which is in the family Hominidae, which is in the order Primates, in the class Mammalia. Other examples of mammal families are dogs (Canidae), cats (Felidae), and mice (Muridae).

35. D. L. Royer, "CO_2-forced climate thresholds during the Phanerozoic," *Geochimica et Cosmochimica Acta* 70 (2006):5665–75.

Chapter 12. Skeleton Crew

1. Quote from F373 (page sequence 150) in C. R. Darwin, *On the origin of species by means of natural selection, or the preservation of favoured races in the strug-*

gle for life (London: John Murray [1st edition, 1st issue],1859), online edition, http://darwin-online.org.uk/content/search-results?sort=date-ascending& pageno=10&freetext=climate&pagesize=50, accessed February 29, 2008.

2. As quoted from an article by Cal Fussman, "It happened in Jersey," *Esquire Magazine* (August 2005). Thanks to Kevin Padian for calling my attention to this quote—Kevin has it at the bottom of most of the e-mails he sends.

3. See endnote 34, Chapter 11.

4. The story of the Burgess Shale and its fossils was popularized by Stephen Jay Gould, *Wonderful Life* (New York: W. W. Norton and Co., 1989). See the following Web site for more information about Cambrian time: http://www. ucmp.berkeley.edu/cambrian/camb.html, accessed March 6, 2008.

5. In Darwin's time, evolution was a theory about how life might have arisen; now it is a fact as scientists define the word: "an observation that has been repeatedly confirmed." This definition is from D. Kennedy, et al., *Teaching About Evolution and The Nature Of Science* (Washington, DC: National Academy Press, 1998). See also A. D. Barnosky and B. P. Kraatz, "The role of climatic change in the evolution of mammals," *Bioscience* 57 (2007):523–32. Both of these publications include bibliographies which give the interested reader a gateway into the vast literature on this topic.

6. See endnote 4.

7. See the Web site listed in endnote 4.

8. Gene flow is how genotypes are traded among populations. The way gene pools can change by chance alone is called random drift, and the effectiveness of random drift is strongly influenced by gene flow—too much gene flow, and you don't get much random drift. Random drift is directly related to population size. Basically, if you have just a few interbreeding individuals (a small population), you have a small gene pool. For statistical reasons, just by chance you can get random changes faster in small gene pools, and it is easier for those changes (or any others—for example, those driven by selection) to become permanently fixed in the population, than is the case for large gene pools (because, basically, a newly arriving genotype will not get swamped by the ones already there). Random drift can cause evolutionary change in small populations, but if genetic variation starts out low, there is only so much that random drift can accomplish.

9. "Mistakes" in replicating DNA include things like deletions of base pairs from the original DNA sequence, or insertions of extra base pairs; transitions and transversions, which swap the mates in base pairs; and inversions, where whole pieces of the genome get flipped around.

10. The fossil record suggests that most species persist relatively unchanged (they exhibit stasis) for long periods of time after suddenly arising ("suddenly," that is, in geologic time, which can still be very long in terms of how people normally think about time); Stephen Gould and Niles Eldredge dubbed this phenomenon punctuated equilibrium. "Sudden" is a relative term, technically defined by 1 percent of the time the species exhibits stasis, as explained by Stephen Jay Gould; see "The meaning of punctuated equilibrium and its role in

validating a hierarchical approach to macroevolution," in *Perspectives on Evolution*, ed. R. Milkman (Sunderland, MA: Sinauer, 1982). Since most species persist for upward of a million years (for mammals, the mean persistence of a species is between 1.7 and 2.5 million years; for example, see endnote 6 in Chapter 2), sudden or "geologically instantaneous" in the context of punctuated equilibrium means a minimum of around 20,000 years. In fact, limits imposed by mutation rates suggest that the process of speciation is usually even slower.

11. Regarding speciation of birds, see J. C. Avise, D. Walker, and G. C. Johns, "Speciation durations and Pleistocene effects on vertebrate phylogeography," *Proceedings of the Royal Society of London* B 265 (1998):1707–12.

12. Regarding fossil evidence of speciation rates, see A. D. Barnosky, "Effects of Quaternary climatic change on speciation in mammals," *Journal of Mammalian Evolution* 12 (2005):247–64; A. D. Barnosky, E. A. Hadly, and C. J. Bell, "Mammalian response to global warming on varied temporal scales," *Journal of Mammalogy* 84 (2003):354–68.

13. Barnosky, "Effects of Quaternary climatic change on speciation in mammals," as cited in endnote 12.

14. If you think of the spectrum of variation as a bell-shaped curve, with the average value for a trait (say, the average height of students in the classroom) being the top of the bell, and the extreme values being the left and right edges of the bell (short people the left edge, tall people the right), selection tends to trim out certain parts of the bell. It can trim one side, both sides, or the middle. Trimming the left side, for example, would shift the mean value of the trait to the right. Trimming the middle would tend to make two new bell-shaped curves, one shifted to the left of the original mean, the other to the right. How the trimming occurs depends on exactly what the selective force is. For example, if cold winters are selecting for large bodies in mammals (because large bodies retain heat better), then animals with smaller bodies are "trimmed" off the left side of the bell-shaped curve and the average body size in the population shifts to the right (toward bigger sizes).

15. W. E. Bradshaw and C. M. Holzapfel, "Genetic response to rapid climate change: it's seasonal timing that matters," *Molecular Ecology* 17 (2008):157–66.

16. Denis Réale, Andrew G. McAdam, Stan Boutin, and Dominique Berteaux, "Genetic and Plastic Responses of a Northern Mammal to Climate Change," *Proceedings: Biological Sciences* 270, no. 1515 (2003):591–96.

17. After a hundred thousand years or so, DNA becomes so degraded that obtaining sufficiently long strands to replicate is virtually impossible, even under the best of preservational circumstances. So far there has been little, if any, success in extracting DNA from specimens older than a few tens of thousands of years, and that success generally has been from fossils frozen in permafrost or otherwise exceptionally preserved in dry, cool caves.

18. E. A. Hadly, M. H. Kohn, J. A. Leonard, and R. K. Wayne, "A genetic record of population isolation in pocket gophers during Holocene climatic change," *Proceedings of the U. S. National Academy of Sciences* 95 (1998):6893–96.

19. E. A. Hadly, U. Ramakrishnan, Y. L. Chan, M. van Tuinen, K. O'Keefe,

P. Spaeth, C. J. Conroy, "Genetic response to climatic change: Insights from ancient DNA and phylochronology," *PLoS Biology* 2, no. 10 (2004):e290.

20. Thorsten B. H. Reusch, Anneli Ehlers, August Hämmerli, and Boris Worm, "Ecosystem recovery after climatic extremes enhanced by genotypic diversity," *Proceedings of the U.S. National Academy of Science* 102 (2005): 2826–31; Jennifer B. Hughes, Gretchen C. Daily, Paul R. Ehrlich, "Population Diversity: Its Extent and Extinction," *Science* 278 (1997):689–92.

21. See http://nationalzoo.si.edu/Animals/AfricanSavanna/fact-cheetah.cfm, accessed March 10, 2008.

22. A. R. Hoelzel, J. Halley, S. J. O'Brien, C. Campagna, T. Ambom, B. Le Boeuf, K. Rails, and G. A. Dover, "Elephant Seal Genetic Variation and the Use of Simulation Models to Investigate Historical Population Bottlenecks," *Journal of Heredity* 84 (1993):443–49.

23. Eric Post, Nils Christian Stenseth, Rolf Langvatn, and Jean-Marc Fromentin, "Global climate change and phenotypic variation among red deer cohorts," *Proceedings of the Royal Society of London* B 264 (1997):1317–24.

24. Elizabeth A. Hadly, "Evolutionary and ecological response of pocket gophers (*Thomomys talpoides*) to late-Holocene climatic change," *Biological Journal of the Linnean Society* 60 (1997):277–96.

25. Francisco Pulido and Peter Berthold, "Microevolutionary response to climatic change," *Advances in Ecological Research* 35 (2004):151–83.

26. David T. Booth, "Influence of Incubation Temperature on Hatchling Phenotype in Reptiles," *Physiological and Biochemical Zoology* 79 (2006):274–81; N. Mrosovsky, Sally R. Hopkins-Murphy, James I. Richardson, "Sex Ratio of Sea Turtles: Seasonal Changes," *Science* 225 (1984):739–41.

27. Elizabeth P. Lacey and David Herr, "Phenotypic plasticity, parental effects, and parental care in plants? I. An examination of spike reflectance in *Plantago lanceolata* (Plantaginaceae)," *American Journal of Botany* 92 (2005):920–30.

28. Julie R. Etterson, "Evolutionary potential of *Chamaecrista fasciculata* in relation to climate change. II. Genetic architecture of three populations reciprocally planted along an environmental gradient in the Great Plains," *Evolution* 58 (2004):1459–71; Julie R. Etterson and Ruth G. Shaw, "Constraint to adaptive evolution in response to global warming," *Science* 294 (2001):151–54.

29. Joan Balanyá, Josep M. Oller, Raymond B. Huey, George W. Gilchrist, and Luis Serra, "Global genetic change tracks global climate warming in *Drosophila*," *Science* 313 (2006):1773–75; and Bradshaw and Holzapfel (see endnote 15).

30. David Jablonski, "Lessons from the past, evolutionary impacts of mass extinctions," *Proceedings of the U.S. National Academy of Sciences* 98 (2001):5393–98; David Jablonski, "Survival without recovery after mass extinctions," *Proceedings of the U. S. National Academy of Sciences* 99 (2002):8139–44.

31. David Jablonski and David M. Raup, "Selectivity of end-Cretaceous marine bivalve extinctions," *Science* 268 (1995):389–91.

32. James W. Kirchner and Anne Weil, "Delayed biological recovery from extinctions throughout the fossil record," *Nature* 404 (2000):177–80.

Chapter 13. Bad Company

1. Brian Maurer, "Relating human population growth to the loss of biodiversity," *Biodiversity Letters* 3 (1996):1–5.

2. Quote from F20 (page sequence 298), C. R. Darwin, *Journal of researches into the natural history and geology of the countries visited during the voyage of H.M.S. Beagle round the world, under the command of Capt. Fitz Roy R.N.* (London: John Murray, 1860); online version, http://darwin-online.org.uk/content/search-results? sort=date-ascending&pageno=2&freetext=Osorno&pagesize=50, accessed February 29, 2008.

3. Tom D. Dillehay, *Monte Verde, A Late Pleistocene Settlement in Chile, Volume 2: The Archaeological Context and Interpretation* (Washington, DC, and London: Smithsonian Institution Press, 1997); Tom D. Dillehay, C. Ramírez, M. Pino, M. B. Collins, J. Rossen, J. D. Pino-Navarro, "Monte Verde: Seaweed, Food, Medicine, and the Peopling of South America," *Science* 320 (2008): 784–86.

4. As an example of whole landscapes being transformed by introduced species, when we drove from Puerto Montt toward Monte Verde on a spring day the scotch broom outlined every roadside and carpeted wide swaths of river valleys bright yellow. Scotch broom (*Cytisus scoparius*) is a shrub of the pea family that was native to central and southern Europe. Immigrants brought it as a little piece of home not only to Chile, but also to India, Iran, Australia, New Zealand, South Africa, and North America (where it is listed as a noxious weed). Darwin, two hundred and fifty years ago, was already commenting on how thistles that came in with the Spaniards had transformed the South American landscape in Argentina (see The Complete Work of Charles Darwin Online, EHBeagleDiary [pp. 380–401], Charles Robert Darwin 1831.00.00—1836.00.00, online version, http://darwin-online.org.uk/content/search-results?freetext=thistle, accessed March 3, 2008). In *A Plague of Rats and Rubber Vines: The Growing Threat of Species Invasions* (Washington, DC: Island Press, 2002), Yvonne Baskin summed up the additional changes visible today: "Darwin would find all the world's temperate grasslands, from South America and Australia to western North America, utterly transformed by invasive plants. If he were to return to the Galapagos, he would find landscapes denuded by goats and pigs and choked with guava and quinine trees and blackberry thickets, with new pests and pathogens arriving continually to threaten the well-being of the giant tortoises, iguanas, finches, and other unique living things that set him to pondering the origins of species" (p. 41).

5. With regard to the harm caused by non-native species, the introduction of new predators, herbivores, or plants that outcompete natives is not a small problem: invasive species contribute to dwindling numbers in about 20 percent of all endangered animals, as well as being a major extinction threat to plants (Yvonne Baskin, p. 79; see full citation in endnote 4). Economically the toll of invasive species is staggering: $137 billion per year in the United States, $7 billion in South Africa, $12 billion in the United Kingdom, $13 billion in Australia, $50 billion in Brazil, and $116 billion in India (Yvonne Baskin, p. 51). See also Jen-

nifer Molnar, Rebecca L. Gambos, Carmen Ravenga, and Mark D. Spalding, "Assessing the global threat of invasive species to marine biodiversity," *Frontiers in Ecology and the Environment* 6 (2008):doi 10.1890/070064.

6. That salmon, like other introduced species, inevitably escape and go wild is well documented. In Alaska, where there is a strict ban on salmon farms, Atlantic salmon that escaped from farms in Canada and Washington State have been turning up in fishermen's nets and establishing themselves in Alaska's freshwater streams ("Escaped Farmed Salmon Find Home in Alaska," *Arctic Science Journeys Radio Script* [2004], http://seagrant.uaf.edu/news/04ASJ/08.27.04 salmon-escape.html, accessed March 2, 2008). In Puerto Montt's Lago Llanquihue, which hosts 33 percent of Chile's salmon and trout smolt farms (the salmon must be born in freshwater before being moved to Chiloé's feeding pens in the ocean), salmon and trout are what sportfishermen catch (I. Arismendi and L. Nahuelhual, "Non-native Salmon and Trout Recreational Fishing in Lake Llanquihue, Southern Chile: Economic Benefits and Management Implications," *Reviews in Fisheries Science* 15 [2007]:311–25). Throughout southern Patagonia, Chinook salmon (a northern-hemisphere Pacific species also introduced for salmon farming and sport fishery) are now spreading through rivers that drain into the Atlantic on the Argentina side and the southern-hemisphere Pacific on the Chile side, displacing fish that were there before them, which also are non-native, the result of earlier sportfishing introductions (Cristián Correa and Mart R. Gross, "Chinook salmon invade southern South America," *Biological Invasions* (2007):doi 10.1007/s10530-007-9157-2).

7. Benjamin Witte, "Marine Harvest Feels Ill Effects of Chile Salmon Disease," *The Patagonia Times* (February 19, 2008), http://www.patagoniatimes. cl/content/view/403/1/, accessed March 1, 2008; Benjamin Witte, "Chile Salmon Strike Far From Over," *The Patagonia Times* (February 18, 2008), http://www.patagoniatimes.cl/content/view/401/1/, accessed March 1, 2008; Steve Anderson and Julia Thompson, "Chile Salmon Strike Quashed," *The Santiago Times* (January 25, 2008), http://www.santiagotimes.cl/santiagotimes/news/ business-news/salmon-leader-puchi-concerned-that-more-labor-agitation-is-on-the-way.html, accessed March 1, 2008; Alexei Barrionuevo, "Salmon Virus Indicts Chile's Fishing Methods," *New York Times* (March 27, 2008), http:// www.nytimes.com/2008/03/27/world/americas/27salmon.html?_r=1&ref=science&pagewanted=print, accessed March 27, 2008.

8. ISA Info Bullets, Livestock Extension Office, University of Maine, Orono, published online at http://www.umaine.edu/livestock/Publications/isa.htm, accessed March 1, 2008.

9. BC Briefing Note, "Sea Lice and Salmon," *Coastal Alliance for Aquaculture Reform* (October 2005), published online at http://64.233.169.104/search?q= cache:d2nlEj7j8fgJ:www.watershed-watch.org/publications/files/SeaLice_Brief-ingNote_Oct2005.pdf+sea+lice+ISA&hl=en&ct=clnk&cd=2&client=safari, accessed March 1, 2008.

10. "Timeline of Salmon Aquaculture," *Seaweb*, published online at http://

www.seaweb.org/resources/aquaculturecenter/documents/Salmon_Timeline.pdf, accessed March 1, 2008.

11. Benjamin Witte, "Second Major Salmon Company Admits Chile ISA Problems," *Santiago Times* (November 22, 2007), http://www.santiagotimes.cl/santiagotimes/index2.php?option=com_content&task=view&id=12319&pop=1&page=0&Itemid=1, accessed February 29, 2008.

12. Ibid.

13. Patagonia Times Staff, "Salmon Disease Detected in Chile's Aysén Region," *Patagonia Times* (December 21, 2007), http://www.santiagotimes.cl/santiagotimes/2007122012587/news/business-news/salmon-disease-detected-in-chile-s-aysen-region.html, accessed May 20, 2008.

14. M. McManus, N. Schneeberger, R. Reardon, and G. Mason, "Gypsy Moth," *U.S. Department of Agriculture Forest Service Forest Insect and Disease Leaflet 162* (August, 1992), published online at http://www.na.fs.fed.us/spfo/pubs/fidls/gypsymoth/gypsy.htm, accessed March 2, 2008.

15. Ibid., endnote 24 in Chapter 11.

16. As Yvonne Baskin put it (pg. 6; see full citation in endnote 4), in summarizing years of study by many scientists who work on the ecology of invasive species, "unique, rare, and localized species have been replaced by a cosmopolitan set of species that can be found the world over: eucalyptus and Monterey pines, brown trout and mosquito fish, starlings and bulbuls, Medflies and gypsy moths, black rats and feral goats, lantana and water hyacinth."

17. The new species that tend to take over ecosystems are the ones that are most effective at grabbing ecological energy fast, which by definition are "weeds." Which explains the intimate connection between habitat disruption and invasive species like knapweed, cheatgrass, and bindweed in overgrazed pastures in the American West, and tamarisk along the rivers and streams there. Those weedy energy grabbers have reproductive strategies that establish them quickly in newly disturbed ground, which means they proliferate like crazy, and thereby co-opt a large proportion of the available ecological energy from the natives. The same can hold true for certain animals, like rats.

18. P. M. Vitousek, P. R. Ehrlich, A. H. Ehrlich, and P. A. Matson, "Human appropriation of the products of photosynthesis," *Bioscience* 36 (1986):368–73; P. M. Vitousek, H. A. Mooney, J. Lubchenco, and J. M. Melillo, "Human domination of earth's ecosystems," *Science* (1997) 277:494–99. See also C. N. McDaniel and D. N. Borton, "Increased Human Energy Use Causes Biological Diversity Loss and Undermines Prospects for Sustainability," *Bioscience* 52 (2002), 929–36.

19. Technically, NPP is "the net flux of carbon from the atmosphere into green plants per unit of time" (Distributed Active Archive Center for Biogeochemical Dynamics, "Net Primary Productivity Methods," *Oak Ridge National Laboratory*, published online at http://daac.ornl.gov/NPP/html_docs/npp_est.html, accessed February 28, 2007). Practically, it is calculated by measuring or estimating the rate of formation of new organic matter per unit of Earth's surface

per unit of time, reported either as calories per square meter per year (a measure of energy) or, more typically in global-scale studies, as petagrams of biomass (i.e., organic matter) per area (a measure of weight).

20. The most comprehensive examinations of how global warming will affect primary productivity used eleven different models to examine what would happen under the IPCC A2 scenario (see Chapter 10 for explanation of the scenarios), as summarized in: P. Friedlingstein, P. Cox, R. Betts, L. Bopp, W. Von Bloh, V. Brovkin, P. Cadule, S. Doney, M. Eby, I. Fung, G. Bala, J. John, C. Jones, F. Joos, T. Kato, M. Kawamiya, W. Knorr, K. Lindsay, H. D. Matthews, T. Raddatz, P. Rayner, C. Reick, E. Roeckner, K.-G. Schnitzler, R. Schnur, K. Strassmann, A. J. Weaver, C. Yoshikawa, and N. Zeng, "Climate-carbon cycle feedback analysis: results from the (CMIP)-M-4 model intercomparison," *Journal of Climate* 19 (2006):3337–53; and Yiqi Luo, "Terrestrial Carbon-Cycle Feedback to Climate Warming," *Annual Review of Ecology Evolution and Systematics* 38 (2007): 683–712. Two models showed very minor increases in NPP by 2100, five models showed little change from the present, and four models showed large decreases in NPP. Estimating how NPP will change with global warming is sensitive to many different assumptions; thus it is no surprise that the eleven different models used to evaluate potential changes produced widely varying answers. They all agree on one thing though: NPP will not be substantially increasing with global warming.

21. See endnote 18.

22. See Figure 4.5, IPCC Special Report on Emissions Scenarios, authored by Nebojsa Nakicenovic, Joseph Alcamo, Gerald Davis, Bert de Vries, Joergen Fenhann, Stuart Gaffin, Kenneth Gregory, Arnulf Grübler, Tae Yong Jung, Tom Kram, Emilio Lebre La Rovere, Laurie Michaelis, Shunsuke Mori, Tsuneyuki Morita, William Pepper, Hugh Pitcher, Lynn Price, Keywan Riahi, Alexander Roehrl, Hans-Holger Rogner, Alexei Sankovski, Michael Schlesinger, Priyadarshi Shukla, Steven Smith, Robert Swart, Sascha van Rooijen, Nadejda Victor, and Zhou Dadi, published online at http://www.grida.no/climate/ipcc/emission/099.htm, accessed February 28, 2008.

23. Jared Diamond, *Collapse: How Societies Choose to Fail or Succeed* (New York: Viking Press, 2005).

24. A. D. Barnosky, "Megafauna biomass tradeoff as a driver of Quaternary and future extinctions," *Proceedings of the U. S. National Academy of Science* 105, supplement 1 (2008):115–48, for details of the biomass tradeoff discussion presented here. The salient points are as follows. Estimates of human population size going back hundreds of thousands of years can be obtained from combining information from the archaeological record with population-growth calculations constrained by how many people are on Earth today, and how long our species and close ancestors have been on Earth. Those estimates suggest that population sizes of humans remained low from the time *Homo sapiens* first appeared, up to somewhere between 50,000 and 100,000 years ago. In that interval, the trajectory of the line graphing the population growth begins to steepen. By 30,000 years ago, the line is really beginning to shoot upward, and by 10,000 years ago,

it is skyrocketing. It is possible to multiply the number of bodies implied by those estimates by the average weight of a human and come up with another graph, this one of human biomass through time.

The second part of the thought exercise is to estimate the weight of all those 178 species of megafauna that went extinct during the interval that human population sizes were dramatically increasing. That number is called the nonhuman biomass. It's necessarily a rough number, because we don't know exactly how many animals there were, or the exact weight of each animal. Nevertheless, we can estimate the average weight of each animal by using equations that relate parts of a fossilized skeleton to the live weight of a whole animal, as determined from live animals that we can measure and weigh. We can also estimate how many animals there were, at least roughly, because it turns out that there are other equations relating the size of an animal to how many of those animals occupy a square kilometer, and to the percentage of a continent their geographic range typically covers. We multiply estimated weight times estimated animals per square kilometer times estimated total square kilometers of geographic range for each species, add up the weights for all of them, and get a total biomass for the megafauna that went extinct and the megafauna that survived. Put together the biomass numbers for humans (which are themselves a megafauna species, because an average adult person weighs more than 44 kilograms, or about 100 pounds), the biomass numbers for extinct megafuana, and the biomass numbers for megafauna still on Earth, including the domestic animals that support humans, and you can then chart total megafauna biomass through time. The line that tracks megafauna biomass through time is straight and level at first, showing least 100,000 years of more or less constant biomass. Then it takes a precipitous downward trajectory that looks like a cliff as the megafauna biomass crashed around 11,500 yeas ago; a gradual buildup to pre-crash levels takes more than 9,000 years. Then, beginning with the onset of the industrial revolution, the line suddenly skyrockets way above the pre-crash "normal" biomass level.

25. E. Galoppini, "Artificial Photosynthesis / Alternative Energy Sources," *Eighteenth Annual U. S. Kavli Frontiers of Science Symposium, National Academy of Sciences* (Irvine, CA: November 2–4, 2006).

Chapter 14. Geography of Hope

1. The original context in which Margaret Mead made this famous quote is lost to history, but is believed to have been "through a newspaper report of something said spontaneously and informally," as explained on The Institute of Intercultural Studies Web page, http://www.interculturalstudies.org/faq.html#quote, accessed October 8, 2008. Use of the quote here is courtesy of The Institute for Intercultural Studies, Inc., New York.

2. Wallace Stegner, "Wilderness Letter" (December 3, 1960), published online by the Wilderness Society, http://www.wilderness.org/OurIssues/Wilderness/wildernessletter.cfm, accessed March 18, 2008.

3. See the IPCC report: "Summary for Policymakers," in *Climate Change 2007: The Physical Science Basis. Contribution of Working Group I to the Fourth*

Assessment Report of the Intergovernmental Panel on Climate Change, ed. S. Solomon, D. Qin, M. Manning, Z. Chen, M. Marquis, K. B. Averyt, M. Tignor, and H. L. Miller (Cambridge University Press, 2007), available online at http://www.ipcc.ch/, accessed April 1, 2008; T. M. L. Wigley, "The Climate Change Commitment," *Science* 307 (205):1766–69; Gerald A. Meehl, Warren M. Washington, William D. Collins, Julie M. Arblaster, Aixue Hu, Lawrence E. Buja, Warren G. Strand, and Haiyan Teng, "How Much More Global Warming and Sea Level Rise?" *Science* 307 (2005):1769–72.

4. See for example http://dictionary.reference.com/browse/nature, accessed June 11, 2008.

5. By some estimates, wilderness as defined by low human population density (fewer than five people per square kilometer), having at least 70 percent original vegetation intact, and covering at least 10,000 square kilometers (3,861 square miles) potentially exists in as much as 46 percent of the Earth's land surface (see: Russell Mittermeier, Cristina Goettsch Mittermeier, Patricio Robles Gil, Gustavo Fonseca, Thomas Brooks, John Pilgrim, and William R. Konstant, *Wilderness: Earth's Last Wild Places* [University of Chicago Press, 2003]); however, less than 12 percent of land is in some way protected as national parks, reserves, or other areas (World Conservation Union, as reported in *National Geographic* in October 2006, available online at http://ngm.nationalgeographic.com/ngm/0610/feature1/map.html, accessed July 13, 2008).

6. Stegner, "Wilderness Letter." (For complete citation see endnote 2).

7. Ibid.

8. For a good, up-to-date summary of the way species migrations are being disrupted by the Gang of Four, see David S. Wilcove, *No Way Home: The Decline of the World's Great Animal Migrations* (Washington, DC: Island Press, 2008).

9. Carl Zimmer, "A Radical Step to Preserve a Species: Assisted Migration," *New York Times* (January 23, 2007), http://www.nytimes.com/2007/01/23/science/23migrate.html, accessed March 18, 2008; Jason S. McLachlan, Jessica J. Hellmann, and Mark W. Schwartz, "A Framework for Debate of Assisted Migration in an Era of Climate Change," *Conservation Biology* 21 (2007):297–302.

10. C. Josh Donlan, Joel Berger, Carl E. Bock, Jane H. Bock, David A. Burney, James A. Estes, Dave Foreman, Paul S. Martin, Gary W. Roemer, Felisa A. Smith, Michael E. Soulé and Harry W. Greene, "Pleistocene Rewilding: An Optimistic Agenda for Twenty-First-Century Conservation," *American Naturalist* 168 (2006):660–81; C. J. Donlan, Harry W. Green, Joel Berger, Carl E. Bock, Jane H. Bock, David A. Burney, James A. Estes, Dave Foreman, Paul S. Martin, Gary W. Roemer, Felisa A. Smith, and Michael E. Soulé, "Re-wilding North America," *Nature* 436 (2005):913–14; C. Josh Donlan, "Restoring America's Big Wild Animals," *Scientific American* 296 (2007):70–77.

11. Paul S. Martin, *Twilight of the Mammoths* (Berkeley: University of California Press, 2005), p. 199.

12. Dustin R. Rubenstein, "America's ecosystems have evolved since the Pleistocene; the consequences of introductions of exotic megafauna to the continent cannot be predicted," *Scientific American* 297 (2007):12; Dustin R. Ruben-

stein, Daniel I. Rubenstein, Paul W. Sherman, and Thomas A. Gavin, "Pleistocene park: Does re-wilding North America represent sound conservation for the 21st century?" *Biological Conservation* 132 (2006):232–38; Tim Caro, "The Pleistocene re-wilding gambit," *Trends in Ecology and Evolution* 22 (2007): 281–83.

13. See, for example, the Leopold Report, a defining document in conservation biology and park management, which states: ". . . the biotic associations within each park [should] be maintained, or where necessary recreated, as nearly as possible in the condition that prevailed when the area was first visited. . . ." A. S. Leopold (Chairman), S. A. Cain, C. M. Cottam, I. N. Gabrielson, and T. Kimball (Advisory Board on Wildlife Management appointed by Secretary of the Interior Udall), *Wildlife Management in the National Parks: The Leopold Report*, 1963, published online by the National Park Service at http://www. nps.gov/history/history/online_books/leopold/leopold.htm, accessed October 9, 2008.

14. Gretchen C. Daily and Katherine Ellison, *The New Economy of Nature: The Quest to Make Conservation Profitable* (Washington, DC: Island Press, 2002).

15. Ibid.

16. Michael L. Rosenzweig, *Win-Win Ecology: How the Earth's Species Can Survive in the Midst of Human Enterprise* (New York: Oxford University Press, 2003).

17. See also Taylor H. Ricketts, Gretchen C. Daily, Paul R. Ehrlich, and Charles D. Michener, "Economic value of tropical forest to coffee production," *Proceedings of the U.S. National Academy of Sciences* 101 (2004):12579–82.

18. Rosenzweig, p. 8. (For full citation see endnote16.)

19. IUCN, *Forest Landscape Restoration: Broadening the Vision of West African Forests* (Gland, Switzerland, and Cambridge, UK: International Union for Conservation of Nature and Natural Resources, 2005), published online at http://www.iucn.org/dbtw-wpd/edocs/Folder-001.pdf, accessed June 12, 2008.

20. William Conway, *Act Three In Patagonia* (Washington, DC: Island Press, 2005).

21. Stegner, "Wilderness Letter." (See endnote 2 for complete citation.)

Appendix: Slowing Down Global Warming

1. See the following for detailed discussions of how you can help the global warming problem:

Tim Flannery, *The Weather Makers* (New York: Atlantic Monthly Press, 2005).

Al Gore, *An Inconvenient Truth: The Planetary Emergence of Global Warming and What We Can Do About It* (Emmaus, PA: Rodale Press, 2006).

National Resource Defense Council, "How to Fight Global Warming," published online at http://www.nrdc.org/globalWarming/gsteps.asp, accessed March 15, 2008.

Larry West, "Top Ten Things You Can Do to Reduce Global Warming," published online at http://environment.about.com/od/globalwarming/tp/globalwarmtips.htm, accessed March 15, 2008.

Emily Main and P. W. McRandle, "A calculated loss: How to reduce your global warming emissions," *National Geographic* 119 (March/April 2007), published online at http://www.thegreenguide.com/doc/119/calculator, accessed April 7, 2008.

"Stop Global Warming.Org," published online at http://www.stopglobalwarming.org/sgw_actionitems.asp, accessed March 15, 2008.

"Climate Change Kids Site," published online at http://epa.gov/climatechange/kids/difference.html, accessed March 15, 2008.

"The Global Warming Survival Guide, 51 Things We Can Do to Save the Environment," published online at http://www.time.com/time/specials/2007/environment/, accessed June 12, 2008.

You can find a variety of other resources by using your Internet search engine with search words like "global warming help".

2. Examples of Web-based calculators for you to determine your own carbon footprint include the following. You can find more by using your Internet search engine to search for "calculate carbon footprint" and similar search terms.

"CoolClimateCalculator," online at http://bie.berkeley.edu/calculator.html, accessed March 17, 2008.

"Calculate Your Impact," online at http://www.climatecrisis.net/takeaction/carboncalculator/, accessed March 15, 2008.

"Reducing Your Impact Carbon Footprint Calculator," online at http://www.carbonfootprint.com/calculator.aspx, accessed March 15, 2008.

"Personal Emissions Calculator," online at http://www.epa.gov/climatechange/emissions/ind_calculator.html, accessed March 15, 2008.

3. On average a 1,000-megawatt coal-fired power plant pumps about four megatons of CO_2 into the atmosphere each year (see science writer Jennifer Ouellette's blog "Carbon, Carbon, Everywhere," covering the American Institute of Physics Industrial Physics Forum on "The Energy Challenge," which took place October 14–16, 2007, in Seattle, Washington [October 17, 2007], http://blogs.physicstoday.org/industry07/2007/10/carbon_carbon_everywhere.html, accessed April 1, 2008). How much carbon output you save by replacing bulbs depends of course on the wattage of the incandescent bulb you're replacing, the wattage of the CFL bulb you replace it with, and how long you leave the light turned on. Estimates reported here are roughly based on the assumption that each of 110 million U.S. households replaces 15 75-watt and 15 100-watt incandescent bulbs with a 19-watt CFL, that on average each bulb is turned on for four hours per day, and that the carbon contribution of incandescent and CFL light bulbs are as reported by Emily Main and P. W. McRandle, "A calculated loss: How to reduce your global warming emissions," *National Geographic* 119 (March/April 2007), http://www.thegreenguide.com/doc/119/calculator, accessed April 7, 2008). I further assume that there is no difference in the energy used to produce CFLs and incandescent bulbs—not strictly true, but close enough (you win back the extra energy used to produce a CFL in the first 50

hours of their 6,000-hour to 15,000-hour lifetime—see "Compact Fluorescent Light Bulbs—a Tale from Dust to Dust," published online at http://thewatt.com/node/175, accessed April 6, 2008).

4. See United Nations Framework Convention on Climate Change, available online at http://unfccc.int/2860.php, accessed March 24, 2008.

5. Matthew L. Wald, "Venture Capital Rushes Into Alternative Energy," *New York Times* (April 30, 2007), http://www.nytimes.com/2007/04/30/business/30energy.html, accessed March 18, 2008; Marianne Lavelle, "Power Revolution," *U.S. News and World Report* (October 26, 2007), http://www.usnews.com/articles/business/economy/2007/10/26/power-revolution.html, accessed March 18, 2008.

Index

About Island Press

Since 1984, the nonprofit Island Press has been stimulating, shaping, and communicating the ideas that are essential for solving environmental problems worldwide. With more than 800 titles in print and some 40 new releases each year, we are the nation's leading publisher on environmental issues. We identify innovative thinkers and emerging trends in the environmental field. We work with world-renowned experts and authors to develop cross-disciplinary solutions to environmental challenges.

Island Press designs and implements coordinated book publication campaigns in order to communicate our critical messages in print, in person, and online using the latest technologies, programs, and the media. Our goal: to reach targeted audiences—scientists, policymakers, environmental advocates, the media, and concerned citizens—who can and will take action to protect the plants and animals that enrich our world, the ecosystems we need to survive, the water we drink, and the air we breathe.

Island Press gratefully acknowledges the support of its work by the Agua Fund, Inc., Annenberg Foundation, The Christensen Fund, The Nathan Cummings Foundation, The Geraldine R. Dodge Foundation, Doris Duke Charitable Foundation, The Educational Foundation of America, Betsy and Jesse Fink Foundation, The William and Flora Hewlett Foundation, The Kendeda Fund, The Andrew W. Mellon Foundation, The Curtis and Edith Munson Foundation, Oak Foundation, The Overbrook Foundation, the David and Lucile Packard Foundation, The Summit Fund of Washington, Trust for Architectural Easements, Wallace Global Fund, The Winslow Foundation, and other generous donors.

The opinions expressed in this book are those of the author(s) and do not necessarily reflect the views of our donors.